Narrative Truth
and Historical Truth

Narrative Truth
and Historical Truth

MEANING AND INTERPRETATION
IN PSYCHOANALYSIS

Donald P. Spence

W·W·NORTON & COMPANY · NEW YORK·LONDON

First Edition

Library of Congress Cataloging in Publication Data
Spence, Donald Pond, 1926–
Narrative truth and historical truth.

Includes bibliographical references and index.
1. Psychoanalytic interpretation. 2. Meaning
(Psychology) 3. Truth—Psychological aspects.
4. Psychotherapist and patient. 5. Psychotherapy—
Research. I. Title.
RC506.S66 1982 150.19′5 81-22311

W. W. Norton & Company, Inc. 500 Fifth Avenue, New York, N.Y.
10110
W. W. Norton & Company Ltd. 37 Great Russell Street, London
WC1B 3NU
1 2 3 4 5 6 7 8 9 0

ISBN 0–393–01588–2 AACR2

TO MARY

Contents

Foreword

For more than a decade now, theoretical writing in psycho-analysis—at least in America—has been preoccupied with what I have come to call "the great metapsychology debate." "Leading psychoanalytic theoreticians, some of them once colleagues and collaborators of Heinz Hartmann and David Rapaport, those chief architects of modern-day ego psychology in its fullest American development, have called for the whole-sale reconsideration, the major revision (albeit along widely different parameters) and, even in the extreme, the total elim-ination, of the whole fabric of metapsychology as an inherently flawed and doomed effort to (inappropriately) create a "gen-eral" (and natural science-linked) theory of psychoanalysis where only a "special" or totally *clinical* theory can be properly sustained by the psychoanalytic data. Needless to say, other theoreticians have equally vigorously defended the metapsy-chological or the general-theoretical structure of psycho-analysis on a variety of heuristic, utilitarian, or more comprehensively philosophy-of-science grounds. Curiously, however, both the attackers and the defenders of the metapsychological structure as a presumed essential explanatory framework for the effort at the scientific conceptualization of the phenomena of psychoanalysis share almost completely their guiding assumptions about the nature of the basic data. These assumptions are in fact very much *taken for granted,* not just by theoreticians, but, even more universally, by the psychoanalytic body of clinicians, as if, whatever the scientific status of the overarching explanatory theory (i.e., the general theory, the metapsychology), at least the data themselves are "self-evident" and, therefore, in analogy with Freud's favorite quotation from F. T. Vischer that "What is moral is self-evident," require no special explanation.

It is precisely at this point that Donald Spence's book is so disturbing—and so revolutionary, in the sense of essaying so radical and fundamental a critique of our most central clinical and theoretical operating assumptions. For Spence is signally one of the very few among us who reminds us that our "data" are not so self-evident, their nature not at all to be taken for granted, and who in fact calls into question our entire sense of the stability, the accessibility, and the face-meaningfulness of the verbal interchanges of the consulting room upon which our total enterprise, clinical, educational, and, even to a large extent, research is made to rest. Granted our somewhat sophisticated awareness of all the shading and amplification (and distortion) of meaning revealed by enlarged attention to tone and inflection and the "music" of the spoken exchanges, and to the various dimensions of nonverbal behaviors, paralinguistic, attitudinal, kinesthetic, postural, etc., as well as our fundamental awareness developed to such depth by Freud that things (words) are not necessarily what they seem, able to be taken at face value with one unvarying definitional truth value, but rather are varyingly transparent or obscure bridges between surface manifest meaning and underlying latent meaning; granted all this, our psychoanalytic enterprise does nonetheless centrally assume that the words of the analytic text of the consulting room, however we capture them, are in themselves the basic clues that can lead to the unraveling of the psychoanalytic (historical) truths.

It is this guiding set of suppositions that Spence squarely challenges, those assumptions grounded centrally in Freud's archeological and/or historical model of the mind, a mind that bears the (distorted) imprint of all its pasts in its variously presenting presents, to be rendered comprehensively accessible—i.e., thoroughly intelligible—to a properly reconstructive and unfolding archeological (historical) digging and unpeeling of those words through their layers of lifetime accretions. Spence's basic counterargument starts with the inevitable difficulties of even the most verbal and articulate among us, that we for the most part quite unwittingly gloss over, of putting things (thoughts), and even more so, of putting pictures, visual images—especially the ambiguous and jumbled images that are our dreams—into precise words; as well as all the inevitable slippages between memories of any kind, thoughts, feelings, fantasies, dreams, etc., and a language of intelligible description, and slippage again between the intended or understood meaning of the speaker and the supposedly shared, perceived, or imputed meaning inferred by the listener. This argument, developed by Spence so deftly and many-sidedly—and convincingly—leads clearly to his disconcerting persuasion that it is through the happenstance of the choice of a particular linguistic construction, whether by analysand or by analyst, that we have fixed in a sharable language the form of the event or the memory we are explaining or seeking, and that once we have decided on that particular construction, we come to see and we in fact determine the past in a particular manner—so that, pushed to its logical extreme, the verbal construction that we create not only shapes (our view of) the past, but, indeed, it, a creation of the present, *becomes* the past.

The logic of all this leads us (if we are willing to follow Spence in all his complexly ramifying argument) to a whole series of transformations of our usual analytic thought conventions: of reconstruction into (new) construction, of acts of discovery into acts of creation, of historical truth into narrative fit, of pattern finding into pattern making, of veridical interpretation into creative interpretation, of all interpretation into a species of (more or less) inexact interpretation, of analysis essentially as a science of recovery of the past into a science of choice and of creation in the present and future, and of psychoanalyst as archeologist and historian, into psychoanalyst as poet, artist, and aestheticist. What this fundamentally does to us, and for us, is both to transform the nature of the scientific (or are they indeed more truly artistic and aesthetic?) problems that our field can properly—i.e., appropriately—address, as well as to transplace the first and most urgent priority level of conceptual and empirical inquiry from the inferential structure created by clinician, theoretician, and researcher out of the psychoanalytic discourse to the more elemental building blocks that go into the very process of formation and shaping of that discourse itself.

Spence charts his own working prescription for that task that he sets us: to transform what he calls *normative competence* (based on both the "public assumptions" that bind the field in its shared psychoanalytic theory and in the presumed clinical competence of its practitioners coming from their comparable clinical experiences, but also based, disturbingly, on the "private assumptions" derived idiosyncratically from the particular individual's own hope and fear-inspired context-giving) that every knowledgeable psychoanalytic scholar brings, albeit therefore differently, to the study of psychoanalytic texts, into what he calls *privileged competence* (that detailed knowledge of context, of personal meaning, of explicated allusion and history that only those two who have together created the particular text in their consulting-room dialogue can even claim to begin to comprehend comprehensively). The path to this specified clinical and research task of transforming the *normative* knowledge that necessarily limits the comprehension of any outsider to the duo in the particular psychoanalytic dialogue into the *privileged* knowledge that would put the third party—supervisor, researcher, clinician reader, theoretician student, etc.—into the *same* comprehending frame as the two principal parties is the process that Spence calls "naturalizing" or "glossing" or "unpacking" the text, and, as he hints, it is a most laborious undertaking that has only been essayed in the most fragmentary manner in our clinical and research literature dealing with our bedrock phenomena, our clinical data.

More than that, however, it is also a most problematic undertaking in the sense that Spence may be (guardedly) optimistic more than is inherently warranted by the nature of the case that he himself has built concerning the possibility (let alone the feasibility) of truly unpacking the psychoanalytic text adequately enough so that all those with requisite normative psychoanalytic competence can read it enough the same way without imposing the distorting lenses of personal "unwitting interpretations" that stem out of private historical (and, therefore, idiosyncratically countertransferentially colored) experiences. Should all this not be reasonably feasible, and that at least is an empirical question that Spence asks that we seriously address, we would indeed be left with extraordinarily disturbing implications for our discipline in its struggles to be a science, to conduct meaningful and incrementally useful empirical research, and to construct explanatory and incrementally useful theory, capable of ordering our clinical phenomena and our research findings within our field and of articulating relevantly with cognate disciplines devoted across common borders to other dimensions of intelligence of man. On this most central issue, Spence does not convincingly answer his own troubling question, nor can we just on reading his book. This is why, however, I consider it so disturbing a book for us in its potential implications that could call for such far-reaching revisions in our conceptualization of the nature of our data, of our research enterprise, and of our possibilities for proper theory building. This is why I think we should at least all read this book and ponder the degree to which we each want—and need—to incorporate its message into our own psychoanalytic scheme of things.

Robert S. Wallerstein, M.D.
May 1981

ACKNOWLEDGMENTS

First, thanks go to Dr. Karl Schick, who initially suggested that I write the book. I am also grateful for the encouragement of Drs. Jack Block, Jim Blight, Marshall Edelson, David Mayer, and Gudmund Smith, who have seen earlier versions; to Jerry Wakefield, who gave me a philosophical perspective; to the Trustees and Dean of Rutgers Medical School–UMDNJ, who made possible a much needed sabbatical; and to Dr. Robert Wallerstein for providing office space and library facilities at the University of California, San Francisco, where so much of the final work was carried out.

My thanks go also to the *International Journal of Psycho-analysis* for permission to reprint material that first appeared in that journal, and to the Louvre, the Prado, and the Print Collection of the New York Public Library for permission to reproduce materials from their collections.

Finally, I wish to thank Mrs. Charlotte Hardy, who, with unfailing good humor, typed the final manuscript and all earlier drafts. She has my warmest gratitude.

Even the simple act which we describe as "seeing someone we know" is, to some extent, an intellectual process. We pack the physical outline of the creature we see with all the ideas we already formed about him, and in the complete picture of him which we compose in our minds those ideas have certainly the principal place. In the end they come to fill out so completely the curve of his cheeks, to follow so exactly the line of his nose, they blend so harmoniously in the sound of his voice that these seem to be no more than a transparent envelope, so that each time we see the face or hear the voice it is our own ideas of him which we recognize and to which we listen.

—Proust, *Swann's Way*

Narrative Truth
and Historical Truth

•————————————————————

CHAPTER I

The Narrative Tradition

Freud, the first psycho*analyst,* was also one of the first great synthesizers. He was a master at taking pieces of the patient's associations, dreams, and memories and weaving them into a coherent pattern that is compelling, persuasive, and seemingly complete, a pattern that allows us to make important discoveries about the patient's life and to make sense out of previously random happenings. Freud's most impressive achievements (in *The Interpretation of Dreams* and in his well-known case histories) are lasting accomplishments of innovative synthesis, and we have been heavily influenced by this tradition. Freud made us aware of the persuasive power of a coherent narrative—in particular, of the way in which an aptly chosen reconstruction can fill the gap between two apparently unrelated events and, in the process, make sense out of nonsense. There seems no doubt but that a well-constructed story possesses a kind of narrative truth that is real and immediate and carries an important significance for the process of therapeutic change. Although Freud would later argue that every

21

effective interpretation must also contain a piece of historical truth, it is by no means certain whether this is always the case; narrative truth by itself seems to have a significant impact on the clinical process.

We are still discovering for ourselves the important ingredients of the narrative tradition in psychoanalysis. Schafer (1980) has provided us with a wide-ranging appreciation of the role of narration in the psychoanalytic dialogue and Sherwood (1969) has emphasized the importance of continuity, coherence, and comprehensiveness in narrative explanation. But Freud's most effective case histories also possess an important literary quality that can best be defined as a masterful control of style and content. The facts alone are not sufficient; they must also be presented in a context that allows their full significance to be appreciated even by the reader who has no other information about the case. We can assume that the same definition would hold for an interpretation: the framing of the formulation is just as important as its content.

The importance of the narrative tradition in Freud's view of the clinical process has sensitized all of us in the therapeutic community to the importance of narrative connection, and it can be argued that it has significantly influenced the way in which we listen to patients.* If our goal is to discover the underlying thread of the patient's story and eventually to be in a position to match Freud's examples of narrative persuasion, we necessarily will listen with an ear tuned to sequence, coherence, and transformation. To an extent that has not been appreciated up to now, the narrative tradition has turned us all into searchers after meaning and, to a significant degree, has prevented us from following Freud's rule of listening with evenly hovering attention. The search for coherence and con-

---

*Schafer has played an essential role in making us aware of the narrative tradition—see in particular Schafer (1979) and Schafer (1980).

tinuity might be described as an important aspect of our psy-choanalytic competence.

The narrative tradition has also had a significant influence on our patients. Some may even feel that they are competing with Freud's more famous cases and have fantasies of seeing their own history in published form; as a result, their effort to associate freely may always be tinged with an effort to show their best narrative voice and thus ensure their place among the clinical immortals. But, of course, narrative closure can easily get in the way of free report, and in an effort after coher-ence, both analyst and patient may collude in an attempt to prematurely streamline a chaotic life.

The narrative tradition has had an important influence on our literature as well. Following Freud, we tend to conceive of clinical papers as being quasi-literary efforts in which form and style are just as important as content. Because the raw data have no secure place in this tradition, they tend to be left out; and as we will see in later chapters, streamlined case reports have tended to take the place of the original data, and our basic observations, until very recently, have tended to dis-appear once they were uttered. As a result, the path from observation to theory can never be retraced; thus we have no way to confirm or disconfirm an observation, much less com-bine old observations in a new formulation.

Even before our papers appear in print, the narrative tradi-tion has had an influence on our ability as observers. Func-tioning as artists and storytellers in the analytic hour, it is in our interest to build a seamless web of belief (to borrow a phrase from Quine and Ullian, 1970) in which all findings can be captured; we necessarily pay more attention to continuity and coherence than to their opposites. But the tradition can easily interfere with our role as data gatherers. Assuming a more scientific stance, we cannot allow form to prejudge content and must be near-ruthless in our capacity to take down everything in its original order. Thus our role as keeper of the narrative tradition is bound to conflict with our role as clinical reporter and keeper of the archives, and it seems likely that many clinical findings have not been reported simply because they could not be fitted into the prevailing narrative.

We are always wearing two hats. Inside the hour, we try to create continuity and coherence and make what sense we can from the emerging findings, not caring very much whether any particular memory or interpretation can be corroborated in any precise manner. We are comfortable with the rather loose fit between an early childhood event and its repetition in the transference, or between an early memory of the father, for example, and the patient's current reaction to the analyst. To match early and late variations on the same pattern in any more precise a manner would seem ridiculous and out of place; it might easily interfere with the process of treatment. But a different kind of standard is needed for sifting over the data of a completed case to create general laws for a general theory; once the context of discovery has given way to the context of justification (see Reichenbach, 1951) we must be concerned about the precise pattern match, replication, and external validation. Speaking as scientists, outside the hour, we must give up the familiar narrative tradition and adopt more conventional rules of truth finding.

Although a narrative sensitivity seems to be a familiar part of what might be called the competence of the practicing psychoanalyst, the narrative tradition is more implicit than explicit in Freud's writings and in the general theory of psychoanalysis. Indeed, the few rules of technique proposed by Freud would seem to make an opposite argument. To introduce the concept of free association, Freud compared the patient in psychoanalysis with a passenger on a train. His job is to look at the passing scene and describe all of its features to his companion (the analyst), who cannot see out the window. Everything must be described—nothing left out. If the patient is properly following the rule of free association, he is merely reporting what he "sees" in the outside "window"; the emphasis is clearly on providing the analyst with a near-complete description of the passing scene, without, in Freud's words, "criticism or selection." The analyst, for his part, assumes a role that complements that of the patient; he tries to listen with "evenly-hovering attention" and, by so doing, tries to reconstruct the scene outside. The analyst also listens without criticism or selection, and the symmetry of the two roles is brought out clearly in Freud's statement that "the rule of giving equal notice to everything is the necessary counterpart to the demand made on the patient that he should communicate everything that occurs to him" (Freud, 1912, p. 112).

The model of the patient as unbiased reporter and the analyst as unbiased listener suggests a kind of naïve realism that is hard to imagine, harder to practice, and runs counter to everything we have learned about the way we come to understand the world. The model persists because it heightens the special virtues of the analytic situation and tempts us to believe that under the special conditions that prevail, the patient does indeed have privileged access to the past and the analyst, by virtue of his special training, is in fact a rather special reporter of a kind that makes almost no mistakes. The mischief is further compounded by the underlying narrative tradition. If we assume that the analyst, at least part of the time, is listening with what he assumes is evenly hovering attention, then it follows that the "story" he "hears" will be understood as being a good approximation of the story told by the patient. The more he believes that he is following Freud's model, the more he will believe in his "hearing" of the material; the more he believes in the model, the less he will look for alternative constructions of the same material. But because he is probably listening with a bias toward coherence and continuity, what he "hears" comes to resemble a finished narrative, further reinforcing his belief that no other alternatives need be considered. Although the implications of the narrative tradition are clearly at odds with the implications of Freud's more explicit models, in practice the two can be combined in a way that gives the uncritical analyst the best of both worlds: he or she hears a satisfactory story and assumes that this is the only story there is to hear.

One clue that this kind of confusion is fairly endemic comes from the fact that the psychoanalytic literature makes no provision for alternative explanations of the same data. A case report is presented as a record of the facts, not as an interpretation of some of the data; this convention is a natural consequence of the assumption that the analyst functions as a largely unbiased reporter. (For a rare exception, see Schafer, 1980, and his suggestion that perhaps "there are no objective, autonomous, or pure psychoanalytic data which, as Freud was fond of saying, compel one to draw certain conclusions" [p. 30].) A case report, by virtue of the assumption that no selection is being exercised by either patient or analyst, is understood to represent a near-undistorted record of a clinical event. If there is no distortion, then there is no need to preserve the original data, and for this reason, case reports have tended to replace the data in the analytic literature.

If the narrative tradition were less compelling or less functional, the flaws in Freud's model would have far less serious consequences; the cases where free-floating attention or free association were less than optimal would quickly come to our attention, and we might ask questions about the conditions under which the two models do and do not apply. But given the force of the narrative tradition, this question never gets raised because there are no inconsistencies in the data. What starts out (in the clinical encounter) as a discontinuity or a lack of closure or a failure to make sense is inevitably smoothed over by the narrative tradition with the result that by the time it takes shape in process notes or published reports, it has acquired a narrative polish that makes it look unexceptional.

As we will discover in later chapters, this narrative polish may make a significant contribution to its narrative truth and thereby to its therapeutic significance. As such, it plays an important role in the treatment process. But the inadvertent narrative smoothing may blur the distinction between the idiosyncratic event that needs careful replication and a more lawful finding; if the initial account is appropriately smoothed by the narrative tradition, it may seem to have all the properties of a general law and may become prematurely incorporated in our general theory. This consequence applies in particular to clinical events that seem to fit an accepted formulation; given the force of the narrative tradition, we have no way of knowing whether they should be considered as true examples of the formulation or as overzealous attempts on the part of the reporting analyst to fit the findings to the theory.

Coupling the narrative tradition with the Freudian model leads to a failure to distinguish between two kinds of truth. Freud had a fondness for thinking of himself as a kind of archeologist, believing that in the process of psychoanalysis he was always uncovering pieces of the past. If the patient is assumed, by virtue of his free-associating stance, to have privileged access to the past, and if the story we hear is assumed to be the same as the story he is telling, then it is tempting to conclude that we are hearing a piece of his history, an account of the "way things were." Narrative truth is confused with historical truth, and the very coherence of an account may lead us to believe that we are making contact with an actual happening. Moreover, what is effective for a given patient in a particular hour (the narrative truth of an interpretation) may be mistakenly attributed to its historical foundations. Out of this confusion grew Freud's belief that every interpretation always contains a piece of historical truth and that this "kernel of truth," as he called it, is what makes the interpretation effective. Even if this rule were true part of the time, we are still left with no systematic way of separating historical from narrative truth; thus the metaphor about the ever-present kernel of truth is not very useful as a rule of thumb. Furthermore, it may obscure the fact that narrative truth has a special significance in its own right and that making contact with the actual past may be of far less significance than creating a coherent and consistent account of a particular set of events.

If we assume that the patient is also under the influence of the narrative tradition, that he is always trying to participate in the analytic "conversation" by presenting the analyst with a partly finished story, and that his wishes to be understood and appreciated tend to bias his utterances toward what is sayable and away from what "really" happened—if we assume all this, then we have further reason to question the privileged status of free association. As a consequence, we need to be even more skeptical about the role of historical truth in the psychoanalytic process. It is one of the central assumptions of the chapters to follow that the associations of a patient have no one-to-one correspondence with his memories and dreams, much less with his unconscious thoughts. In his model of the passenger on the train, innocently reporting everything he sees, Freud tended to underemphasize the enormous difficulty we face in using language to describe a visual event. Much of what is visual cannot be put into words; certain kinds of stylized images may be captured, but the complex visual scene represented by a dream or an early memory can probably never be completely realized by language. As a result, the particular words used in the report may distort the significance of what is being "reported." But there is a further problem—the problem of uncontrolled context. If the patient's verbal presentation of a dream or memory is, by definition, incomplete, then we must assume that further context must be supplied in order for understanding to take place. The context may come from the patient, who is elaborating on the remembered dream, or it may come from the analyst, who, hearing the dream report, is unwittingly supplying details of his own to make it somehow coherent. Under the influence of the narrative tradition, the analyst may add a wide range of missing items, always assuming that he is doing justice to the material and merely supplying what the patient would have said had he been asked. Here is where the narrative tradition creates the most mischief because it comes into play between the time the patient speaks and the time the analyst has understood. To put it more precisely, context must be supplied *in order that* understanding takes place. We will argue that to listen with *only* free-floating attention to a patient who is truly free in his associations is to run the risk of hearing nothing more than a series of words. To register the utterance with some kind of understanding, we must supply a wide range of background assumptions and listen in an active, constructive manner, making assumptions about incomplete sentences, filling out ambiguous references, and otherwise supplying what the patient leaves out. Thus the tradition of narrative listening comes into particular prominence at those times when the patient is following Freud's rule of free association and speaking in half sentences wrapped around incomplete thoughts.

This line of reasoning suggests that the relation between the associative stance of the patient and the listening stance of the analyst is a good deal more complex than Freud had assumed. In contrast to Freud, who believed that free-floating attention was the complement of free association, we will argue that passive reporting on the part of the patient may actually *prevent* passive listening on the part of the analyst. If the patient is truly free-associating, he is supplying content but little context, and the analyst, therefore, must supply a wide range of background assumptions simply in order to understand. If the patient, on the other hand, is not following Freud's model and is providing us with a finished narrative, he is supplying both content and context, and the analyst can indeed listen with evenly hovering attention. To the extent that the patient follows the narrative tradition rather than Freud's model, the analyst can follow Freud's model and give up the narrative tradition. Thus, free-floating attention would seem to alternate with, not complement, free association.

Just as the analyst must listen constructively and actively much of the time, supplying his own meaning to a large part of the analytic "conversation," so the outside reader must supply many of his own assumptions when he tries to understand the transcribed text of an hour or read a published report of a case. The treating analyst understands by supplying his background assumptions to the clinical material, but these assumptions, with only rare exceptions, are never made a part of the clinical record. Because the necessary context is not supplied, the outside reader must supply his own; as a result, even the fully transcribed session will mean something quite different to the outside reader unless specific steps are taken to add the background assumptions of the treating analyst. We will call this step the *naturalization* or *unpacking* of the transcript. We can extend the argument to the problem of understanding the psychoanalytic literature. We will argue that reading more often than not leads to *misunderstanding* because the outside reader reads the published case report against his own set of private assumptions, which rarely, if ever, match those of the author. Thus the problem of becoming an intelligent consumer of the literature shares many of the problems faced by the treating analyst in trying to understand his patient and many of the problems faced by the patient in trying to verbalize his dream or early memory. At every step of the way, we project our own meanings onto the clinical material. The narrative tradition, hovering in the background, guides this projection and thus determines our individual sense of the state of the psychoanalytic enterprise.

A few final words about the difference between narrative truth and historical truth. One way of appreciating this distinction is to compare the French and the English titles of Proust's masterpiece. In the French original, *À la recherche du temps perdu,* the emphasis is placed on the search through time, an adventure of discovery in which the author tries to make sense of what had once happened. In the process, he comes to realize that the same event can take on different meanings depending on the conditions under which it is remembered, and his model can be expressed in the passage quoted at the beginning of this book. We recover the past much as we go about recognizing a face, filling in a vague outline (the domain of "lost time") with the specific thoughts and feelings of the remembering moment. The form of these creative efforts is guided by the narrative tradition; as the vague outlines take on form and substance, they also acquire a coherence and representational appeal, which give them a certain kind of reality. Narrative truth can be defined as the criterion we use to decide when a certain experience has been captured to our satisfaction; it depends on continuity and closure and the extent to which the fit of the pieces takes on an aesthetic finality. Narrative truth is what we have in mind when we say that such and such is a good story, that a given explanation carries conviction, that *one* solution to a mystery must be true. Once a given construction has acquired narrative truth, it becomes just as real as any other kind of truth; this new reality becomes a significant part of the psychoanalytic cure.

The English translation of Proust puts the focus on historical truth. To use the phrase *Remembrance of Things Past* (a phrase, it turns out, that was borrowed from Shakespeare), the translator has put the emphasis on concrete objects and events that happened at some earlier period and that can be brought forward to the present. The focus is on the act of remembering, which, when properly carried out, will give us an accurate transcription of "things past." In his attempt to perform this task, the narrator functions like a historian. The English title makes Proust's classic sound like a kind of oral history that attempts to recapture a certain time and place before it is too late; it says nothing about the multiple layers of memory that may refer to the same triggering episode or to the way in which past becomes fused with present to generate something that is essentially time-free. Historical truth is time-bound and is dedicated to the strict observance of correspondence rules; our aim is to come as close as possible to what "really" happened. Historical truth is not satisfied with coherence for its own sake; we must have some assurance that the pieces being fitted into the puzzle also belong to a certain time and place and that this belonging can be corroborated in some systematic manner.

If we followed what Freud says in his writings, we would find ourselves looking for historical truth. This emphasis comes out most clearly in his many references to archeology as the guiding metaphor, and in his persistent belief in the curative effects of the "kernel of truth"—historical truth being clearly intended. Freud's specific recommendations to patient and analyst on how to associate and how to listen are clearly in the service of providing conditions that will allow the emergence of the historical truth. To function in this tradition was, as we shall see, not only to function as a dispassionate scientist; it also provided the best protection against the charge of suggestion and the best defense against the doubts of the incredulous nonbelievers. Early findings were indeed shocking and outrageous, but if it could be shown that the analyst was merely an archeologist, putting the pieces together as they became visible, then he could not be held responsible for the strange stories coming to light.

On the other hand, if we look at what Freud does, at how he writes, how he interprets, and how he assembles his explanations, we see the strong influence of the narrative tradition and we learn from him the clinical importance of narrative truth. Interpretations are persuasive, as we shall see, not because of their evidential value but because of their rhetorical appeal; conviction emerges because the fit is good, not because we have necessarily made contact with the past. As analysts, we may try to listen with evenly hovering attention, but we are also heavily, if unofficially, guided by the narrative tradition, and what registers may more often represent a good pattern than what precisely was said. And until recently, the good pattern tended to prevail; we are only just beginning to look at the actual record and to explore the ways in which what "really happened" does not always correspond with what was remembered.

Because narrative truth works so well within the clinical setting and because we are heavily influenced by Freud's success with the narrative tradition, we may have tried to extend the paradigm into regions where it does not belong. As analysts, we appeal to narrative truth when we describe our cases, when we publish our reports, and when we find evidence for corroborating theory, but these enterprises cannot function on narrative truth alone. As analysts, we may tend to confuse the context of discovery—the moment of excitement within the hour when a particular formulation came to life in a way that explained for the first time some long-standing symptom—with the context of justification. What works for a particular patient at a particular time and place does not necessarily become a candidate for the general theory of psychoanalysis. Freud failed to make a distinction between clinical happenings and general truths, and we have tended to follow in his footsteps; one-time insights tend to be inflated into general laws. If we confuse narrative truth with historical (and, more generally, with theoretical) truth, we will never make the necessary distinction, and our theory will never rise much above the level of metaphor. Here is why it becomes particularly important to recognize the difference between the narrative and historical tradition; by recognizing the particular virtues of the former, we also recognize its limitations. If the limitations are clear, we are then in a much better position to get on with the task of building lasting theory.

A LOOK AHEAD

We begin by looking at the problem faced by the author in putting things into words, and Chapter II compares two pieces of prose that differ in the extent to which they supply us with the necessary context. We will see how content alone is not sufficient for understanding and will begin to appreciate how the reader unwittingly supplies his own context when the author leaves it out. Chapter III takes up the problem of translating visual detail into language. Because language is necessarily incomplete, the assumptions provided by the reader become all the more important. Much of the clinical material presented by the patient is inherently visual, and because it is almost never presented in its original visual form, we are uncomfortably dependent on an approximate verbal translation. In Chapter III we will look at some of the more obvious consequences of this state of affairs.

In Chapter IV we apply what we have learned to the problems faced by the associating patient in trying to free-associate and to the problems faced by the analyst who is trying to listen with evenly hovering attention. We will explore the extent to which background assumptions are necessary for the process of understanding and how the use of these assumptions seems to vary inversely with the fluency of the patient's productions. We will call these assumptions *unwitting interpretations* and make the claim that they are necessary for any kind of understanding; that they are triggered in particular by truly free associations; and that they provide the foundation for the more formal, visible interpretation which is given to the patient. The unwitting interpretation, furthermore, almost never becomes part of the record.

In the next chapter (V), we take a careful look at the form and content of formal interpretations in an effort to understand their link to unwitting interpretations and the grounds of their appeal. We will claim that the historical truth of an interpretation is less important than is usually assumed; that it may have no necessary relation to the actual past; and that Freud's well-known temptation to compare psychoanalysis with archeology may be a substantially misleading analogy. If anything, psychoanalysis is an archeology of *descriptions* rather than *forms*, and there are some important differences between the two kinds of data that bear on the problem of putting pictures into words. Because our clinical data are "softer" than we usually like to assume, it seems more appropriate to conceive of an interpretation as a *construction*—a creative proposition—rather than as a *reconstruction* that is supposed to correspond to something in the past. We will enlarge on this distinction by returning to the two kinds of truth—historical truth and narrative truth—and the contributions of Viderman and Loch. The discussion is continued in Chapter VI.

In Chapter VII, we move from the problem of understanding the patient to the problem of understanding the text of the hour, and we will see that just as the analyst must listen constructively and creatively, so the outside reader must supply many of his own assumptions when he looks at any piece of clinical material. Thus the outside reader is continually supplying his own set of unwitting interpretations to anything he reads. In this chapter, we introduce the distinction between two kinds of competence—*privileged* competence, which belongs to the treating analyst at the time when the session takes place, and *normative* competence, which belongs to the outsider with full psychoanalytic training but no specific knowledge of the case in question. Understanding with only normative competence means, by definition, understanding without the background assumptions (unwitting interpretations) which were active in the treating analyst at the time of treatment; as a result, the transcribed session as it is being read and understood multiplies into a universe of different "texts," the number of texts corresponding to the number of persons reading. We will argue that some way must be found to provide the necessary context in order to eliminate these spurious texts and in order for real communication to take place. We will call this step the *naturalization* of the transcript.

In Chapter VIII we discuss the problem of naturalization in more detail and explore a variety of ways by which the context of the treating analyst can be recovered and presented to the outside reader in a way that will allow him to share his assumptions and burdens, his private hopes and fears. If this step is properly carried out, we have a way of closing the gap between normative and privileged competence. But how do we begin? We not only have a problem of presenting certain kinds of information but the more difficult problem of how to *dramatize* this information in a way that will give the outside reader the same experience as that possessed by the treating analyst. It may be necessary to develop a specific genre for clinical reporting—a genre that goes beyond the usual kind of reportorial account we are used to reading and comes closer to Freud's more impressionistic, almost novelistic presentations. This genre will capture the critical units of a clinical encounter and present them in a way that can be understood by anyone with the necessary background and training. This genre would somehow make visible the important background assumptions of patient and analyst and provide us with the full "text" of the hour. It is clear that a sound and video transcript barely approximates this "text."

In Chapter IX we discuss two alternative ways of looking at a formal interpretation. Rather than see it as a statement with some kind of historical truth, in keeping with Freud's fondness for *reconstructions* and the archeological model, we will argue for thinking of the interpretation as a specific kind of proposition, called a pragmatic statement. We will suggest that the analyst has a belief in the proposition but not necessarily a belief in its referent, and we will explore the implications of this conception. In a second approach to the problem, we will suggest that an interpretation can be seen as a kind of artistic product, and as such, it becomes possible to consider its effect on the patient as a kind of aesthetic experience. What might be called its "beauty" need have no necessary relation to its "truth." Both alternative formulations leave room for the important contribution of background assumptions and expand on the concept of narrative truth.

The final chapter brings together the main strands of the argument and returns to the central issue of narrative truth versus historical truth.

CHAPTER II

Putting Things into Words

How do we put things into words? We can begin with the
following formulation:

> Verbalizing seems to be a two-sided process in which both sides
> are simultaneously active. On the one hand human experience
> includes an infinite variety of shades and patterns of feeling, atti-
> tude, desire, interest and discrimination. On the other hand lan-
> guage provides a vast range of subtle ways by which to refer to
> such experiences. When we speak or write, experience in some
> way merges with, and emerges in the form of, patterns of lan-
> guage. But in some minds the language processes reflect not
> only the main experience, in statements that could be more or
> less paraphrased, but also much subtler features of the preverbal
> experience, and features of which the writer may have no aware-
> ness except through the overtones of what he finds himself writ-
> ing. Even then he may well fail to notice what he has said.
> (Harding, 1963)

It is clear that the names for things are not exactly lying around, waiting to be picked up and placed in sentences; every word marks a specific decision by the author and every sentence represents a particular overall combination of these words. The author is faced with the problem of how to express his view of the world in a string of words that will convey the same representation to someone who may have shared none of the experience. He must encode his view of reality in such a way that it can be decoded by the reader; if the coding and decoding (writing and reading) are properly carried out, the reader will come away with approximately the same view of reality that the author had when first starting to write.

Two kinds of choices, as Harding makes clear, enter into the encoding part of this process. On the one hand, the author must choose what aspect of his experience he wishes to transform into words—where does he wish to focus his view, and how should it be organized? At the same time, he must decide which words he needs and in what order to convey these impressions. The two activities are simultaneous because, to some extent, the words, as Whorf (1956) has made clear, influence how we see the world; and our choice of categories to write about will determine which words are relevant.

What do I see and how shall I describe it? This is the author's problem. If he is successful, the finished product will be accessible to the reader in such a way that he can recapture the author's original view. For this to happen, style will inform content in such a way that the core meaning of the text is enhanced by the way it is presented. When style and content combine in a mutually reinforcing fashion, we have something that approximates reality and that is sometimes called literature. But content alone is apparently not enough; a bare description of a scene conveys much less information than the same description conveyed in the appropriate style.

Exactly why this is true is not completely clear, but we can sketch out a partial answer. Good literature approximates reality because it provides the reader with just enough of the right kind of information in just the right sequence to permit a controlled appreciation of the passage in question. Good literature controls both the content of the passage and the background of associations against which it is read; it provides a context that helps to determine how it is sensed and what associations it brings to mind. A finished piece of writing, because it controls the background associations of the reader, will bring about a roughly similar series of reactions in all readers; we say that it is *publicly accessible*. A less finished piece of writing—and this includes the raw transcript of the patient-analyst dialogue, as we will see in Chapter VII—is less accessible and more likely to generate quite different reactions, depending on the hopes and fears of the individual reader.

We have chosen to begin with an analysis of the task of writing because the problems faced by the writer are, in many ways, the problems faced by the patient. In parallel fashion, the problems of the reader—and particularly the critical reader—are those faced by the analyst. Freud tended to underestimate the difficulty of putting things into words and spoke as if associations were already formed, simply waiting to emerge as soon as the usual restraints were relaxed. Lacan (1977), in his metaphor of the unconscious as a language, talks as if the lexical units were already formed and only remained to be spoken. But the unconscious is not a language; it is a set of experiences waiting to be expressed. The same applies to the patient's past or present life. Many of these experiences are simply too fleeting to be captured; they disappear from awareness before we can find the proper language. Others can perhaps be captured in words but not formed into sentences; they quickly drop out of sight because the patient feels the requirement to make sense as he is speaking and will probably choose a coherent thought over an incomplete fragment.

When we contrast the analytic conversation to the collaboration between reader and author, we are struck by what might be called a lack of craft. Because he is not experienced in the ways of putting things into words, the patient does not know how to signal such critical variables as point of view, genre, or any of the other skills that are part of the writer's trade. The message is further disguised by the changing assumptions about the listener; now the analyst is his father, now his mother, now his football coach. Each of these listeners may require a different style of speaking, perhaps even a different dialect; each may require a different genre. Before one style of speaking can be clearly identified and organized around the significant persons in the patient's history who may be responsible, it is replaced by a different style with a different (implied) cast of characters. Because the patient has neither the time nor the experience to properly signal these changes and mark their characteristic features, many of the significant leitmotifs in his message are never heard.

The gifted author, by contrast, tells us what to see and how to see it. If he is successful in the second part of his mission, he will arouse in the reader a particular set of images and associations which will add a certain texture and tone to what is being described—the chordal accompaniment, so to speak, to the melodic line. Consider the following sentence from Henry James, the very beginning of *The Ambassadors:*

> Strether's first question, when he reached the hotel, was about his friend; yet on his learning that Waymarsh was apparently not to arrive till evening he was not wholly disconcerted.

What is being said? This question is the subject of a well-known essay by Watt (1969), and we will summarize his main points. In the first place, by not reporting it as direct speech, James can bring in a narrator who is then in a position to comment on the scene and provide a neutral context. By putting the event in the past, he provides additional perspective; and lastly, by making the question the subject of the sentence,

James brings into focus the psychological aspects of the scene and puts into the background the more behavioral details. Watt elaborates on this transformation as follows:

> The primary location of the narrative in a mental rather than a physical continuum gives the narrative a great freedom from the restrictions of particular time and place. . . . we feel ourselves to be spectators, rather specifically, of Strether's thought processes, which easily and imperceptibly range forwards and backwards both in time and space. (Watt, p. 272)

Now we can return to the problem of putting things into words. James wished to tell a certain story, but, at the same time, he wished to tell it in a certain way and from a certain point of view. Always disdainful of the bare facts, as Watt makes clear, James wished to go beyond the concrete happening and generalize to the more abstract aspects of the human condition. He makes a clear decision to present the event in a way that will sharpen the focus on Strether's ambivalence and, more generally, on what was happening inside his mind. Many of the words used in this sentence—"question," "learning," "disconcerted"—serve to enhance the psychological focus, as do the relatively small proportion of concrete nouns.

How, then, is the sentence produced? James begins with the bare particulars of the story—Strether, Waymarsh, and the hotel—and then embeds these facts in a construction that alludes to the scene being described while concentrating primarily on Strether's reaction. We have the impression of maximum deliberation in word choice and word sequence. At the end of the sentence we are left with a vague impression of time, place, and person but a clear sense of what that person, whoever he is, happens to be thinking. The structure of the sentence follows the structure of the book—now revealing, now concealing—with a pattern, in Watt's phrase, of "progressive and yet artfully delayed clarification," which is central to

James's belief that a good story must have surprise, development, and tension (Watt, 1969, p. 279). Thus we come away from this particular sentence with three kinds of information: a vague notion of how and where the story begins; a somewhat clearer picture of the hero's reaction to this scene; and the beginning of a feeling for James's views on fiction. A single, not particularly long or elaborate sentence combines all three levels of meaning.

This example shows just how far the author's decisions can shape the structure of his language. And we see something else: *only* by shaping the sentence as he did could James convey the mixture of scene impression and mental activity which, for him, is a core aspect of experience.

By stressing the psychic reality of the event, James prepares us for a psychological novel. His opening sentence sensitizes the reader to issues of perception and understanding and uncertainty as opposed to issues of concrete action. By not telling us about time and place, he wards off associations to a particular locale and increases the chance that we will "see" the scene with a certain ambiguity and remoteness.

Now let us turn to the opposite kind of fragment. Where James succeeds in establishing a certain tone and expectation, the next passage, because it is not as carefully crafted, does not control the background associations that are being aroused in the reader; as a result, it appears somewhat awkward and incomplete. Its sense of strangeness, its inappropriate emphasis and somewhat arbitrary construction is a mark of how different the author's assumptions were from our own; because of differences in custom and value, we sense that he is writing from a different context. But this context is not available as part of the text; it does not form the kind of accompaniment that James's style gives to his opening sentence in *The Ambassadors*. Without access to the writer's governing assumptions, we are confronted with a text which is not fully accessible and in our effort to discover its meaning, we will necessarily read into it our own private associations.

Here is the passage; it comes from *The Education of Henry Adams*:

> He had been some weeks in London when he received a telegram from his brother-in-law at the Bagni Di Lucca [a town in Italy] telling him that his sister had been thrown from a cab and injured, and that he had better come on. He started that night, and reached the Bagni di Lucca on the second day. Tetanus had already set in. . . . He found his sister, a woman of forty, as gay and brilliant in the terrors of lockjaw as she had been in the careless fun of 1859, lying in bed in consequence of a miserable cab accident that had bruised her foot. Hour by hour the muscles grew rigid, while the mind remained bright, until after ten days of fiendish torture she died in convulsions. (Adams, 1918, p. 287)

We first sense that we are in a different time period when we read, at the end of the first sentence, that Adams is told he had "better come" to the scene of the accident; apparently the accident is more serious than it appears. We become more convinced on reading that the journey from London takes two days; and when we are told, without elaboration, that tetanus had set in, we know that the passage must come from another era. This complication is presented as something that follows inevitably from the accident—a comment on nineteenth-century medicine. Also, we note the passivity and helplessness of Adams in the face of misfortune—nothing could be done except to wait for the end, nothing could be done to relieve the pain.

Adams's account is clear but rather stark because it seems to leave out many facts that we assume would be added. By reading between the lines we can infer that nothing more could be done to save his sister, and further, that accidents of this kind were not particularly uncommon because Adams does not see the need to emphasize the idea that this was an exceptional happening.

Somewhat later in his account we find this passage:

> Death took features altogether new to him, in these rich and sensual surroundings. Nature enjoyed it, played with it, the horror added to her charm, she liked the torture and smothered her victim with caresses. Never had one seen her so winning. The hot Italian sun brooded outside, over the market place and the picturesque peasants, and, in the singular color of the Tuscan atmosphere, the hills and vineyards of the Apennines seemed bursting with midsummer blood. The sick room itself glowed with the Italian joy of life; friends filled it; no harsh northern lights pierced the soft shadows; even the dying woman shared the sense of the Italian summer, the soft, velvet air, the humor, the courage, the sensual fulness of Nature and man. She faced death, as women mostly do, bravely and even gaily, racked slowly to unconsciousness, but yielding only to violence, as a soldier sabred in battle. For many thousands of years, on these hills and plains, Nature had gone on sabring men and women with the same air of sensual pleasure. (p. 288)

This passage seems even more dated: how strange to emphasize the sensuous qualities of the scene when he is referring, after all, to the death of his sister! And how strange to stress nature's success rather than medicine's failure! From our modern perspective of scientific accomplishment, the reverential tone seems wrong because it is clearly a medical mistake and not an occasion for poetic imagery.

Adams, inadvertently, makes us see the gap between writing and the real world. At the time he was writing this passage, he must have felt that he was telling a simple story in straightforward language. Our difficulty in reading it today, and our sense of unreality and strangeness, all suggest that the text is not a simple copy of the real world but a rather complicated transformation. The passage of time has made it no longer accessible; we need the writer (or a more modern substitute) to somehow carry us back into that time and place, for only then can we really understand the passage. Without that kind of assisting gloss, the text remains an exotic curiosity; given such a gloss, it becomes accessible once more.

We begin to see how Adams's account is colored by his own view of the world and how the categories he takes for granted play a role in selecting and organizing his observations. But these categories can be only dimly sensed—and that is the root problem of imperfect fragments. Because Adams is a lesser craftsman than James, he has not perfectly controlled the background associations through which we read the passage. He seems to assume that we will see it through his eyes; because we read it with a different set of assumptions and associations, we experience a radically different text. Much of its strange flavor is a direct result of the failure to provide the reader with an adequate context.

Two additional examples of the way in which context can influence understanding come from the contemporary play, *Jumpers,* by Tom Stoppard. In the first, a man has been murdered, and Crouch, the porter, is wondering who did it. George, an absent-minded professor, is unaware of the murder but is trying to find out what happened to his pet rabbit. The following dialogue ensues:

GEORGE: Who killed him?

CROUCH: Well, I wouldn't like to say for certain . . . I mean I heard a bang, and when I looked, there he was crawling on the floor . . . (George winces) . . . and there was Miss Moore . . . well—

GEORGE: Do you realize she's in there now, *eating* him?

CROUCH: (pause): You mean—*raw?*

GEORGE: (crossly): No, of course not!—cooked—with gravy and mashed potatoes.

CROUCH: (pause): I thought she was on the mend, sir.

GEORGE: Do you think I'm being too sentimental about the whole thing?

CROUCH: (firmly): I do not, sir. I think it's a police matter. (Stoppard, 1972, p. 76)

Crouch is thinking of the murdered man, George of his pet rabbit; each statement is sensible and appropriate within context but ludicrous and/or funny out of context. Once again we see that understanding always takes place against a particular context. Part of the humor in this example stems from the fact that each character assumes that he knows all there is to know about the situation and that the person he is speaking to knows it too. Thus George, hearing Crouch say "raw," assumes that he is talking about a rabbit, feels offended that rabbit should be eaten in this manner, and adds the comforting words "gravy" and "mashed potatoes." But Crouch, of course, is thinking of the murdered man, and the details only make matters worse. The audience understands both contexts, hears each statement against a mixture of assumptions, and appreciates single, double, and triple entendres. Note that the words alone are not particularly funny; the humor emerges when we appreciate the assumptions that each character brings to the situation.

In the second example from Stoppard, we hear three different sounds in sequence—a fanfare of trumpets, a loud animal bray, and the noise of something falling down a flight of stairs. On first hearing, we are exposed to a bedroom scene and the trumpets are sounded when the woman rises to greet the man—as if to mark a romantic happening. When the pair come closer, we hear the animal bray (as in a mating call). When the scene builds somewhat further with increasing erotic overtones, the man drops a vase and we hear the crash—to mark his astonishment and ecstasy. Everything seems appropriate.

Stoppard soon shows us that this is not the case when he

plays the sounds for the second time. This time we learn that they come from a tape recording designed to illustrate a lecture on moral philosophy. The trumpet fanfare is designed to illustrate a pure ideal of beauty; the animal noise, which turns out to be the mating call of an elephant, illustrates a second kind of beauty (presumably beauty for an elephant); and the third noise—the sound of something falling down stairs—is used to provide a neutral contrast. By using the same sound sequence in two different contexts, Stoppard shows us that meaning does not lie in the stimulus alone and that even rather simple noises acquire a specific significance depending on the viewer's background assumptions. Trumpets in a romantic setting sound quite different from trumpets in a philosophy lecture.

TWO KINDS OF TRANSLATION

From the examples presented in the preceding section, we begin to see how putting experience into words presents the author with a number of insoluble problems. Language is both too rich and too poor to represent experience adequately. In the act of writing, the author is producing a complicated translation of the "text" of the world; we generate a second translation in our attempt to return to the "native tongue of reality."* But since each author translates in his own manner, with his own private language and his private set of rules, we are handicapped in the second translation—from text to reality— because we can never completely know the rules of the first— from reality to text.

The more skillful the author, the more accessible the first translation because more of his rules are made explicit. As we have seen in the example from James, he takes pains to provide the reader with the information necessary to read his text

* See Schafer (1976).

in the most appropriate way. Given this kind of controlled background, the reader is better able to make the second translation—from text to reality—and in so doing, to re-experience the author's view of the world. James provides us with an accessible text. Adams, by contrast, does not give us the appropriate context, and we can never make an adequate second translation. We might guess at his original experience, but the guesses are only approximations; his text, by definition, is relatively inaccessible. Stoppard, by playing with context, permits each of his characters, Crouch and George, to come away with essentially nonoverlapping interpretations.

But even without a formal gloss, we can still make an educated guess about many of Adams's assumptions and in so doing reconstruct some of his original perceptions. In going "behind" the text to the actual journey, in trying to reconstruct Adams's state of mind as he crossed the Channel and, the next day, crossed the Alps, in trying to picture him traveling in the full costume of the period—in all these activities, we are carrying out the second translation, the act of understanding. If we are lucky in our assumptions, in what we select as critical starting points and in what we dismiss as irrelevant side issues, we will reconstruct something that approximates the reality as experienced by Adams when he made the journey. "Where the most thorough possible interpretation occurs," writes George Steiner,

> where our sensibility appropriates its object while, in this appropriation, guarding, quickening that object's autonomous life, the process is one of "original repetition." We re-enact, in the bounds of our own secondary but momentarily heightened, educated consciousness, the creation by the artist. We retrace, both in the image of a man drawing and of one following an uncertain path, the coming into form of the poem. Ultimate connoisseurship is a kind of finite *mimesis:* through it the painting or the literary text is made new. (1967, p. 26)

If we are lucky in our explication, we may recover the original "text." But because there is no one-to-one correspondence between text and reality and because of the range of options outlined by Harding in his analysis of the act of writing, the reader can never be sure of exactly reversing the transformation produced by the author. And there is the further problem that reading is not something we do first, before we begin our interpretation; rather, we are forced to make continual interpretations simply in order to comprehend. We cannot help but read into the text our own assumptions about time, place, and intention because it is only by actively "translating" the original text into a contemporary document (see Steiner, 1975, for a more complete discussion of this idea) that we can begin to participate in the author's experience and go beyond the bare words of the passage. Because we are compelled to interpret as we read, we can make the paradoxical statement that we probably never experience the text in its raw form; the very act of reading sets in motion a translation.

TWO KINDS OF READING

It can be argued that there is a systematic interrelationship between the clarity or transparency of the text and the effort and activity required of the reader. To the extent that sufficient context has been provided, the reader can come to a well-crafted text with no expert knowledge and come away with a good approximation of what has been intended by the author. The text, as we will discuss more fully in Chapter VII, has become a public document and the reader can read it with a minimum of effort and struggle; his experience comes close to what Freud has described as the deployment of "evenly-hovering attention." He puts himself in the author's hands (some have had this experience with great novelists such as Dickens or Tolstoy) and he follows where the author leads.

The real world has vanished and the fictive world has taken its place.

Now consider the other extreme. When we come to a badly crafted text in which context and content are not happily joined, we must struggle to understand, and our sense of what the author intended probably bears little correspondence to his original intention. An out-of-date translation will give us this experience; as we read, we must bring the language up to date, and understanding comes only at the price of a fairly strenuous struggle with the text. Baldly presented content with no frame of reference can provide the same experience; we see the words but have no sense of how they are to be taken. The author who fails to provide the context has mistakenly assumed that his picture of the world is shared by all his readers and fails to realize that supplying the right frame of reference is a critical part of the task of writing.

Presented with a badly crafted text, the reader must read actively and constructively; far from placing himself in the author's hands, he must carry on a constant struggle against an opaque text. Active, constructive reading is needed for any kind of understanding to take place; to merely register the words of such a text is to comprehend next to nothing.

It would seem as if the effort made by the author bears a reciprocal relation to the effort required of the reader. A well-written text, the result of many drafts, is easily read; a hastily written text, dashed off in one sitting, is usually unreadable.

In the chapters to follow, we will show how this relationship between author and reader can be extended to the relationship between patient and analyst. We will make the claim that a truly free and spontaneous piece of association corresponds to a hasty piece of writing and can only be understood by active and constructive listening. Thus it follows that evenly hovering attention is *not* the necessary complement of free association, as Freud claimed on many occasions, and as many analysts still like to assume; on the contrary, we will argue that free association, to be understood in any depth, requires a certain kind of active and constructive listening in which the analyst is continually supplying meanings, choosing from a range of ambiguities, and, in general, imposing his own context on the material. The freer the association, furthermore, the more he must impose structure in order to understand. Since the patient is encouraged to free-associate and because one of the hallmarks of a proper analysis is a free-associating patient, it follows that a large part of the analyst's activity during an analysis takes the form of active, constructive listening.

Only where the associations are controlled can he listen with evenly hovering attention. This mode of listening is most likely to occur at times when the patient is presenting a carefully detailed and organized account in which a large part of the necessary context has been supplied; this presentation would correspond to the traditional piece of classical literature that we read with ease and enjoyment. Because he is provided with the proper mixture of structure and content, the analyst can afford to listen as Freud recommended by "not directing one's notice to anything in particular and . . . maintaining the same evenly-suspended attention . . . in the face of all that one hears" (Freud, 1912, p. 112). In more modern language, the analyst becomes aware of what Barthes has called "le plaisir du texte" (Barthes, 1973).

Thus it would seem as if the analyst can listen with evenly hovering attention only at times when the patient is *not* following the "Basic Rule" of free association. When the patient is associating with any degree of freedom, the analyst must change his stance and listen actively and constructively. Thus his mode of listening would seem to supplement the patient's mode of speaking. Instead of the symmetry assumed by Freud, we find more of a reciprocity between the stance required of the analyst and the stance assumed by the patient. If the analyst is listening constructively much of the time, what needs to be studied are the ways in which he tries to impose his own structure and meaning on the clinical material. We will take up this question in more detail in Chapter IV.

In light of all that has been said, can we ever return to the original "text" of reality? Probably not. But we can identify some of the conditions that make possible a reasonable reconstruction. First, the governing assumptions of the author must not be too different from our own; if the correspondence in values is reasonably close, we will be inclined to translate back much as he translated forward, and end up with a reasonably accurate view of his original impression. Second, given different assumptions, he must use his skill to allow us to somehow share his experience, because only then can he represent the complex mixture of impressions that we call the real world. We have seen that a bare-bones description is not sufficient to capture what we may experience at any particular time and place; unless the experiential surround is provided by the author, we are likely to project our own onto the text and end up by generating a "reality" that has nothing in common with his experience.

Language reveals, but it also conceals. We have noted the fact that we probably never experience the raw text because, in the act of reading, we are already translating. It is probably also true that once we read a passage, we will always "see" it in about the same way. Thus the original decisions made by the author in how he represents his experience and how he presents his message will have a lasting impression on our sense of this experience—for better or worse. Once our impression has formed, no amount of careful explication will change it in any important respect. Thus the author's original stylistic decisions may have a more lasting effect than his choice of content because the former will determine how we "see" the latter and how we combine it with our own experience.

CHAPTER III

• ———————————————————————————————

Putting Pictures into Words

In his landmark paper on the recovery of childhood memories, Kris compares his presentation with a "visit to a familiar scene, repeated after a lapse of time. I propose to pass over a wide and well-mapped-out area and to stop at certain points to see in what way our reaction to the scenery may have changed" (Kris, 1956a, p. 54). The striking visual imagery of this introduction is reminiscent of (and may well have been inspired by) Freud's rather similar comment midway through *The Interpretation of Dreams:*

> When, after passing through a narrow defile, we suddenly emerge upon a piece of high ground, where the path divides and the finest prospects open up on every side, we may pause for a moment and consider in which direction we shall first turn our steps. (Freud, 1900, p. 122)

Each quotation preceded a discussion of either memories or dreams, and it is probably no accident that both authors chose a visual figure of speech to prepare us for arguments about to come. Perhaps not enough attention has been paid to the fact that visual data are among the primary data of an analysis; that in their natural state they are seen *only* by the patient; and that the large part of an analysis must make do with an approximate and largely makeshift verbal translation. Because the clinical phenomena are never seen by the analyst, he is unusually vulnerable to errors of translation.

We choose to put the problem in these terms because language is characteristically helpless in the face of the challenge to express pictures in words.

> It is not that words are imperfect, or that, when confronted by the visible, they prove insuperably inadequate. Neither can be reduced to the other's terms: it is in vain that we say what we see; what we see never resides in what we say. And it is in vain that we attempt to show, by the use of images, metaphors, or similes, what we are saying; the space where they achieve their splendor is not that deployed by our eyes but that defined by the sequential elements of syntax. . . . But if one wishes to keep the relation of language to vision open, if one wishes to treat their incompatibility as a starting-point for speech instead of as an obstacle to be avoided, so as to stay as close as possible to both, then one must erase those proper names [that refer to a specific image] and preserve the infinity of the task. It is perhaps through the medium of this grey, anonymous language, always over-meticulous and repetitive because too broad, that the painting [or any image] may, little by little, release its illuminations. (Foucault, 1973, p. 9)

The very attempt to translate the image will destroy it because, first, the words, as they are chosen, will invariably misrepresent the image (see Langer, 1942; Goodman, 1968; and Barthes, 1977) and, second, because the translation, no matter how approximate, will tend to replace the original. Consider the first problem in more detail. We know that any descriptive term will place an image into a category to which it only partly belongs. Suppose the patient has an image of his mother nursing with breast bare and lights down low—but instead of seeing a blissful expression on her face, he remembers a look of revulsion and disgust. The mixture of sense impressions is uncoordinated and, in some sense, inartistic; it cannot be reduced to a single theme, and thus any description is bound to misrepresent the complete memory. Even if all parts were faithfully described, the resulting impression would probably not duplicate the original impression.

The second difficulty follows from the first. Once a particular term is chosen to describe an aspect of a memory or dream, this term will arouse its own network of associations and these, if they are sufficiently compelling, will tend to supplant the image. We will discuss this problem in more detail in subsequent chapters; it is particularly critical in psychoanalysis because the original images are never available for check and comparison, and once they are "swallowed up" by a particular description, they are probably lost forever.

Part of the difficulty in putting pictures into words stems from the fact that the memories and dreams reported by the patient belong to no particular artistic tradition. Barthes (1977) has made clear how a drawing may be better captured in language than a photograph because a drawing, by definition, was executed with a particular style and represented a particular artistic tradition whereas a photograph may be simply a random slice of reality. Patients' memories, if true, tend to resemble photographs—particularly if they are more or less faithful to the original experience. Screen memories, on the other hand, may be more like drawings or other works of art because they are, by definition, somewhat stereotyped and adjusted to conform with a particular theme or to make a certain kind of impression. It might, therefore, follow that screen memories draw attention to themselves during an analysis not only because they are more defended representations of the past but because they are simply easier to describe. We will come back to this possibility in a later section of this chapter.

We can be more specific and say that because a memory is often a literal reproduction of a piece of life, we are unable to find a convenient way of breaking it up into its natural constituents; this is what Barthes means when he says that a photograph is a continuous message and a message, furthermore, without a code. Whereas an Impressionist painting, for example, can be analyzed into its separate dots and a still life can be described according to well-known principles of design and balance—principles that were used in its construction—a photograph or a memory image is not mediated by any particular tradition and, therefore, stands alone, *sui generis*. In his attempts to describe it, the patient will search for what might be called the natural units of the image, and it could be argued that the patient gradually learns, during the course of the analysis, how to become more sensitive to the "seams" and thereby find ways of putting the visual data into words that do it the least damage. The memories themselves may not actually change. Where we speak of the recovery of childhood memories, it may be more accurate to speak of their more artful description, and we will come back to this issue in the next section.

The popular image of the freely associating patient simply saying "what comes to mind" does not agree with the dilemma we have been describing. What Barthes has called the photographic paradox—that the literal reality of the photograph is impossible to convey through language—faces the patient throughout the analysis. The impossible task of translating visual scenes into verbal descriptions is neither free nor simple, and we will see in the next chapter how much of an effort is required to bring these images into verbal life and, from the standpoint of the analyst, to translate the language back into visual terms. It is sometimes assumed that because psychoanalysis is first and foremost a "talking cure," words are the natural unit of meaning. It would be more accurate to say that words allow us to make contact with the data of experience; these are largely visual data that are accessible only to the patient. It is through language that they become accessible to the analyst. If the language is transparent, it allows us to see the world much as the patient saw it. But the language can easily add a reality of its own—both because the patient's descriptions ("associations") are approximate and incomplete, and because the analyst's interpretations tend to become polished linguistic achievements that are larger than life and, therefore, more compelling. To tell us what comes to mind, the patient must somehow put the visual data into words—and this is a much more difficult task than simply saying "what comes to mind."

TRANSLATING THE VISUAL TEXT

Consider the patient recalling the past. In the language of the last chapter, we can think of his memories as being the result of an earlier translation from reality. His experience has been transformed into a series of discrete visual images that correspond to real life in the way a manifest dream corresponds to the dream thought. It was one of Freud's signal achievements to make clear the illusory quality of memory and to show how the mechanisms of displacement and condensation apply to memory as much as they apply to dreams. Although the memory has a feeling of being closer to the real experience, it was Freud's genius to show how this sense is often illusory and how both memory and dream belong to the same group of wish-determined phenomena.

The patient takes this initial translation—from reality into image—and attempts to put it into words. More exactly, we could say that he is inadvertently presented with a visual text by several authors that he must put into words. Why inadvertent? Because in contrast to the authors described in the previous chapter, he does not fully choose his material; it is presented to him as he attempts to let his associations "come to mind" (although as we will see in the next chapter, he must make critical decisions about which parts to present and how exactly to describe them). Why several authors? Because the "text" of memories is written in collaboration with other selves (the patient when younger or the patient when angry) and in collaboration with other significant objects (family members, friends, and the like).

Since there are no precise terms by which the images can be described—the message, in Barthes's language, has no code—the patient must supply his own phrases from other lexicons. Here is one way in which the image becomes distorted; since there is no appropriate language that would represent the memory without modification, the verbalized utterance is constructed with a "make do" language. Another distortion comes, as we have seen in the preceding chapter, from the fact that full description requires both content and context; the patient presents us with approximate content and haphazard context. Not only is the language badly suited to describe the visual data but the analyst is usually given no instruction as to how to "hear" the utterance. In the absence of an "official" gloss, he must provide his own, private commentary, and we will see in the next chapter how this requirement significantly affects what he hears.

The screen memory, as we have suggested, may lend itself more readily to verbal description because it has already been modified and adjusted to emphasize certain themes and to hide others. A sort of mnemonic cartoon, it can be described as an exaggerated piece of reality in which, as in bad fiction, subtleties are erased, colors are brighter, and outlines bolder—and, indeed, Freud drew attention to the sensory vividness of the screen memory as one of its defining characteristics. True memories, by contrast, will tend to have a more complicated form, be composed of more subtle gradations of light and shade, and in general prove more resistant to being translated into words.

Throughout the analysis, the patient is confronted with the conflict between what is true but hard to describe—the pure memory—and what is describable but somewhat untrue—the screen memory or, more generally, any kind of compromise formation. What Freud called the conditions of representation that allow a memory to appear as a visual image interfere with what might be called the conditions of presentation, the basic difficulty of putting pictures into words. From this point of view, the change in a patient's productions during the course of treatment may have more to do with a change in his descriptive ability than with a change in the memories per se. What has been called the "recovery" of childhood memories may refer to the patient's new-found ability to capture a complex image in words and present it, fully fledged, in language that for the first time conveys its true complexity in a way that we can understand. Kris, in his paper on the conditions of recovery, made the observation that many times the new memory will emerge almost silently, without attracting our attention. "The patient may have mentioned the particular recollection in an aside, as something he had always remembered. When the importance of the memory has gradually become acceptable to him, he may show some disappointment which seems most marked in training analyses" (1956a, p. 78). He also refers to the situation of *déjà raconté,* in which the patient has the experience of having already reported the memory. Both of these observations would agree with the hypothesis that the memory was available from the beginning of treatment in more or less fixed form and that what changes is not the memory but the patient's ability to describe it. This formulation allows us to understand the lack of surprise referred to by Kris; there is no surprise because there is no revelation. To put it another way, the surprise belongs to the analyst because he is the one who is presented with new information; from the patient's perspective, the image has been there all along.

If the perennial conflict facing the patient is between what is true and what is describable, we can arrive at a new definition of the task of the analyst: to provide whatever conditions are necessary to allow the patient to feel safe enough to risk the impossible and to describe what he really sees. The patient, for his part, will always be tempted to forsake the true image and use whatever words are available to come up with an approximation: to present the screen memory, because it lends itself more readily to verbal description, and to present the secondary revision of his dream, because it is more easily expressed. Language is the persistent seduction—giving way to language is perhaps the central resistance.

The conflict between what is true and what is describable also affects the analyst. We have seen that the true, because of its complex visual component, can only be haltingly described; therefore, an elegant interpretation is very likely untrue. Whereas *any* interpretation, because it is language-based, runs the risk of blurring the image that the patient is trying to represent, the elegant interpretation is particularly suspect. For the analyst, the conflict is experienced as the choice between a halting attempt to get "behind" the patient's utterance and recover the original image and the much easier solution of elaborating on the utterance and leaving the image far behind. We have seen that to put a picture into words is to run the risk of never seeing it again, and this danger applies with particular force to elegant interpretations and to overly abstract formulations.

If the analyst, on the other hand, resists the temptation to replace image with language, his interpretation can often result in a clearer sense of the original experience, much as a good critic helps us see the painting in more detail. An interpretation of a dream or an early memory can be thought of as a text that "quickens" the image, to use an expression from Barthes

(1977, p. 25). The linguistic message guides the interpretation of the visual data; it selects from the multiple meanings of the image some fraction of items for emphasis and focus. To come back to the earlier formulation of a message without a code, we can say that a good interpretation supplies the code through which we can understand the original image. "The text [interpretation] helps to identify purely and simply the elements of the scene and the scene itself. . . . [It results in] an anchorage of all the possible meanings of the object by recourse to a nomenclature . . . it permits me to focus not simply my gaze but also my understanding" (Barthes, 1977, p. 39). An interpretation, we might say, provides a useful gloss on something that is, by definition, indescribable.

Barthes was referring to the way in which a caption on a newspaper photograph can alert the viewer to critical parts of the image and enable him to make sense out of what may seem disorganized or random. But it must be remembered that the images of memories and dreams are never visible and that the analyst is always working with third-order data, two steps removed from the target experience: the associations of the patient are approximations of memories which are, in turn, wishful representations of reality. If he is lucky, the analyst's interpretation will allow the patient to produce a better description of the unseen memory or dream. This goal is achieved, as we noted above, by somehow allowing the patient to "see" the image for the first time in all of its intricate complexity. Once again, we can describe the process in two ways. In the usual formulation, the conditions of the treatment allow the patient to regress and make contact with previously warded-off associations. On the other hand, we can just as easily say that the conditions of treatment allow him to feel that now, for the first time, he can take the risk of describing the indescribable, and that what makes it indescribable is not its awesomeness and readiness to arouse anxiety but, rather, its pictorial character and the fact that pictures do not change easily into words. Putting the problem in this manner is reminiscent of Schachtel's explanation for infantile amnesia (see Schachtel, 1947). He argued that early memories are forgotten because, as we get older, we no longer have the language necessary to describe them properly. By extension then, one of the achievements of a good interpretation is to somehow make available the appropriate lexicon that will permit the patient to describe his images in a way that we can see them, too.

The dilemma of the analyst stems from the fact that he can easily supply the patient with the wrong lexicon. And since he never knows what exactly is needed in the way of words because he never sees the memory or dream, he must always choose his lexicon from second-order data. Part of the wisdom in the traditional recommendation to interpret surface rather than depth may stem from the fact that preconscious material, when it appears, alerts us to the general nature of the patient's concern and permits us to provide him with a more appropriate lexicon. The premature or the inexact interpretation, on the other hand, runs the risk of supplying the patient with an irrelevant lexicon; as a result, the target image is permanently distorted by language that comes from a separate domain. Because the wrong interpretation can easily be substituted for the target image, part of the patient's past is now placed forever out of reach.

A mistaken interpretation does something even more serious. By supplying words that are irrelevant to the image in question, the analyst is conveying the message that image and word are only loosely coupled and that even an approximate description will suffice. The patient never learns how to fit word to object and never improves in his ability to capture the image in precise language because he sees only examples of language as an encumbrance.

UNRAVELING THE DREAM

Many of the difficulties in translating from image to word are expected to be solved by the method of free association. The patient is told to say "what comes to mind" on the assumption that associations will lead us back to the critical images of the past. The unit of treatment is the association; the psychoanalytic process concerns itself exclusively with what is "capable of being said," according to Ricoeur (1977, p. 836). "This restriction of language," he continues, "is first of all an inherent restriction on the analytic technique . . . facts in psychoanalysis are in no way facts of observable behavior. They are 'reports.' We know dreams only as told upon awakening; and even symptoms, although they are partially observable, enter into the field of analysis only in relation to other forces verbalized in the 'report' " (pp. 836–37).

The medium is clearly language; the "facts" must be sayable; and yet the subject of the psychoanalytic "conversation" is only approximated by words. We expect the patient, as he regresses and learns to associate more freely, to lead us ever closer to what cannot be put into words. But there are several reasons to be skeptical of this assumption. Free association in its pure form is guided by the rules of the primary process; thinking is no longer logical but heavily influenced by the mechanisms of condensation and displacement. The patient is encouraged to move freely from topic to topic, using whatever linkages come to mind: meaning, sound, sensory attribute, and the like. From primary process thinking we hope to reconstruct the patient's images. But fragmentary associations are more apt to give us fragmentary impressions. As we will see in the next section, a comprehensive verbal analysis of an image is, in fact, a highly controlled endeavor which, to be effective, must be systematic and exhausive—adjectives we would hardly apply to free association. Putting pictures into words, as we have tried to argue in this chapter, is inherently difficult (some would say impossible), and the task does not seem any easier under more regressed conditions.

What is the rationale for the model of free association? In the seventh chapter of *The Interpretation of Dreams* where Freud attempts to explain the dream process, he uses the concept of regression to describe the translation of dream thought into image. He argues that whereas, during normal waking thought, there is an unimpeded flow of thoughts into consciousness, during sleep this pathway is interrupted. The dream image results from the "effect of a resistance opposing the progress of a thought into consciousness along the normal path, and of a simultaneous attraction exercised upon the thought by the presence of memories possessing great sensory force" (1900, p. 547).

The dream, then, is the outcome of a regressive process whereby the dream thought is transformed into a visual image. How does free association give us access to these images? Freud argued that the freely associating patient is also regressed, and hypothesized that the regression brought about by the conditions of treatment is equivalent to the regression that produced the dream. Thus the patient is in a privileged position to describe and interpret the visual data of dreams— and by extension, of memories. He is in a position "to unravel what the dream work has woven" (Freud, 1901, p. 114) because the process of association is seen as taking apart in the waking state what was put together in sleep. Freud makes the symmetry even clearer in the following passage. Free association is defined as

the establishment of a psychical state which, in its distribution of psychical energy (that is, of mobile attention) bears some analogy to the state before falling asleep—and no doubt also to hypnosis. As we fall asleep, "involuntary ideas" emerge, owing to the relaxation of a certain deliberate (and no doubt also critical) activity which we allow to influence the course of our ideas while we are awake. . . . As the involuntary ideas emerge they change into visual and acoustic images. . . . In the state used for the analysis of dreams and pathological ideas, the patient purposely and deliberately abandons this activity [of pursuing a single train of thought] and employs the psychical energy thus saved (or a portion of it) in attentively following the involuntary thoughts which now emerge and which—and here the situation differs from that of falling asleep—retain the character of ideas. (Freud, 1900, p. 102)

To what extent was Freud justified in conceptualizing free association as the converse of dream formation? He speaks of the process as if it were as automatic as dream formation and seems to assume that once the patient begins to associate to his dream, provided the associations are sufficiently free, he will necessarily "unravel what the dream work has woven." But where are the threads? The dream does not appear as a pattern of pieces, waiting to be disassembled; rather, the patient must partition the dream as he sees fit, and it can be seen that the units chosen for association will depend heavily on the way he partitions the image. Choice of fragment controls the flow of association which, in turn, affects our picture of the dream. In contrast to the systematic and exhaustive analysis of a painting (to be described in the next section), the typical dream analysis is capricious and selective, significantly influenced by the way the image is first partitioned.

Not only is the partitioning apt to reveal one or more specific decisions and thus introduce an element of conscious control into what is assumed to be a largely unconscious and automatic process, but, in addition, the very fact of fragmentation does damage to the integrity of the dream. Once broken into pieces for analysis—and notice that no claim is made that the partitioning is either systematic or exhaustive—the associations that emerge are likely to subtly influence the remembered form of the dream. A good example of how this might happen is provided by the change in the way Freud reported his dream of the botanical monograph. He describes the dream in three places in *The Interpretation of Dreams*. Here are the three reports:

(1) I had written a MONOGRAPH [sic] on a certain (indistinct) species of plant. (1900, p. 165)

(2) I had written a monograph on a certain plant. The book lay before me and I was at the moment turning over a folded colored plate. Bound up in each copy there was a dried specimen of the plant, as though it had been taken from a herbarium. (p. 169)

(3) I had written a monograph on an (unspecified) genus of plants. The book lay before me and I was at the moment turning over a folded colored plate. Bound up in the copy there was a dried specimen of the plant. (p. 282)

In the first dream report (admittedly incomplete because of the requirements of the surrounding passage), the plant is indistinct; in the second, it becomes recognizable (and presumably capable of being identified); in the third, it seems distinct but no longer classifiable. In the first and third reports, there appears to be only one copy of the monograph whereas the word *each* in the second report suggests that the dream portrays more than one. In the third report, the phrase about the herbarium has been omitted.

The multiple descriptions of a single dream illustrate the general problem of putting pictures into words. The different reports may also illustrate the way in which subsequent associations can influence the memory of the original image. In Freud's first report of the dream, the nature of the plant is indistinct and no associations are given following the report; in the second report, he provides us with a full set of associations and conveys the feeling of fully understanding the dream (see Freud, 1900, pp. 169–77). The resulting clarity of understanding may have increased the clarity of memory and caused him to report the specimen as a specific plant in contrast to an indistinct species. The idea of several copies (introduced in the second report) may have been the result of his associations to that report; these included thoughts about his days as a medical student when he "succeeded in getting hold of a number of volumes of the proceedings of medical societies"; there may be significance in the theme of many volumes. The herbarium mentioned in the second report triggered a memory of failing an examination in botany, a clearly unpleasant experience; the negative associations aroused by this failure may have led to the omission of the triggering event in the third report.

Whether or not our analysis is correct, it is clear that the formal properties of the dream image changed substantially during the time that Freud was writing the dream book. It is also clear that the form of the dream report is going to influence the way in which it is partitioned; if no herbarium is mentioned, for example, we will have no associations to examination failure. And there is some evidence for assuming that the changes in the dream report were specifically influenced by the nature of the subsequent associations, or, more generally, that the specific words used to describe a scene may come to influence the memory of that scene. We will see further examples of this phenomenon in the next chapter.

What should be emphasized at this time is the fact that Freud's method of free association is not the simple converse of the process of dream formation. Rather than give us privileged access to the dream and its possible meanings, "unraveling it" into its constituent threads, the method of free association would seem to arbitrarily fragment the received image and run the risk of making it impossible to ever put it back together again. Free association would seem to facilitate the easy transition from dream fragment to verbal association; it would also seem to facilitate the easy shifting from theme to theme and from one mode of observation to another. But the very freedom of this kind of thought tends to emphasize the uncontrolled partitioning of the dream; to emphasize part instead of whole; and (because of its verbal character) to emphasize word over image. As we pointed out at the beginning of the chapter, one of the problems in putting a picture into words is the tendency for the description to replace the image. Once the patient forms a particular association to a dream fragment, it becomes somewhat more difficult to go back to that fragment at a later time and see it in purely visual terms because the association has left a particular impression. Because there is no "official version" of the dream image to which we can refer all disputes, the process of association would seem to inevitably erode the visual texture and the integrity of the original dream.

By way of contrast, we would like to present another kind of attempt to put a picture into words. The subject is a painting by Velásquez, and the analysis shows how far it is possible to be faithful to the original image. It may be the best attempt we have to create a verbal translation of a visual stimulus.

AN ANALYSIS OF A SPECIMEN PAINTING

In the first chapter of his book *The Order of Things,* the French philosopher Foucault has provided us with a detailed analysis of Velásquez's painting *The Family of Philip IV* (see Plate A). We now present a few excerpts from his analysis to give the flavor of his approach:

> The painter is standing a little back from his canvas. He is glancing at his model; perhaps he is considering whether to add some finishing touch, though it is also possible that the first stroke has not yet been made. The arm holding the brush is bent to the left, towards the palette; it is motionless, for an instant, between canvas and paints. The skilled hand is suspended in mid-air, arrested in rapt attention on the painter's gaze; and the gaze, in return, waits upon the arrested gesture. (Foucault, 1973, p. 3)

Plate A. Valásquez, *The Family of Philip IV* ("*Las Meninas*") (1656).

By standing back a little, the painter has placed himself to one side of the painting on which he is working. That is, for the spectator at present observing him he is to the right of his canvas, while the latter, the canvas, takes up the whole of the extreme left. And the canvas has its back turned to that spectator; he can see nothing of it but the reverse side, together with the huge frame on which it is stretched. The painter, on the other hand, is perfectly visible in his full height. (p. 3).

As soon as they place the spectator in the field of their gaze, the painter's eyes seize hold of him, force him to enter the picture, assign him a place at once privileged and inescapable, levy their luminous and visible tribute from him, and project it upon the inaccessible surface of the canvas within the picture. He sees his invisibility made visible to the painter and transposed into an image forever invisible to himself. (p. 5)

What is being attempted here is an exhaustive analysis of all parts of the painting which tries to stay within the painting and to use the "gray language" of observation rather than the more vivid language of association. The description can be defined as *centripetal,* preferring to stay within the visual stimulus, rather than *centrifugal,* in the manner of Freud's method, which fragments the image and follows each association wherever it leads. Foucault at one point explicitly considers and rejects the possibility of knowing *who* the picture is about because to do so would detract from the purely visual aspect of the painting, which is the object of his analysis (see Foucault, 1973, p. 10).

His description is exhaustive—and exhausting. To systematically explore the surface of the painting, the analysis must move at an extremely slow pace. But this very fact tells us something about the problem. When looking at an image, we take in much more information than we realize, and to express the multiple features of the image in serial language is to produce a text—Foucault's description—that seems infinitely more complex than the original image.

Three points stand out in Foucault's analysis. First, as already noted, he tries to discover a neutral language that stays with the painting as a visual specimen. In addition to the figures in the painting, he makes use of the arrangement of the figures with respect to periphery and center; he tries to find ways of describing the forms within the painting—a large X or a St. Andrew's cross; he pays particular attention to the use of light and shade; and in other ways shows an awareness of the painter's idiom. Second, he tries, as far as possible, to give us an exhaustive analysis of the painting. To carry out this goal, he proceeds systematically by first describing the painter, then his model, then the canvas, which both records and conceals the painter's work, and then the other figures in the scene. Third, he takes advantage of the fact that the painting is visible to the reader; this fact allows him to use language as a pointer, helping us to focus on a particular part of the painting and then letting us continue the analysis beyond the point where language can take us. The fact that the painting *must* be available is shown by a simple experiment. Try to read the Foucault description without looking at the painting and it (the description) becomes rather vague and confusing—a testimony to his claim that a visual stimulus cannot be put into words.

Freud, by contrast, does not focus on the dream as a visual specimen, and in few of his dream interpretations do we have the feeling of knowing with any certainty the specific appearance of the visual stimulus. And while he does (particularly in the Irma dream) attempt to exhaustively analyze the verbal report, he makes no particular attempt to exhaust the visual stimulus; on the contrary, we are left with the feeling that what is not described is not important. Since we never see the dream itself, this claim is hard to contest, but a moment's study of any one of Freud's dream reports will show the loose coupling between report and dream. The Botanical Monograph dream is only one example; there are many others.

What might be called the fidelity of the verbal report depends, first, on the size of the descriptive unit. The unit chosen depends, in turn, on the descriptive model. Foucault uses the model of the visual scan and writes as if he were looking at the painting as he formulates his description. "Starting from the painter's gaze, which constitutes an off-center center to the left, we perceive first of all the back of the canvas, then the paintings hung on the wall, with the mirror in their center, then the open doorway, then more pictures, of which . . . we can see no more than the edges of the frames" (Foucault, 1973, p. 11). The units are visual, and his descriptive pace tries to approximate a fairly methodical visual scan.

His refusal to associate to the details of the painting helps to facilitate this kind of analysis—and to maintain the consistency of the unit. For as soon as we adopt the associative model and use a fragment of the visual stimulus to trigger further thoughts, we are likely to change our unit once we return for the next fragment. Associations aroused by the first fragment can affect our sense of what the dream is about and thus affect our choice of the next unit.

A second factor influencing the verbal report is what might be called the visual presence of the dream. In some dream reports we are impressed by the frequent use of such expressions as "I saw . . . ," "I noticed . . . ," and other phrases having to do specifically with the act of looking. Other dreams, by contrast, seem to be collections of thoughts with no visual element. We can see that the second type of dream report is much less faithful to the details of the visual image than the first.

The patient in analysis may be told that dreams are important, but he is rarely told how they are to be described. Partly because Freud did not emphasize this methodological issue (in contrast, for example, to the way he instructed the patient to free associate), subsequent analysts have not considered the issue in any detail. As a result, we have no standard method of description, and the form of dream report chosen by the patient depends on his particular model of what a patient is supposed to say. Some choose to emphasize the visual element whereas others do not; some choose to summarize all visual details whereas others will be more selective; some are consistent in their choice of units whereas others keep changing. The variety is almost unlimited—and essentially undocumented.

Now it might be argued that it is the dream report, after all, that should receive our attention and that the dream as dreamt is of no particular psychological importance. We deal with what the patient makes of his dream. But this argument assumes that what is not reported is not significant, and we can easily see the flaws in this hypothesis; if we take the pleasure principle seriously, we would assume that details that go unreported are apt to be particularly significant. To rely on the method of free association is simply not sufficient to guarantee a report of all significant aspects of the dream.

But perhaps the most important significance of the visual

detail of the dream stems from the fact that the *formal* features of a dream prove to have important implications for the treatment. As we will see in Chapter V, it is the outward appearance of dreams, memories, and symptoms which are used as a clue to their underlying meanings. Unless a systematic effort is made to assess (and exhaust) their visual characteristics, we can hardly rely on the formal properties that emerge, much less make claims about their particular significance with respect to other kinds of visual data. The assertion that the form of a particular dream or memory *corresponds* in some significant way with some other data requires us either to produce the original visual stimulus or to demonstrate that our mode of translation is exhaustive and systematic and captures *all* essential features of the image.

We never have the former—and can only rarely claim the latter. To show why this is so, we can refer to a well-known painting by Manet, *Le Déjeuner sur l'herbe* (see Plate B, p. 152). It has been described by Rosenberg as follows:

> A realistically painted scene that consists of a completely naked woman sitting on the grass with two fully dressed young men near the remains of a picnic, while in the background another girl in a pink chemise is gracefully picking something off the ground. (Rosenberg, 1975, p. 155)

This passage would seem to be a fairly complete description of the essential features of the painting—and yet it gives us no inkling of one of its most striking features. We are referring to the formal similarity between the group of figures in the Manet painting and a group in the lower right corner of an earlier painting by Raimondi (see Plate C, p. 152). The striking similarity between the two paintings has led critics to believe that the first was inspired by the second (see Gombrich, 1972). Nevertheless, the similarity is not even mentioned by Rosenberg, presumably because it was not relevant to his purposes at the time—and yet his description seems more or less complete. The point is that we have no standards by which we can say that a given description covers all the important features of a painting, just as we have no way of knowing whether the patient, in reporting a dream or memory, has exhausted all relevant information.

But there is a further problem. The similarity we are discussing here—the fact that the two paintings in Plates B and C show the same arrangement of three figures, a resemblance so good that we assume that it did not occur by chance—cannot be established by words alone. Gombrich's book, *Symbolic Images,* is a collection of many such examples, but conviction comes *only* from looking at the plates, not from reading the text. Words can help us focus on certain features of the painting in question, but the final instant of recognition—the feeling that this arrangement of figures, for example, *must* have been inspired by a prior painting—comes *only* from inspecting the visual evidence. Words alone are simply not sufficient to establish a correspondence, and it is probably for that reason that art histories are necessarily crowded with plates. Once the formal similarity has been established, it seems possible to accept it as a given and refer to it in language, but language alone is not sufficient to establish the similarity in the first place.

This failure of language—another example of its inability to capture certain kinds of visual truths—has important implications for psychoanalysis. As we will see in Chapter V, we often use the psychoanalytic method to discover hidden commonalities of meaning by searching for similarity of form, and since we never have a copy of the experienced dream or memory, we must rely on the patient's verbal report. But the patient, as noted, has received no instruction in how to represent that image; therefore, what we hear as verbal translation can only be loosely coupled to the original image. Nevertheless, we rely heavily on these translations—and on his subsequent associations—to reconstruct an image of the dream or memory. From that (largely imaginary) image we may select a particular formal property, look for its reappearance in some other data, and draw extended conclusions from a discovery of similarity. But this discovery can hardly be conclusive; it is more likely only another example of how language muddies more than it mediates.

There is gathering evidence to show that the cognitive processing of mental images follows the same rules as the processing of visual stimuli; the kinds of visual illusions found in sensory psychology are also found in the description of images (see Finke, 1980). A dream or memory, as it is being reported and as it triggers the patient's associations, is represented as a mental image. It, therefore, follows that the rules that control the description of photographs and paintings also control the description of the dream or memory. If formal equivalence is hard to document from descriptions of paintings, it is even harder to justify from free associations, and in the large proportion of cases, the information gathered from dreams and memories is heavily—and unwittingly—influenced by the lexicon that happened to be available at the time of description and by the needs of the patient at the time he forms the utterance. As we have seen, the similarity between Manet and Raimondi was omitted from Rosenberg's description—despite its striking character—because Rosenberg had other points to make. In the same way, we might worry about what is omitted in our patients' reports, particularly because we have no way of checking them against the "original copy" and because they receive no instruction in how to proceed. We can hardly depend, despite Freud's argument to the contrary, on the pure freedom of the analytic method to recover the all-important visual dimensions of memories and dreams.

Gombrich provides us with a telling example of the danger. As part of his attempt to explore the role of expectation in perception, he asked a child to copy a landscape by Constable.

"As expected," Gombrich writes, "the child translated the picture into a simpler language of pictorial symbols. The copy is really a tidy enumeration of the principal items of the picture, particularly those which would interest a child—the cows, the trees, the swans on the lake, the fence, the house behind the lake. What has been missed, or much underrated, are the modifications which these classes of things undergo when seen from different angles or in different light. The house, therefore, is much larger than in Constable's picture and the swans are gigantic. . . . Each object has its own and proper color, the lake is dark blue, the lawn green, and such modifications as there are are due to impatience and accident rather than intention" (Gombrich, 1969, pp. 293–94).

Suppose the original painting by Constable had been a memory; suppose the child in the experiment were a patient; and suppose the memory report was the child's translation just quoted. It seems doubtful whether we would be able to recognize the original memory. In the usual psychoanalytic view, the failure may be unimportant because time is on our side; we become interested in the way the memory is presented, analyze the associations to the cows, the trees, the swans, and similar fragments, and assume that subsequent attempts to recall that scene would bring us closer to the original Constable painting (memory). But is there any reason to assume that we would know when that moment had been reached? Because the patient is not schooled in careful reporting, and because we have no heuristic by which we can tell when a scene is or is not being accurately portrayed, we are forced to take each report as it comes. The same uncertainty applies to dreams. We have no clear way of knowing whether the dreamer has left out an important section or even whether his verbal report corresponds in any significant way with the dream as dreamt. Errors of omission and commission are bound to occur, and in the end we are left with unchecked verbal translations of highly significant clinical phenomena. There is no reason to assume that associations—no matter how free—will necessarily lead us back to the original image, and it would clearly seem a mistake to assume that report and image are one and the same.

Freud was perfectly right in showing us that memory is not veridical and that valuable information is contained in the distortions. But he was too hopeful in his assumption that the analytic process would eventually remove the distortions and bring us back to the original image. The same kind of error can be seen in his conception of dreams. The reports are significant sources of revealing information but it is less clear whether the associative process will systematically return us to the original image. Nor is it clear to what extent the act of reporting a distorted version will necessarily interfere with subsequent discoveries; the very method of free report, in other words, may stand in the way of ever uncovering the basic data.

It would be equally wrong to assume that the analyst, listening to a dream report in a state of free-floating attention, is in any way privileged to reconstruct its essential visual form. He can only use what he is told, and if the patient makes no reference to significant details, the analyst can only rarely retrieve them from what he hears—and such attempts may often contribute more error than insight. We have seen how the report of a visual stimulus is determined by point of view; if the patient concentrates on content, we will not hear much in the way of form; if the patient gives us details, we can only approximate the overall Gestalt. To listen with evenly hovering attention does not give us automatic access to a complex dream which was unevenly reported, despite Freud's claim that the listening stance of the analyst is the complement (and by implication, shares many of the features) of the associative stance of the patient. The reverse would seem closer to the truth: if free association leads to inaccurate reporting, free-floating attention is equally vulnerable.

CHAPTER IV

Unwitting Interpretation

THE PATIENT'S CONTRIBUTION

In one of his early papers on technique, Freud (1913) gives his most complete statement of what has come to be called the "Basic Rule" of psychoanalysis:

> One thing more before you start. What you tell me must differ in one respect from an ordinary conversation. Ordinarily you rightly try to keep a connecting thread running through your remarks and you exclude any intrusive ideas that may occur to you and any side-issues, so as not to wander too far from the point. But in this case you must proceed differently. You will notice that as you relate things various thoughts will occur to you which you would like to put aside on the ground of certain criticisms and objections. You will be tempted to say to yourself that this or that is irrelevant here, or is quite unimportant, or nonsensical, so that there is no need to say it. You must never give in to these criticisms, but must say it in spite of them—indeed, you must say it precisely *because* you feel an aversion to doing so. Later on you will find out and learn to understand the reason for this injunc-

tion, which is really the only one you have to follow. So say whatever goes through your mind. Act as though, for instance, you were a traveler sitting next to the window of a railway carriage and describing to someone inside the carriage the changing views which you see outside. Finally, never forget that you have promised to be absolutely honest, and never leave anything out because, for some reason or other, it is unpleasant to tell it. (Freud, 1913, pp. 134–35)

Noteworthy in this wording is the visual metaphor. In assuming that the patient is merely "looking" at a changing "landscape" of thoughts, Freud underemphasized the problem—raised in Chapter III—of putting pictures into words. The task of presenting the traveling companion with a complete picture of the passing scene is far more complex—as we have seen—than Freud's metaphor would imply. Similar problems—as we have seen in Chapter II—are raised by the task of putting thoughts into words.

"To speak," argues Merleau-Ponty, "is not to put a word under each thought. . . . Language signifies when instead of copying thought it lets itself be taken apart and put together again by thought. Language bears the meaning of thoughts as a footprint signifies the movement and effort of the body" (1964, p. 44). Where Freud's metaphor makes it sound as if each thought did, indeed, have a word attached to it, Merleau-Ponty emphasizes the essential slippage between thought and language. Within this framework, to speak is to attempt to produce a construction of words that will come as close as we are able to represent the partly formed thought we are trying to experience; speech is an active task that, as Merleau-Ponty is fond of pointing out, never quite succeeds. Much more than simply reporting on what is "outside the window," speech may be necessary for the speaker to know what he thinks. "To think [and we can substitute speak] is not to possess the objects of thought; it is to use them to mark out a realm to think about which we therefore are not yet thinking about" (p. 160).

The slippage between thought and words can be partly appreciated by going back to the first sentence of *The Ambassadors* in Chapter II. The core message is not produced by simply lumping the words together, as would be the case if each word carried a piece of the final thought. Our sense of what Henry James is trying to say is informed by the sentence but actually goes beyond the mere words; we cannot break the sentence apart and point to the contribution of each word to the final thought. "All signs [words] together allude to a signification which is always in abeyance when they are considered singly" (Merleau-Ponty, p. 88). The words must be put together in a certain sequence to convey the final meaning; once that is accomplished, the words themselves take on somewhat different meanings. In much the same way, the associating patient forms his thoughts into words; he is actively constructing something that will somehow approximate what he has in mind but will never quite contain it all; and once the words are expressed, they take on a particular color from the thought. Rather than being aware of a field of words in his mind's eye, waiting to be named, it is more as if the patient is conscious of bits and pieces of experience, "written" in a variety of languages (not always in words). He must continually translate from the private language of experience into the common language of speech.

Expressed in these terms, free association is hardly free and the patient is hardly passive. The patient is probably not as diligent as the writer and usually not trying to find the exact word (an essentially impossible task and, therefore, a convenient resistance); but viewing speech in this manner puts a different interpretation on the task of the patient. It makes free association much less similar to passively reporting the passing scene and much closer to active composition; and it gives the common expression "tell me what comes to mind" an ironic twist because, from the patient's point of view, the mind is often empty of words until the patient makes an effort to find them. Silence, in this view, is therefore not a resistance but the base-line condition; to be a truthful reporter, putting a strict meaning on *truthful,* the patient might not speak at all.

But, of course, the patient does speak; he contributes the greater part of the analytic conversation. What does his speech tell us about the patient? First of all, he speaks predominantly in sentences, and right away we can sense something of how much active effort is required in free association. The sentences are usually well formed, syntactically correct, and, therefore, obeying the necessary rules of grammar. Within the sentence frame, the "Basic Rule" is in abeyance; once the sentence is under way, the sequence of words is determined by the demands of grammar and the successive words are ordered rather than free. And as the sentences accumulate, we have the impression that coherent paragraphs are being formed; sentences are not randomly arranged. We have a sense of an overriding organization at work. Is the "Basic Rule" being broken? In the strict sense, yes; sentences and paragraphs, at the very least, tell us that thoughts are not being freely spoken but contained in some kind of frame. But this is a requirement of communication, and it is clear that Freud's initial instruction to the patient implies communication as well as freedom. The patient's contribution must "differ in one respect from an ordinary conversation"—namely, in its freedom to wander—but in all other respects, it must remain the same and, therefore, adhere to the usual conversational rules of making sense and being responsive to the other person in the dialogue.

If the conversational part of the requirement becomes too relaxed, the patient will be likely to err in at least two directions. He cannot be truly free in his associations because then his sentences would disappear; and he cannot be too accurate in his choice of language because he could easily be misunderstood. The more seriously he takes his task and the more carefully he tries to find language that will truly capture his thoughts, the more likely he is to make no sense at all. The more accurately he represents his own experience, the more we will become aware of the way in which his mind differs from our own; the more faithful he is to his own individual thoughts and feelings, the more he will construct a unique representation that is so unlike our own that we are no longer able to understand it. Here another paradox intervenes: faithful and conscientious efforts to approximate his solipsistic self will cause the patient to speak in bursts of words that no one can understand and which, at first hearing, may be put down to some kind of resistance. The more faithfully he takes his task of matching his language exactly to his thoughts, the more the conversation will suffer. Thus we see that the analytic conversation can flourish only at the cost of unfaithful reporting.

We begin to see that Freud's fundamental rule is composed of two contradictory instructions. On the one hand, to join in the conversation, the patient cannot be truly introspective; on the other hand, to accurately represent his innermost thoughts, he cannot carry on a conversation. If he is truly free and veridical in his reporting, he cannot be understood; if he is understood, he is not freely reporting.

How is this paradox resolved? What seems to happen in a successful treatment is that a shared language develops over time. Words which we initially hear in their common meaning without fully understanding their sentences gradually acquire, as we hear them in different contexts with varying degrees of understanding, the sense intended by the patient. But for this to happen, both parties in the conversation must make an active effort to achieve a negotiated understanding. The patient, like the poet, must always be searching for just the right word and the analyst, using one of the conventions of analytic competence (see below), must empathically try to construe the patient's intended meaning. If the patient speaks only in a conversational mode—that is, speaks only to be understood— the right words will never appear. His attempt to be *only* understood will result in his never being understood because he does not dare risk misunderstanding. Only by risking silence or confusion on the part of the listening analyst will the patient's world emerge clearly. Here is another paradox, and it applies with particular force to the narcissistic patient. He has the most to tell us about his private world (see Schwaber, 1979) and yet the most to lose by being misunderstood.

Recalling the Past We have seen how the patient must continuously translate the private sensations of experience into the common language of speech. We can distinguish two rather different modes of reporting. One concerns recall of the distant past which comes down to us in the form of discrete and disconnected memories, primarily visual and having the appearance of isolated scenes or pictures—what Virginia Woolf (Schulkind, 1976) would call "moments of being." The second concerns recall of the present and recent past, and here the experience is not only visual but influenced by a mixture of cognitive and affective sensations as well. Recent memories usually convey a strong sense of coherence and connection between impressions. They are usually felt to be more or less continuous with the ongoing present; William James's metaphor, the stream of consciousness, applies particularly well to this mode of recall, and the patient is apt to be aware of the flowing sense of impressions. By contrast, distant memories seem disconnected, are often hard to place in a convincing sequence, and may even seem to come into consciousness unbidden, outside of the patient's control. The role of selection, then, is different in the different modes of recall. When early memories are being reported, the patient is more apt to feel at the mercy of the scene being described and may have the experience of being only a passive observer, Freud's passenger on the train. When the recent past is being reported, a greater number of impressions seem available and the role of choice and construction assumes more importance; at times, the patient may be overwhelmed by the wealth of impressions and not know where to begin; at other times, he may move quickly from one impression to the next. However, as we shall see, the patient also exerts a strong selective influence on early memories despite the strong impression that he is at the "mercy" of the material.

Freud's image of the passenger on the train seems particularly appropriate for describing the visual quality of the distant past. It does seem as if we simply let the memory come to mind and "read off" its contents from the image in our mind's eye. Something of this experience is conveyed by Virginia Woolf in describing her first memory:

> This was of red and purple flowers on a black ground—my mother's dress; and she was sitting either in a train or in an omnibus, and I was on her lap. I therefore saw the flowers she was wearing very close; and can still see purple and red and blue, I think, against the black; they must have been anemones, I suppose. (Schulkind, 1976, p. 64)

But of course the parallel between a memory and a picture is sometimes illusory, despite the strong sense of a veridical visual experience. Freud recognized the illusory aspect of early memories in one of his earliest papers, cautioned against the compelling sense of reality contained in certain early memories, and even suggested a converse hypothesis: the more intense the visual experience, the more likely that the memory was a composite of two or more events. The number of participating elements, in a direct additive fashion, would each contribute something to the final intensity of the image; thus, the more intense the color or the form of a particular detail, the greater the number of contributing factors. The psychoanalyst, on reading Virginia Woolf's memoirs, is apt to be struck by the sensory vividness of her first memory, mumble something about screen memories, and wonder what "really happened" on her mother's lap and where in her childhood experience the intense colors can be found.

A good specimen of the way in which memories can be seen as amalgams of discrete experiences can be found in Freud's initial paper on screen memories (1899). He describes a recurring memory in which he sees a piece of meadow, thickly green and strewn with yellow dandelions, which impresses him with its vivid color—and by the rather trivial nature of the scene. Why, he wonders, does he go on remembering it? In the memory, Freud (aged around three) is picking flowers with two cousins—a boy and a girl. He and the boy snatch away the girl's bouquet; she runs off in tears to some nearby women who give her a piece of bread. Freud and his cousin follow; they also get bread, and he is impressed by its delicious taste.

Subsequent reflection led him to assume, first, that the memory did not happen in exactly that way; rather, that it was selectively distorted by the influence of subsequent fantasies which were linked to the memory by virtue of commonalities in theme or place. He argues further that by remembering the scene in such vivid detail, he is protected from becoming aware of these fantasies; thus, the memory serves as a screen which wards off feelings of remorse, disappointment, lost opportunity, and the like. Two details bear particular mention. The bread, with its delicious taste, seems to stand for the sweetness of settling into a family job in the country (a "bread and butter" occupation), perhaps marrying a country girl and leading a peaceful, rustic life that would have none of the tension and discontent he was then experiencing in beginning a new practice with an unknown method. The center of the memory, taking away flowers from the girl, is thought to symbolize a sexual experience ("deflowering") with a later reincarnation of this girl, an adolescent he met some years later in the same region of the country about whom he had strong and unrequited sexual feelings and from whom he was suddenly separated. After the separation, he was accustomed to taking long walks in and around the meadow of his memory; thus the scene becomes associated with rather vivid sexual thoughts. These thoughts are later transformed into the intense sensory impressions of the screen memory, and we assume that these become substitutes for his repressed sexual feelings. We can further assume that the memory is gradually generated during the time the sexual thoughts are being repressed, and that it may be triggered at times when its referent—sexual associations—have been aroused by some ongoing event.

Attempts to get behind the screen and reconstruct its contributing *anlagen* are subject to the same criticism as attempts to "unravel" a dream, and the results are usually inconclusive. Freud was never able to provide a clear rule that would allow us to separate the "real" memory—the central, veridical core—from the subsequent distortions. (For example, when is a particular memory detail no longer vivid?) Thus we can never be sure when to stop in our attempts to deconstruct the screen. Second, the suggestions of the analyst are easily incorporated into the memory; as Loftus (1979) has shown in some detail, the way in which we talk about a memory and the kind of questions we ask of it can easily become part of the original memory. Because Loftus's research has such obvious implications for the discussion of early memories, we now present four of her studies in greater detail.

Experimental Research on Memory   In one of Loftus's experiments, a group of subjects saw a series of color slides showing people walking, talking, arguing, reading, and engaging in other ordinary activities. One slide—the critical stimulus—showed a person reading a book with a *green* cover (keep the color in mind). Next, the subject was asked a series of questions that alluded to some other color not in the slide—thus he might be asked whether the person reading the book with the *blue* cover was wearing a hat. Finally, the subjects were given a color test that covered items in the original slides. Under conditions where the suggested color (e.g., blue) was different from the true color (e.g., green), 44 percent of the subjects believed that they had seen the suggested color in the original slides. Thus the suggestion coming after the slide and after its memory had been formed, seems to have revised the memory for that slide; the new color has been incorporated in the old memory.

In a more graphic experiment, subjects were shown a film of a multiple-car accident in which one car fails to stop at a stop sign and makes a right-hand turn into the mainstream of traffic. To avoid a collision, the cars in the traffic stream stop suddenly, resulting in a five-car accident. The accident lasted for only four seconds. At the end of the film, the subjects were asked a series of ten questions; the first question was asked in two forms:

1. How fast was car A going when it ran the stop sign?
2. How fast was car A going when it turned right?

The last question asked whether the subject had actually seen a stop sign in the film. If the first question mentioned a stop sign (form 1), 53 percent of the subjects reported later that they had seen a stop sign. However, if the first question did not mention the stop sign (form 2), only 35 percent of the subjects claimed to have seen a stop sign in the film.

In a related study, students were presented with a film of an accident followed by a misleading question; the object of the study was to determine whether the content of the question would be incorporated into memory. Some subjects were asked, "How fast was the white sports car going when it passed the barn while traveling along the country road?" Other subjects were asked the same question with no reference to the barn. In fact no barn existed in the film. One week later, subjects were asked whether they had seen a barn. In the group asked the leading question, 17 percent reported seeing a barn; of the group asked the control question (leaving out the barn), only 3 percent reported seeing a barn.

One final experiment will complete our summary of this kind of evidence. In this study, Loftus showed a three-minute film of a classroom being disrupted by 8 student revolutionaries (remember the number). At the end of the film, half the subjects were asked, "Was the leader of the four demonstrators a male?"; the other half were asked, "Was the leader of the twelve demonstrators a male?" One week later all subjects were asked, in a list of other questions, "How many demonstrators did you see entering the classroom?" Subjects who had previously been asked about 4 demonstrators recalled an average of 6.4 people; subjects who had been asked about 12 demonstrators recalled an average of 8.9 people. In each case, the number recalled represented a rough average of the actual number seen in the film—8—and the suggested number—12 or 4. (Fuller descriptions of all four experiments can be found in Loftus, 1979.)

These findings—supported by a large number of studies not reported here but which are included in Loftus (1979)—extend Freud's original observations to a much larger domain. Memory is more fallible than we realize and vulnerable to a wide range of interfering stimuli. Substitute memories are perhaps much more frequent than Freud had assumed, and in fact, one might ask whether any kind of veridical memory exists. (See Loftus and Loftus, 1980, for a recent discussion of the evidence for this question.) Memory experiments of the kind reported here suggest that the distortions are not only contributed by dynamic factors but may simply occur by virtue of the similarity and contiguity of subsequent chance events. If, after I was witness to an accident, someone asks me a suggestive question about what I had just seen, there is good reason to believe that part of its contents will be incorporated into my memory. The onset of this kind of interference is partly a matter of the singularity of the critical event. A certain memory may be preserved unaltered because it happens to be particularly distinct and discrete; nothing like it ever happened again. (Consider your memory of what you were doing when you heard of the Kennedy assassination.) Other memories, perhaps because they are more commonplace, stand a greater chance of being followed by similar but slightly different happenings, which may become mixed into the original memory. What is of interest here is that the distortions can come about for a variety of reasons. Just as we cannot separate what really happened from the distorting screen, so we have no clear way of separating a distortion caused for defensive reasons—as in Freud's example—from a distortion caused by chance overlap.

If we now return to our theme of patient as translator, we can illustrate another kind of possible distortion. We have indicated how many memories are experienced as somewhat vague and nonspecific, a mixture of imprecise sensations. But to be communicated, they must be put into words, and we might ask: What influences the choice of descriptive terms? A variety of incidental factors may play a part; thus a color just noticed in the waiting room may be used to describe the vague color in a memory of a childhood book; a particular adjective used earlier in the session by the analyst may be borrowed to describe an early childhood sensation; one can think of a variety of other possibilities. The point is this: once expressed in a particular set of sentences, the memory itself has changed, and the patient will probably never again have quite the same vague, nonspecific and unspoiled impression. Thus the very act of talking about the past tends to crystallize it in specific but somewhat arbitrary language, and this language serves, in turn, to distort the early memory. More precisely, the new description *becomes* the early memory. In a very real sense, memories are being created in the course of the analysis, and to the extent that the past is always changing (and always out of reach), analysis becomes interminable.

Now, some critic might argue that this kind of influence takes place long after the memory was formed, and is quite different from experiments in which misleading information is introduced immediately after a film has been shown. But this factor—the timing of postevent information—has itself been studied, and the results are cause for concern. Misleading information introduced one week after the presentation of a series of color slides—the critical stimulus—produced more of an alteration in memory than the same information introduced immediately after the stimulus (Loftus, 1979). Following Loftus, we can conclude that allowing an event to fade in memory may make it all the more vulnerable to the influence of misleading—or irrelevant—information.

We have come a long way from the naïve illusion that recalling the past is a simple act of going back to an earlier time and place and reading off the contents of the scene that emerges. Although Freud was fond of describing the process of uncovering the past as a kind of archeology, we have little reason to believe that the memories that emerge can be trusted very far. More than we realized, the past is continuously being reconstructed in the analytic process, influenced by (a) the repressed contents of consciousness; (b) subsequent happenings that are similar in form or content; (c) the words and phrases used by the analyst in eliciting and commenting on the early memories as they emerge; and (d) the language choices made by the patient as he tries to put his experience into words. The past, always in flux, is always being created anew.

Given this view of memory, we begin to see the importance of the early months in an analysis. It is during this period that many of the patient's memories will be expressed for the first time and as we have tried to make clear, their form of expression affects their representation in memory. The specific wording used in that first account—and some of these accounts may occur as early as the first or second screening interview—will be influenced by a number of incidental factors, which, in turn, may become a kind of screen in their own right and stand between the "real event" and the patient's recall. Queries by the analyst of the order of "Was it more like green than blue?"

or "Did it remind you of fall or spring?" may have some unfortunate consequences; what is intended as a clarifying question can easily become incorporated in the revised memory. It becomes clear that impatient analysts, too eager to confirm the theory, may easily see their wish granted; under the pressure of leading questions, the memory all too easily assumes the form which they are expecting.

In the traditional view of the psychoanalytic process, time is supposed to be on the side of truth. The early memories are often hard to understand; the patient's initial sense of his life is presumed to be tentative and distorted by neurotic conflict; clarification will develop as the analytic process unfolds. Where one analysis is inconclusive, we may suggest a second; where three years is indeterminate, we may suggest four or five. Time, we think, is on our side. The first four to six months of treatment, in fact, are often called a "trial analysis" with the implication that the early period is preliminary to the real work, which begins somewhat later. But the view of memory being presented here puts a somewhat different light on this formulation. The early months of treatment are very likely critical because they may determine the past more clearly than even the past itself; and thus the surrounding factors that influence the early reports—the state of the transference, the patient's need to be understood (or the reverse), his facility with language, the pressure to clarify—may irrevocably affect the way in which the past is put into words and, as a consequence, the way it is laid down in long-term memory. The patient's early constructions become the subject matter of the analysis; as they are being formed, they tend to screen out the "real" past and prevent this aspect of the patient's life from ever being studied.

Transference and Recall   One of the background influences on the way in which the past is put into words is the patient's sense of whom he is talking to—in more theoretical terms, the state of the transference. As we know, the "person" being spoken to is always changing and the role assumed by the analyst determines, to some degree, what the patient says and how he puts it into words. If all associations were nominally free, we would expect transference not to make a difference. How does it play a part? Because the patient is speaking to a specific other, his words always carry a rhetorical message, and the limits of that message will wax and wane with the state of the transference. "This other," writes Ricoeur (1977), "can be someone who responds or who refuses to respond, someone who gratifies, or someone who threatens. He may be, above all, real or a fantasy, present or lost, a source of anguish, or the object of a successful mourning" (p. 839).

The tension between the pure freedom of free association and the social constraint of a conversation comes to a focus in the transference. If the rhetorical side of this polarity begins to prevail, the patient's report will be slanted toward the side of persuasion—he speaks in order to win some kind of response from the analyst. Under these conditions, the truth value of what he says may tend to deteriorate. Under the press of a strong transference—either positive or negative—what the patient is saying about the past must be translated into what he is demanding of the present. If he needs to be pitied, for example, he might exaggerate the misery of his childhood; if he wants to be praised for being an exceptional analytic patient, he might generate a crystal-clear memory of an infantile event. These reports have nothing much to do with the past as experienced or with other reports of the same event at different times in the analysis. Rather, they are tokens in a conversational exchange designed to win some kind of response from the analyst. As in any bargaining session, truth takes the back seat; to treat these reports as faithful accounts of some earlier time is to overemphasize the historical side of the analytic process and to underplay its conversational overtones.

Thus we see that recall of the past is a hostage to the transference. The language used to describe an early memory may be subtly influenced by the state of the transference as well as by previous attempts to describe the same referent. The pure form of the early memory is not merely the average of all acounts; it requires a kind of differential weighting of the separate reports with adjustments made for the state of the transference at each moment of reporting. Notice that the roughly veridical account may only appear at times when the transference is partially neutralized; at times, that is, when the conversational constraints are minimal relative to the associational. Note further that if the transference is not properly managed (and here Gill's position [1979] takes on particular significance), the veridical account may never appear. Careful consideration of this "worst case" condition shows why a simple average is not sufficient; if all accounts of a childhood scene are distorted by transference pressures, an attempt to extract what might be called the least common denominator will get no closer to what really happened than an amalgam of screen memories will yield the original, undistorted event.

One of the more frequent conversational needs is the need to impress the analyst by being a good patient and bringing in useful material. One way to add conviction is to introduce a new memory as a kind of linking theme between two isolated events in early childhood, and in the next section we will see how one of the early memories of the Wolf Man provided such a bridge. But, under conditions where the patient has a strong need to impress the analyst, a good fit is less evidence of confirmation than cause for doubt, and the proper interpretative stance should become, in Ricoeur's terms, an exercise of suspicion (1970, p. 32). Where the patient's need to please takes the upper hand, the narrative pressure may have the maximum distorting effect, because what could be more convincing than a memory fragment that fits the larger outlines of the case?

The situation can be reversed, with much the same effect.

If the patient's need to please is uppermost, he may be more than willing to accept a plausible construction, and the limits of plausibility may be stretched pretty far if the transference pressures are extreme. Something of this kind of situation may have been created during the Wolf Man case. Freud's extreme attempts to establish a linking reconstruction—the Grusha incident, to be discussed in the next section—may have been detected by the patient, but if his need to be a good patient was sufficiently strong, he might have raised no objection.

The state of the transference must be continuously sampled because it provides us with a reading of what might be called the context of discovery. If bargaining has achieved the upper hand and the memories are being used to win some kind of interpersonal advantage, the content of what is being recalled is much less important than its rhetorical advantage. But if the conversational demands are relatively subdued, then the content becomes more important. We can imagine a complicated interaction between the truth value of a particular memory and its superficial appearance, because the appearance may determine its strategic importance. When the truth value is high, the descriptive features of the memory may be unimpressive because we are being presented with unembellished recall; as in the *Merchant of Venice,* it is the lead casket that contains the most important message. But when the memory is being used to win some short-term advantage, it may literally glitter with possibilities, and the analyst may need all his native skepticism in order to resist it. Under these conditions, the memory becomes a bribe; the more it sparkles, the more it seems to fill a narrative niche, the more likely it is made of fool's gold. We sample the transference first to decide what to expect; then we examine the memory and either add it to our narrative account or set it aside.

We begin to see at this point some of the necessary preconditions for interpretation proper, a subject to be discussed in more detail in the next chapter. We assume, first, that not all reports are trustworthy. Next, we must decide whether content or rhetoric takes priority. We make this evaluation, first, by assessing the state of the transference and, second, by drawing up a strategic evaluation of the particular memory in that particular context. With respect to the first question, we might ask: Does a particular memory add to our understanding of the past, or does it seem to play a more important role in manipulating the present? If the former is true, an interpretation of content seems in order; if the latter case prevails, the content may be spurious and any interpretation will necessarily be inexact.

A further check on what is happening comes from an analysis of the memory itself. We noted that the lead casket probably contains the most significant message, whereas the more sparkling memory is most likely to be false. Screen memories are most likely to fall into the latter category; in fact, one of their defining characteristics is their sensory vividness. If we feel that a memory may be somewhat beguiling but not obviously a screen, we may check further to see how it is being used in the transference. If it is being used for a here-and-now conversational gambit, we may be a little more suspicious of its content.

If a memory appears in what might be called a conversational context, we can assume that it is partially distorted; we can further assume that the "true" memory may appear at some other time in a more neutral setting. It may be wiser practice, therefore, to disregard the first and wait for the second, as opposed to trying to deconstruct the first into its real and false components. We have seen the problems that appear in trying to make this separation; we can now add a further complication. If we try to analyze the screen memory in a conversational context, each new "insight" raises the suspicion that it, too, is being used for some temporary gain. In other words, we are carrying on a difficult task under the worst possible conditions; each new version of the suspicious memory will be slanted toward what is needed in the current analytic space and further distortions are likely to emerge as a result. If, on the other hand, we wait until the transference climate is more promising, we may have a clearer view of the original event with most of the screens removed.

THE ANALYST'S CONTRIBUTION

We have seen how eyewitnesses are far from objective, even when reporting recent and relatively simple events. What kind of a witness is the analyst? Highly variable, we might assume—but basically reliable. Yet consider the following incident reported by Wallerstein and Sampson (1971):

> A young therapist who regularly brought the tape recordings of his therapy hours for discussion in supervision reported on one occasion that this time he had only an incomplete record because the patient had exercised his option to ask in the middle of the session that the recording machine be turned off so that he could divulge some particularly painful material with less embarrass-ment. After full discussion of the possible dynamic reasons for this circumstance, the recording was turned on to be played up to the point of interruption. It turned out that, faced with the patient's evident reluctances in the hour, the *psychiatrist* had suggested that the patient would feel more comfortable if the recording were turned off. *He had no memory of this.* (p. 21, n.)

Mistakes of this kind are probably rare, but they raise the question of how often registration by the analyst turns into interpretation. Once this issue is raised, we begin to think twice about process notes and case presentations—the heart of the analytic literature. At stake is the problem of how the analyst listens. We have seen in Chapter II how reading is a construc-tive process and how the reader brings to the material infer-ences and suppositions. The less structured the text, the more the reader must contribute, and we can assume that the same principles must apply to listening. Even within the limits of evenly hovering attention, we still must assume that each analyst construes the words of the patient in his own particular fashion. As the patient's contribution begins to approach free association, the contributing structure of syntax and grammar begins to play less of a role and the way is open for the therapist's presuppositions to assume more and more importance.

Consider, to begin with, the problem of describing the quality of a patient's silence. Labels like *easy, angry,* and *troubled silence* all appear in the literature: how much of this labeling is in the mind of the therapist? How much, in other words, of his interpretation rests on the "true" nature of the silence and how much is projected onto it as a reflection of his own easy, angry, or troubled state? Similar kinds of attributions must go on all the time; fragmented associations from the patient are particularly vulnerable to therapist-centered distortion. And the problem is further complicated by the fact that the therapist is not listening merely with evenly hovering attention but, in addition, with a focus already sharpened by theory; material from the patient that happens to fit one or more predetermined categories becomes figure and assumes the center of attention; it probably remains in memory when other details, not anticipated by theory, fade from view. We might assume that what is figure will become, sooner or later, the focus of subsequent queries.

In a later section we will see how unwitting interpretations, operating out of awareness and at variance with Freud's rule of evenly hovering attention, form the background for the official interpretations—interpretations that form the core of the psychoanalytic process. First, however, we must look more closely at specific influences on unwitting interpretation.

Private and Public Language   When you and I have a conversation, we share the same words but not the same meanings.

One of the paradoxes of communication lies in the fact that each person's lexicon is inevitably a product of his own experience; when you say *tree,* I may think of an oak when you have in mind a willow; when you say *argument,* I may think of a tight-lipped interchange when you think of a series of screams and curses. In the most general sense, as George Steiner (1975) has observed,

> no two human beings share an identical associative context. Because such a context is made up of the totality of an individual existence, because it comprehends not only the sum of personal memory and experience but also the reservoir of the particular subconscious, it will differ from person to person. There are no facsimiles of sensibility, no twin psyches. All speech forms and notations, therefore, entail a latent or realized element of individual specificity. They are in part an idiolect. Every counter of communication carries with it a potential or externalized aspect of personal content. (p. 170)

We have seen in Chapter II how reading is an active process; some of this activity consists in adding our private associations to the specific words in the text. Consider the following passage:

> I found each wave, instead of the big, smooth glossy mountain it looks from shore, or from a vessel's deck, was for all the world like any range of hills on the dry land, full of peaks and smooth places and valleys. The coracle, left to herself, turning from side to side, threaded, so to speak, her way through these lower parts, and avoided the steep slopes and higher, toppling summits of the wave. (Stevenson, *Treasure Island,* 1911, p. 168)

As we read this passage, we begin to see the shifting surface of the sea in constant motion, moving the narrator up and down in his small boat; we begin to see the boat "threading" its way between crests, staying dry and afloat; we begin to catch some of the narrator's growing sense of accomplishment and a sense that he will manage to survive and make his passage. We begin to see all these things; but just what picture we form will depend on our experience with the sea and small boats. The more detailed our experience has been, the more likely that pieces of it will be imported into the scene Stevenson is trying to describe. But it should be clear that each piece of private information quietly transforms Stevenson's description into our interpretation.

Listening is an equally active process; registration inevitably becomes interpretation. As the analyst hears his patient describe a time he got lost in Brooklyn, he cannot help but supply images at appropriate places in the story. Mention of Flatbush Avenue might bring to mind the low skyline around Prospect Park, the broken store fronts, and the glass on the street. As the story unfolds and the patient begins to recapture his growing sense of disorientation and bewilderment, the analyst may shift to scenes where he had similar feelings; now he has left Brooklyn and is visualizing the back streets of bombed-out Frankfurt shortly after the end of World War II, wondering how to get back on the Autobahn. There is overlap, of course, but there is also great diversity; what the patient is trying to describe is being constantly reinterpreted and fleshed out with the analyst's memories. At times, the differences may become so extreme that communication breaks down and the description offered by the patient is never registered. Distortions of this kind probably form the basis of many counter-transference reactions; the analyst has stopped listening and is preoccupied with his own memories or conflicts. Unwitting interpretation has reached its peak and the patient may complain of being misunderstood. But even under more ideal conditions, when the analyst is listening empathically, it should be clear that he is still forming a continuous series of unwitting interpretations as he hears the material through the haze of his own experience.

Consider the following example. In the preceding hour, the analyst has announced that he plans to be away for a week but does not say where. Suppose the patient, referring back to this announcement, makes the statement "While you're in California, I plan to visit my sister." Suppose, further, that the analyst had intended to attend a funeral in Colorado; as a result of his own preoccupations, he mishears the patient and mistakenly assumes that he said *Colorado* instead of *California*.

This mistake has two interesting implications. First, the analyst's error, because it was never verbalized, will probably go unnoticed. Second, the mishearing might be used to generate a set of false assumptions about the transference. These assumptions might include the idea that the patient is reading the analyst's mind and the analyst may start searching for other clues to his presumed clairvoyant behavior. Mistakes of this kind can be seen to form the core of many countertransference reactions; the analyst's hopes and fears cause him to hear the material in a certain way, which can then be used to form (erroneous) constructions about the patient.

The analytic situation is particularly vulnerable to this kind of distortion because it does not use the usual conversational conventions for guarding against error. In a normal exchange, each speaker, as he takes his turn, tends to correct the more obvious errors of the speaker who has just finished. In addition, both speakers share a number of assumptions about the course the conversation will take.* Perhaps the most important of these rules for our discussion is the principle of relevance: each speaker assumes that the other will stick with the initial topic unless he explicitly flags a change. Common flags

* See Grice (1967) for a more extended discussion of the conversational rules that are shared by the speakers in normal conversation, and an analysis of how they prevent misunderstanding.

are statements such as "To change the subject . . . ," "By the way," and the like. If the relevance rule is broken, one speaker may say something like "You're getting away from the point," thereby bringing him back to the original focus.

In the analytic situation, however, the rule of relevance is deliberately relaxed. The patient, explicitly instructed to say whatever comes to mind, is allowed to leave the "subject" whenever he likes. Digressions are permitted because we assume that they only appear to be changing the subject. But as a result of the relaxation of the normal conversational constraints, it becomes possible for divergent understandings to develop unchecked.

There is a further problem which stems from the unusual form of the analytic conversation. The patient speaks ad lib; the analyst replies only when he chooses. Many of the patient's remarks meet with no response; when the analyst does speak, he will probably respond only to a partial number of the patient's statements. Because only some of his utterances receive a reply and because the replies are often delayed, the patient is in a poor position to check on their adequacy or truth value, and many unwitting errors may go unchecked. Take the example just mentioned. If the analyst mishears the patient say *Colorado* and begins to build up an image of the patient as mind reader and clairvoyant and silently gathers other evidence to support this hypothesis, the consequences of this mistake may not be revealed for several sessions. If and when they finally culminate in an interpretation, the patient will have no way of knowing that it was initiated by the mishearing of *California*. And to the extent that there is some minimal support for this construction in the form of other evidence, its apparent truthfulness will further reduce the chances of reacting to the original mistake. As we will see in Chapter V, chance overlap is much more the rule than is commonly supposed; approximate similarities in content are relatively easy to find because of the richness of the material. Given this state of affairs, almost anything the analyst says can be justified by a careful selection and combination of past utterances, and the chance of spotting a clear mistake is correspondingly reduced.

We are not arguing that the analyst is deliberately misconstruing the evidence; the problem is both more subtle and, paradoxically, more serious. It starts from the fact that the analytic situation is inadvertently designed to increase the chances of this kind of misunderstanding. Because he is freely associating, the patient is more than likely to use incomplete sentences, to make ambiguous references, and from time to time, let his voice drop to a level where his words are muffled. Mishearing is furthered by the fact that he is facing away from the analyst with his lips out of sight; lip reading is, therefore, out of the question. Body language, often used to supplement an utterance and clarify its ambiguity, is somewhat restricted and partially concealed. Finally, the analyst is reluctant to query each ambiguous utterance because he does not want to interfere more than necessary with the ongoing regression; constant interruptions would only make the patient more aware of what he is saying and place unnecessary reality constraints on his associations.

As a result of this combination of circumstances, the analyst is exposed to a fairly large proportion of ambiguous statements. But because of the active nature of listening, he does not let them remain ambiguous but must necessarily "disambiguate" each incomplete sentence or unclear reference and supply tentative constructions to each. As the material accumulates, he may lose track of which constructions came from the patient and which he supplied by way of a temporary gloss. And because the temporary constructions grow out of his own associations (as in the example cited above, mistaking *Colorado* for *California*), the analyst's own hopes and fears gradually infiltrate the patient's associations.

The full extent of this problem has never been documented—nor can it be eliminated. As we have seen, forming temporary constructions of this kind is a necessary part of active listening; if an incomplete sentence or muffled word is allowed to remain unaltered, it probably goes unheard. Some kind of internal glossing is a requirement for involved listening, but we have no clear awareness of its extent. Part of our ignorance stems from the fact that, although we have recorded sessions, we have no way of matching the transcript with how it is being heard. Since only a part of the patient's utterances result in a response, we have no systematic method of deciding from the transcript which of the ambiguities result in clearly mistaken constructions. It seems more than likely, however, that a substantial portion of the mishearings are silently absorbed into the analyst's slowly accumulating picture of the patient's character, forming a background against which subsequent statements are interpreted.

We will never have an accurate estimate of this kind of mishearing until analysts are trained to systematically unpack each transcript as soon as possible after the hour takes place. The analyst must be trained to give the background for each utterance and, more generally, to show how his own preoccupations influenced his "hearing" of each of the patient's utterances. We will discuss in a later chapter the ways in which this kind of unpacking can be used to naturalize the transcript and make it available to other analysts who are less familiar with the material. Here we are pointing to a second benefit— namely, that systematic unpacking will allow us to make a clear estimate of the amount of inadvertent misunderstanding and how, in turn, this misunderstanding leads to false constructions and what Glover (1931) might call "inexact" interpretations.

Freud was aware of the distortion introduced by premature formulation and in one of his early papers on technique he advised the beginning analyst to make no predictions about the outcome of a case but rather to allow himself to be surprised, as it were, by each new turn of events. He also warned against taking notes during the hour; such mnemonics are unnecessary, he claimed, because the important details would not be forgotten. All the analyst must do, he stated in a famous passage (1912), is to listen by

> not directing one's notice to anything in particular and in main-
> taining the same evenly-suspended attention . . . in the face of
> all that one hears. . . . It will be seen that the rule of giving equal
> notice to everything is the necessary counterpart of the demand
> made on the patient that he should communicate everything that
> occurs to him without criticism or selection. If the doctor behaves
> otherwise, he is throwing away most of the advantage which
> results from the patient's obeying the "fundamental rule of psy-
> choanalysis." (p. 111)

Under certain circumstances, passive listening seems to be the appropriate and necessary response to the patient's mate-rial, and somewhat later in this chapter we will discuss the kinds of material that seem to call for this kind of listening. But Freud seems to have overestimated the usefulness or the suitability of the passive stance. For a number of reasons, a much more active stance is always being forced on the analyst and brings, in its wake, a number of important consequences. We now proceed to identify some specific reasons why active listening is an essential element in the analytic conversation.

Search after Meaning   This has become the analyst's stock in trade. He prides himself on bringing meaning out of chaos; he often feels uncomfortable with persisting ambiguity and finds it difficult to admit to himself that there may be no unifying theme, no simple solution to increasingly complex material. Almost one hundred years of detectivelike search-and-discovery case histories have laid down the implicit rule that there is *always* an underlying thread; that it must emerge sooner or later; and that if the analyst does not find it, someone else will.

The persistent search after meaning tends to subvert the modal stance of free-floating attention and leads to premature structuring of loosely coupled associations. It can also lead directly to incomplete and ill-advised ("inexact") interpretations, which may produce additional resistance and interfere with the analytic process. The search after meaning is especially insidious because it always succeeds. There are essentially two reasons for this: first, the search space can be infinitely expanded until the answer is discovered and, second, there is no possibility of finding a negative solution, of deciding that the search has failed. For example, if the analyst is preoccupied with the fact that he will be going on vacation in two weeks, he can almost surely find some "confirmation" of this possibility in some part of the patient's productions during this two-week period. If, for whatever reason, he fails to find positive confirmation, he can point to the *absence* of evidence as a kind of negative confirmation; if the patient seems reluctant to admit this as evidence, he can point to this *reluctance* as confirmation. Thus the search will always succeed. What Popper (1959) calls falsifiability seems out of the question. It would be difficult, if not impossible, to think of an association that would indicate that the search had failed and that the forthcoming vacation did *not* produce some kind of response in the patient.

Let us carry the example one step further. If the analyst is committed to discovering a response to his vacation, he will be listening with quite a different stance than if he had no preconceptions; he will be screening the material by asking, does it or does it not support this interest, rather than allow it to form new themes or new combinations. If a theme fails to confirm his expectation, it will probably register with much less significance; in extreme cases, it probably will not register at all.

Psychoanalytic Competence The search for connections is part of a larger sensitivity that we will describe here as psychoanalytic competence. This competence grows out of training and experience; it alerts the analyst to specific implications, leads him to form certain expectations, and generally defines the important units of meaning in the material. To understand how psychoanalytic competence bears on clinical listening, consider the way in which literary competence bears on literary appreciation. "To read a text as literature," Culler (1975) has argued,

> is not a make one's mind a *tabula rasa* and approach it without preconceptions; one must bring to it an implicit understanding of the operations of literary discourse which tells one what to look for. Anyone lacking this knowledge, anyone wholly unacquainted with literature and unfamiliar with the conventions by which fictions are read would, for example, be quite baffled if presented with a poem. His knowledge of the language would enable him to understand phrases and sentences, but he would not know, quite literally, what to *make* of this strange concatenation of phrases. He would be unable to read it *as* literature . . . because he lacks the complex "literary competence" which enables others to proceed. He has not internalized the "grammar" of literature which would permit him to convert linguistic sequences into literary structures and meanings. (p. 113)

Psychoanalytic competence has its own set of conventions, formed by clinical training and experience, didactic analysis, and self-analysis. These are conventions that we routinely apply to utterances from the patient in order to go beyond the bare words of the statement and reach an understanding of the manifest content, and which we apply to manifest content in our search for latent content. We will now discuss the most important of these conventions.

First, we have the convention of thematic unity, which leads us to look for commonality among the separate details of an hour, a dream, or a set of fragmented associations. What seems isolated, we tend to unify; what seems unrelated, we try to bring together. If the patient presented three dreams during the hour, we would look for a single underlying theme; if he seemed to change the subject during the hour, we assume that the same theme is being continued. So powerful is this expectation that the analyst may often overlook subtle changes in subject or theme. Because he is trained to supply the missing links in a progression of ideas, the analyst is sometimes ill prepared to evaluate a case presentation; without realizing it, he may overlook critical gaps in the evidence and unwittingly supply his own explanations. If he is too much under the influence of this convention, the analyst may blur critical differences in form or content and make what we will call *soft* pattern matches; as a result, the patient's message may be seriously distorted. We will discuss some of these soft matches in more detail in the next chapter.

Second, we have the convention of therapeutic urgency. It assumes that critical and significant meanings are always being discussed, whatever their external form. Listening with this convention in mind enables the analyst to spot the more obvious kinds of resistance because it leads him to ask why, for example, is he (the analyst) feeling bored or distracted? The assumption of urgency lies behind Freud's recommendation that the analyst listen with "evenly-hovering attention"; if we assume that all material is significant, then it follows that we will listen to everything in the same careful way. If all material is equally significant, the analyst will be more likely to sample the different modes of the message; if the content seems trivial, he may focus attention on context ("Why is he telling me this story at this time?") or on tone ("Why is his voice heavy and halting?") in an effort to discover the underlying significance. This convention promotes a certain flexibility in the analyst's style of listening, prompting him to shift from form to content or from content to form as seems necessary.

Third, we have the convention of multiple meanings, or more precisely, the principle of multiple function. We assume that any single item can have more than one meaning; we assume, with Waelder, that "each psychic act has a multiple function and therefore a multiple meaning" (1936, p. 52). More broadly, any piece of behavior can be understood from a variety of perspectives: at times, the defensive aspect of a symptom may be most apparent while at other times, its drive demands may be uppermost. Listening with this principle in mind, the analyst can identify the faint glimmer of an unconscious impulse in an apparently staid utterance; because he believes that the drives are everywhere present, he can more easily identify continuity and transition. The convention of multiple function allows him to practice the convention of thematic unity.

Fourth comes the convention of transference. This rule leads us to listen to every utterance on at least two levels—as a statement about the manifest referent and as a statement about the doctor-patient relationship. Gill (1979) has proposed that this convention applies to almost every utterance, that a transference meaning can always be detected in every statement made by the patient. Others would take a somewhat more modified stance, perhaps being on the lookout for transference implications but not expecting to find them in the majority of cases. For the moment, we can agree that the transference convention is one of the basic underpinnings of psychoanalytic competence; it leads us to look for the influence of the doctor-patient context on all patient utterances; and it frequently contributes to our search for significance (convention 2) or multiple function (convention 3). It may be the most important of all the conventions with respect to technique because it alerts us to statements that require a response and helps us make decisions with respect to timing and overall strategy.

Fifth and last, we have the convention of empathic listening. A useful introduction to this particular stance can be found in a discussion of the problem of understanding by the philosopher, Merleau-Ponty:

> We begin reading a philosopher by giving the words he makes use of their "common" meaning; and little by little, through what is first an imperceptible reversal, his speech comes to dominate his language, and it is his use of words which ends up assigning them a new and characteristic signification. (1964, p. 91)

Empathic listening takes the same form. As we listen to the patient and become accustomed to his manner of speaking, we learn to hear his store of private meanings reflected in the words he uses. We listen on at least three levels—to the sense of his message, to the words he is using (and misusing), and to the gradually accumulating private meanings that become clear as his "speech comes to dominate his language." Listening in this manner is similar to making a close reading of a poem; it attempts to get "behind" the surface structure of the sentence and to identify with the patient as he is expressing the thought. We must go beyond the words of the sentence because language, by definition, is incomplete. Again, Merleau-Ponty:

> The spoken word . . . is pregnant with a meaning which can be read in the very texture of the linguistic gesture . . . and yet is never contained in that gesture, every expression always appearing to me as a trace, no idea being given to me except in transparency, and every attempt to close our hand on the thought which dwells in the spoken word leaving only a bit of verbal material in our fingers. (1964, p. 89)

Listening in this manner, we try to imagine how the patient is experiencing the world; we then are in a better position to understand his choice of words and to respond to their particular shades and colors. Schwaber (1979) gives the example of a very nearsighted patient who chooses not to wear glasses; knowing this about her experience, we are better able to appreciate her descriptions of specific scenes in her daily life; the words in her account are given an added dimension by the fact (probably not stated) that the images are blurred and the forms indistinct. An occasional sharp detail in her reporting becomes all the more significant against this general myopic background. As we become sensitized to her visual problem, we may become attuned to specific words referring to the act of seeing; even when used in metaphors or dreams they probably take on additional significance because of her myopia.

Notice the parallel with Chapter II: in trying to get "behind" the myopic patient's language and understand the full significance of her words, we are performing exactly the same operation we applied to Henry Adams in our attempt to understand the fragment from his autobiography. Knowing something about the conditions of the times, we can put ourselves in "his shoes" and better appreciate his feelings about his sister's death from tetanus, just as we can better understand our myopic patient by thinking our way into her blurred and out-of-focus world. If carried out successfully, the empathic convention allows us to perform a silent translation of the patient's language as he is speaking so that we use his dictionary rather than ours, supply his references rather than our own, and, in general, come a little closer to seeing his world as it looked in the split second before it was transformed (and distorted) into language.

Evenly Hovering Attention   By this time it should be clear that listening in a perfectly balanced manner is a near impossibility. Freud's ideal stance is constantly being beset by a variety of constraining influences. Again and again we are reminded of the fact that listening is an active, not a passive process; that we are constructing meanings and images all the

time we are registering the patient's words; and the more fragmented the utterances, the more actively the therapist tries to
give them form and meaning. To this basic requirement of all
listening, the analyst brings the specific conventions implied
by analytic competence that provide additional form and
meaning to what is being registered. (Schwaber, 1979, makes
a special point of the active nature of empathic listening.)

Passive, evenly-hovering listening, as we argued in Chapter
II, may come into its own at those times in the analysis when
the patient is presenting us with a completely finished, well-
crafted "text." When this kind of material is emerging, the
analyst is then in a position to adopt a fairly passive stance and
allow a construction gradually to take shape that parallels our
response to a piece of literature. Consider the following passage from Faulkner:

> It was a summer of wisteria. The twilight was full of it and of the
> smell of his father's cigar as they sat on the front gallery after
> supper until it would be time for Quentin to start, while in the
> deep shaggy lawn below the veranda the fireflies blew and drifted
> in soft random—the odor, the scent, which five months later Mr.
> Compson's letter would carry up from Mississippi and over the
> long iron New England snow and into Quentin's sitting room at
> Harvard. (*Absalom, Absalom!*, p. 31; quoted in G. L. Dillon, 1978,
> p. 130)

The incomplete clauses in this passage, the ambiguous references, the attempt to create a mood rather than specify a
particular happening—all these aspects can be best appreciated by a passive stance, which allows the details to gradually
cohere in some large, unspecified image that takes shape over
time. Notice that the composite image is not organized by the
sentence structure of the passage but, rather, is allowed to
happen in the reader's mind and to be influenced, we would
suspect, by each reader's private associations.

We need to emphasize the assumption that passive, free-floating listening can take place *only* when the stimulus is a fully controlled piece of exposition. The usual kind of fragmentary utterances provided by patients may require, as we have seen, a more active style of listening because we must supply our own constructions to counteract the ambiguity. Thus we have a paradox: truly "free" associations may require active, constructive listening whereas the more controlled, literary, carefully crafted narrative requires only free-floating attention. Evenly hovering attention is apparently *not* the complement of free association, Freud's model notwithstanding. Instead, it would seem as if freedom and control are negatively associated. We are faced with a critical asymmetry between style of talking and style of listening.

Because the bulk of the patient's utterances are loosely integrated, the exercise of passive, evenly hovering attention seems to be the exception rather than the rule. During occasional, overcontrolled sections of the hour, the analyst may be able to carry out Freud's recommendation and listen without prejudice and without selection to all utterances. But in response to most utterances, some kind of internal picture will begin to form in the analyst's mind which only partly corresponds to what is being said, and once this happens, the listener has shifted from registration to interpretation. Perhaps a name is mentioned—one of the patient's friends; some kind of image will very likely come to mind. Perhaps the patient mentions a movie; if the analyst has seen it too, it has already acquired a cluster of private associations that are now aroused and help to color what the patient is saying. This gradually emerging, unwitting interpretation is necessarily different from what is in the patient's mind as he is describing the movie; and even if the analyst has never seen the movie, his picture of what the patient is telling is necessarily colored by his own associations. As his elaboration becomes more fully developed, it takes on its own organization with figure and ground which are necessarily different from the figure and ground assumed by the patient.

One of Alfred Hitchcock's favorite devices for creating suspense was to use the literary convention of dramatic irony and give the viewer more information than he provided the characters in the film; thus he might make it clear in some earlier sequence that the man riding in the train compartment was inadvertently carrying a bomb in his suitcase. Hitchcock counted on the fact that this information was necessarily projected onto the scene, coloring even the more innocent references with a kind of tragic ambiguity. Suppose the porter comes by and offers to take the suitcase up to the front of the car as they are coming into the station; the audience breathes a sigh of relief. But suppose the owner, concerned about its safety, decides to keep the suitcase and carry it off himself; the relief is replaced by foreboding. Suppose the train pulls into a siding to let another train go by; the audience, knowing about the bomb, automatically invests this delay with horror.

In much the same way, the analyst listens to his patient. There may be no bomb in the suitcase but the analyst cannot fail to form his own reactions to each of the patient's utterances. Some of these responses may organize themselves into explicit hypotheses, and we will see in the next chapter how unwitting interpretation develops into official interpretation. But before that stage is reached, the unwitting interpretations are continually influencing how the analyst listens and casting a kind of private tint over all the patient's responses.

There is a paradox here that deserves to be noted. Sensitive, empathic listening can probably take place *only* if the words spoken by one speaker are invested with private meanings by the other. Unless some kind of internal elaboration takes place, the listener hears only words—we can imagine our response to a long monologue in a completely foreign tongue—and communication fails. To listen with understanding and involvement requires the listener to be constantly forming hypotheses about the next word, the next sentence, the reference for a recent pronoun, or the color of the bride's eyes, because it is only in the midst of this kind of activity that words take on some kind of meaning. We might even argue that to carry out Freud's recommendation to the letter is to run the risk of losing the meaning and hearing only the words.

The Wolf Man Reconstruction   A good example of the perils of active listening can be found in one section of the well-known Wolf Man case (Freud, 1918; I am indebted to a paper by Jacobsen and Steele [1979] for alerting me to this incident). In an effort to make sense out of a particular sequence of clinical events, Freud supplied the hypothesis that something more had happened than was contained in the patient's memory. This reconstruction quickly became absorbed into the memory itself; what began as an hypothesis about the past became part of the past. This example points up one of the consequences of active listening; it not only affects our understanding of the patient's associations *as they are being formed,* but also affects the way they are *laid down in memory* (in keeping with the implications of Loftus's memory studies) and thus the way in which they are accessed during subsequent sessions.

At one point in the Wolf Man analysis, the patient remembers

> a scene, incomplete, but, so far as it was preserved, definite. Grusha [a maid] was kneeling on the floor, and beside her a pail and a short broom made of a bundle of twigs; he was also there, and she was teasing him or scolding him. (Freud, 1918, p. 91)

Freud goes on to describe how the patient, at some other time, had told of his interest in the John Huss legend and how impressed he had been by the story that he was burned at the stake. He makes the connection between the bundles of fire-wood needed for the execution and the bundle of twigs in the maid's room. Freud adds the assertion that Huss is frequently the "hero" of sufferers from enuresis, and uses this assertion to generate the following reconstruction:

> This material fitted together spontaneously and served to fill in the gaps in the patient's memory of the scene with Grusha. When he saw the girl scrubbing the floor, he had micturated in the room and she had rejoined, no doubt jokingly, with a threat of castration. (p. 92)

Freud rather quickly loses sight of the tentative nature of this reconstruction. Two paragraphs later, we find this analysis:

> When he saw the girl on the floor engaged in scrubbing it, and kneeling down, with her buttocks projecting and her back horizontal, he was faced once again with the posture which his mother had assumed in the copulation scene. She became his mother to him; he was seized with sexual excitement owing to the activation of this picture; and, like his father (whose action he can only have regarded at the time as micturition), he behaved in a masculine way toward her. *His micturition on the floor* was in reality an attempt at a seduction, and the girl replied to it with a threat of castration, just as though she had understood what he meant. (p. 92, my italics)

The micturition has now become a valid piece of the memory, on a par with the image of Grusha scrubbing the floor; and her tease or scold has been turned into a castration threat. From its original incomplete status, as reported by the patient, the memory has been transformed into a specific event. The new memory is now accepted as fact—consider the following quotation four pages later:

The question now arises whether we are justified in regarding the fact [sic] that the boy micturated, while he stood looking at the girl on her knees scrubbing the floor, as a proof of sexual excitement on his part. . . . Or are we to conclude that the situation as regards Grusha was entirely innocent, that the *child's emptying his bladder* [my italics] was purely accidental . . .? (p. 96)

Supposition has become assertion; the tentative status of the micturition construction has become a conviction and background for a new speculation—whether or not the patient had been sexually aroused. But in truth, the idea that the boy had urinated is no more a fact on page 96 than it was earlier on page 92; no confirming material has intervened to change its truth value. Instead, what seems to have happened is that, as Freud's argument developed, the evidential need for such a fact became stronger and micturition was incorporated into his recall of the patient's memory, much as the early memories of his patients were retrospectively distorted by ongoing concerns. By page 107, the revised memory has been fully established as a part of the record, and Freud summarizes the scene with Grusha as representing an "identification with his father, and urethal erotism representing masculinity" (p. 107). In a subsequent footnote we find the following extraordinary disclaimer:

The Grusha scene was, as I have said, a spontaneous product of the patient's memory, and *no construction or stimulation by the physician played* any part in evoking it [my italics]. The gaps in it were filled up by the analysis in a fashion which must be regarded as unexceptionable, if any value at all is attached to the analytic method of work. (p. 112, n.)

In fact, the original memory was insufficient; only by adding the details of micturition and castration threat could it be satisfactorily incorporated into a narrative explanation that would link the presumed primal scene with the nightmare of the wolves, a dream that marked the onset of the patient's phobia. Freud's memory of the patient's memory has been selectively distorted outside of awareness, and we can assume that the clarifying nature of this distortion—the way in which it helps to round out a dynamic explanation of the case—would tend to add to his sense of conviction. It must be true—therefore, it is true. The more skeptical analyst might take the opposite position: if it must be true, then some kind of selective remembering must be at work.

The Wolf Man history presents us with a chain of constructions: (1) the patient's memory of the Grusha incident, set forth in language which may have been influenced by the ongoing analytic process, but of which we have no record; (2) Freud's "reading" of this account, influenced in part by his theoretical assumptions; and (3) Freud's subsequent reconstruction of this reading at the time he wrote up the case history, influenced in part by the theme of his exposition. We have no record of the original event (meeting Grusha when the patient was two and a half), and a careful reading of the case shows how the third reconstruction was gradually substituted for this original record so that by the end of the history Freud is talking confidently about a little boy who has urinated and been threatened with castration. But this is not a fact, as Jacobsen and Steele (1979) make clear; it is more accurately a third-generation gloss on the original memory, which is forever out of reach.

Memory is fragile because we only know about it through language. We sometimes lose sight of the fact that our patients' reports are colored by the words they use to report them; and further, as we will see in the next section, by our attempts to understand them. Ambiguous reports are quickly cast into the form we would like to hear, and in the bulk of the examples reported in the clinical literature, we have no way of knowing just how the memory was first expressed. In the case of the Wolf Man, we are at the mercy of Freud's constructions;

because they seem plausible and because it is always tempting to substitute a known quality for an unknown ambiguity, we are easily persuaded to substitute reconstruction for fact.

In the course of a long analysis, each attempt at recalling the past sets in motion a chain of updated memories; they all refer to the same referent but their form is gradually and unwittingly changing as a result of ongoing language choices. Because there is no memory on record, no museum copy to refer to when in doubt, the subsequent rememberings are all the more likely to undergo gradual and subtle changes in wording and emphasis. What was introduced as tentative may become definite (as in the Grusha incident); what was introduced in passing, as in the use of a color from the waiting room, may become a specific part of the scene and generate specific associations. As the elaborated memory is traded back and forth over the course of several hundred hours, it can easily become something quite different from the patient's initial report. Some attempts at a revision of the past are a specific part of analytic technique—an effort to construct something specific from something vague. But these deliberate efforts after meaning must be distinguished from the gradual erosion of memory over time. This kind of change is not deliberate, would probably surprise both analyst and patient in its extent, and plays an important part in the shaping of the treatment. For example, a series of unwitting changes in the language used to describe a crucial early memory may change an elephant into a giraffe; accepted as the original memory, the giraffe then becomes the subject of an official interpretation, much as the revised memory of Grusha became part of the official record of the Wolf Man.

Occasionally, the change is noticed—but the explanation for the change may be incorrect. As an early memory becomes more distinct, the analyst may see the alteration as the logical consequence of a piece of analytic work and congratulate himself on his ability to bring about change. What he may not realize is that changes in the patient's report have been subtly prefigured by alterations in the analyst's description, alterations which were brought into play by the fact that he had a particular image of the early memory which went beyond the patient's description and influenced his account. We have seen how listening is an active process in which meaning is constantly being introduced into the material in order to make sense out of it. The same interpolated meanings can also affect the analyst's memory of a particular event. Each time the memory is discussed, it may be subtly influenced by these background meanings. We have no verbatim transcripts of Freud's sessions with the Wolf Man, but we can be reasonably sure that as his conception of the Grusha incident gradually changed over time, his manner of presenting the memory—emphasis and wording—also changed; very likely the patient responded with changes of his own.

But, of course, more than wording is involved. Changes in the description of a memory directly affect the visual image of the scene, and, as Loftus (1979) has shown, incidental changes in language may have a significant effect on the memory image. Here, again, there is no check, no family snapshot clipped in the patient's folder that can be retrieved from time to time to correct our recollections; both the memory and its description are always in flux, and change in one interacts with change in the other. Here again, a subtle distorting process is at work; as the patient hears a new description of an old event, he is probably not aware of the ways in which his image of the scene automatically adapts to minor changes in wording; as the new image becomes crystallized and he attempts to put it into words at some later time, he is probably unaware of the slippage between visual image and verbal description—a slippage that paves the way for the next round of alterations.

Once the process of accommodation is set in motion, it is very hard to reverse. Sherwood (1969) has gone to some length to emphasize the importance of narrative explanation in psychoanalysis, and, indeed, one of the analyst's tasks is to turn the patient's life into a meaningful story. The larger themes of this narrative account impose a certain kind of hermeneutic pressure on the isolated events of the patient's life; once they have been elaborated or otherwise adjusted to fit the larger frame, it is almost impossible to go back to their original innocent, unformed state. A good fit of memory with narrative is often applauded but perhaps for the wrong reasons; it may not suggest a successful recovery of an infantile experience but, rather, a gradual (and unwitting) distortion in line with expectations. But a good fit for the wrong reasons effectively precludes a bad fit for the right reasons; once a smooth narrative has been provided to the patient, it becomes very difficult to disrupt the sequence in order to introduce one or more disconcerting details.

What we are suggesting is that the successive accounts of a patient's early experiences often undergo a kind of progressive distortion apart from the work of deliberate reconstruction. Accommodations of memory to the unfolding narrative of the patient's life will take place automatically, given sufficient time; they are evidence more of a general preference for closure and good fit than for the effectiveness of the technique or the usefulness of the theory. At times, of course, the fit may be genuine, but just as we have no clear way of decomposing a screen memory into its real and illusory components, so we have no way of determining which newly recalled memory is truly a report of the past and which is the consequence of ongoing narrative pressure.

But wait, says the critic. Don't we assume that psychic reality has privileged status? Don't we assume that whether or not something "really" happened is partly irrelevant to the analytic work? The argument doesn't hold because of the critical difference between a deliberate reconstruction—which may or may not be true—and an unwitting distortion, brought about by the narrative pressure and unintended by either patient or analyst. The first may lead to insight; the second probably makes for mischief.

UNWITTING INTERPRETATION AND CHOICE OF GENRE

We have seen how the patient, always speaking to another, is always under the obligation to make sense. The demand may be projected onto the analyst so that his silence is understood to be imposing this requirement, or it may actually appear in specific attempts by the patient to select, organize, or otherwise clarify the material. Either way, the freedom implied by free association is always being inhibited by the interpersonal character of the analytic space. Our protocols might be quite different if the patients were alone, and it is worth noting that few analytic protocols have the freedom of some experimental studies of subjects speaking under conditions of sensory deprivation (see Kammerman, 1977).

The demand to make sense can be understood as the conversational requirement of the analytic situation, and we have shown in some detail how it can influence the form and content of the protocol. This requirement is constantly interfering with the pure freedom of free association. But, as we have shown, it is much more than simply the natural consequence of a social situation. Only rarely do we find a patient speaking to the analyst in a two-person dialogue; rather, the patient is speaking with multiple voices to a variety of loosely defined "others," and the conditions of the conversation—who is speaking to whom and for what reason—become critical determinants of what is being said. The parties, always shifting, are rarely labeled; the analyst (and eventually the patient) must deduce, from the form and content of the utterance, who is being addressed, and he must make this deduction quickly, before a new "speaker" appears and all clues have vanished.

The identity of the "speaker" and his demands always seem to take precedence over what is being said. Whereas in the usual conversation we take the speakers for granted and focus on the content, in the analytic situation we are often more concerned to know "*who*" is "speaking" and for what reason. The shifting emphasis from "what" to "who" and "why" can be seen as the logical outcome of Freud's early discovery that not all patients' memories were to be trusted. His gradually appearing skepticism about early reports of seduction slowly developed into a recognition of how the immediate demands of the analytic situation influenced what was being said—a conception that later became elaborated into the concept of transference. It is worth noting—in passing—that Freud's skepticism did not keep pace with his reformulation; thus we find an occasional return (as in the Wolf Man case, for example) to what might be called a state of rather naïve credulity. Put another way, we can say that the full implications of the transference model were not always maintained in his case presentations; when it suited him, Freud would sometimes relax his skeptical stance, as when he transformed the Wolf Man's rather vague early memory into an elaborately detailed primal scene.

Freud's readiness to listen to (and believe in) the patient's associations can be seen as another kind of conversational constraint. Credulous listening is, after all, the hallmark of any dialogue; in only a few exceptional conversations do we try to remain skeptical. But if we take the position that "who" the patient is speaking to determines what is being said, we see that much of the associational content had better be disregarded—or at least heard with a skeptical ear. Given the pressure of the transference at any given time, it is easy to see why the truth value of any given statement must be relative at best.

We can summarize this chapter by considering in more systematic fashion just how the conversational requirements of the analytic situation impose themselves on the idealized freedom of free association. Consider first the initial demand on the patient to put his thoughts into words. We have seen (in

Chapter II) that this translation is composed of at least two steps: he must first translate experience into thought, and second, he must find language to translate thought into words. Which part of his experience he selects is clearly under the influence of the transference demands of the session; a patient who has not paid her bill may be reluctant—perhaps even unable—to discuss plans to take the Concorde to Paris because the contradiction between having money for the trip and no money for the analyst may effectively prevent both topics from appearing. The patient who thinks the analyst has no ear for music may feel unable to fully describe her thoughts about a recent concert because the sense of being listened to, understood, and appreciated must have a bearing on how her thoughts are presented. In this second example, we have an illustration of how the transference affects the language because if the patient feels she is talking to a musician, she may use a different lexicon than if she were talking to a painter.

Transference assumptions may affect choice of topic and choice of language; more common conversational constraints would seem to play a role in modulating what might be called the paragraphing of the response. Subtle clues that the analyst is listening—occasional comments, requests for clarification, and the like—may easily be heard as signs that he is also interested and wishes the patient to continue, whereas the onset of complete and total silence may easily bring the topic to a close. A sense of the analyst as listener, apart from his particular role in the transference, may affect the patient's need to continue the same topic or go on using the same lexicon; if he is cast in a musician's role and seems to be listening intently, the patient may even increase her use of musical terms on the assumption that there is now even less risk of misunderstanding than there was before. In extreme circumstances, truth may once again give way to language; the event being talked about may be quite real, but the language used to describe it may be added primarily for the benefit of the imaginary "other" and have nothing much to do with either the event or the patient's abilities to describe it properly. If, for example, the patient believes she is talking to a music lover and is trying to describe a recent concert experience, she may find herself elaborating on changes of tonality which (a) never took place, and (b) which she couldn't recognize even if they did. But unless the analyst was present at the same concert, he has no way of identifying either of these distortions. What is happening here is that the patient, in speaking to the analyst-as-music-lover, is no longer freely associating but rather is constructing a picture of an event that is partly true (there was a concert) and partly imaginary (it wasn't heard in quite the way being described) in the interests of winning from the analyst a certain kind of sympathy, perhaps even admiration and—at some future time, perhaps—an informed response that would continue the conversation along musical lines.

We can begin to see the range of possible distortions when we consider in how many different ways a particular event can be described. Is the focus on the action, as in Hemingway, or on the witness and his perception, as in James? Is it on the scene itself or its implications? Is there first a long prologue to put it in some kind of setting? Is it described in some psychological context so that the patient tries to look for motivation and defense, or is it seen as a pure happening? Each of these views of experience represents a choice that may be influenced by the patient's assumptions about whom he is talking to and what he wants to hear. Just as the writer may first make up his mind about which audience he is writing for, so the patient tries to gauge "who" is listening.

It may be helpful to think of the range of descriptive options open to the patient as comparable to the different genres open to the writer. Genre affects content; if we are writing satire, we have a more limited choice of topics than if we are writing poetry. In similar fashion, if the patient wants to speak in an ironical tongue, he will be forced to choose certain pieces of his experience and ignore others. Here is another example of how associations are less than free; once the patient "decides" on a genre, he is limited severely in topic. And we can assume that choice of genre is heavily influenced by the transference, that is, by what might be called the extended conversational constraints of the analytic situation.

We can now return to the problem of unwitting interpretation. The patient chooses whatever genre will maximize his conversational impact on the listening analyst. Once he chooses his genre, the patient has substantially narrowed his choice of topic and, by extension, his associative freedom. He has interpreted free association to mean, try to talk about this range of topics using this particular approach and in a language that will maximize its effect on the listener.

The analyst, for his part, must continuously attempt to identify the genre in order to understand the content, because genre affects interpretation. His decision as to which genre is being used becomes a kind of unwitting interpretation because it takes place, most of the time, in the fringes of awareness. But it is obviously critical for determining how he will listen to the material. If we assume that the patient is speaking truthfully, we will place much greater significance on his early memories than if we assume that the patient is trying to impress us with his marvelous early recall. In the first case, early memories will be treated as data and used to reconstruct the patient's early history; in the second case, they might be treated as screens, having the same "truth" value as dreams or fantasies, but not inserted into the patient's early history. Notice how choice of genre affects how the material will be heard and how it will be treated; here we begin to see how an initial, unwitting interpretation can pave the way for an official interpretation. If the analyst decides that a particular memory is probably true, he may conceptualize it as the *trigger* for a later clinical event and shape his interpretation accordingly. On the other hand, if he decides that it is probably a delusion, he may decide that it is the *consequence* of some previous occurrence, and his interpretation would reflect this evaluation.

How exactly does genre affect interpretation? "The interpreter," as described by Hirsch (1967),

> has to make a guess about the kind of meaning he confronts, since without this guess he possesses no way of grounding and unifying his transient encounters with details. An individual trait will be rootless and meaningless unless it is perceived as a component in a whole meaning, and this kind of whole must be a more or less explicit guess about the kind of utterance being interpreted. Genre ideas, then, have a necessary heuristic function in interpretation. (p. 78)

We can read "analyst" for "interpreter" and assume that he is constantly making decisions about the form and status of the patient's material. The specific listening conventions described in the preceding section help to guide these decisions. If, for example, the analyst assumes that contiguity indicates causality, then he will hear a sequence of disconnected statements as a causal chain; at some later time, he might make an interpretation that would make this assumption explicit. If he assumes that transference predominates and that the patient is always talking, in more or less disguised fashion, about the analyst, then he will "hear" the material in that way and make some kind of ongoing evaluation of the state of the transference.

The patient chooses from a different range of possibilities, and for different reasons. Where the analyst chooses a genre in order to maximize understanding and chooses it from a range of possibilities derived from theory, the patient seeks to maximize his need to make sense, to win a temporary response, or—more generally—to affect the conversation. He chooses his genre unconsciously and unaffected by theory—rather, he selects from his own particular store of significant people in his life. This decision affects "who" he is speaking *as* and "whom" he is speaking *to;* as we have seen, it affects which thoughts he presents and how he presents them. It informs not only the form and content of his associations; it also affects how he will hear the responses from the analyst. He is constantly searching for signs that he is being understood in the particular stance he has chosen; if he is speaking as a prodigal son, he will be looking for signs of forgiveness; if he is speaking as a painter, he will be listening for clues that his listener can discriminate tempera from oil. Again we can make reference to Hirsch:

> Even when the meaning which the speaker [patient] wishes to convey is unusual (and some aspects of his conveyed meaning will almost always be unique), he knows that in order to convey his meaning he must take into account his interpreter's probable understanding. If his interpreter's system of expectations and associations is to correspond to his own, he must adopt usages which will fulfill not only his own expectations but also those of his interpreter. This imaginative transference from the speaker to the interpreter parallels that from the interpreter to the speaker and is called by Bally *dédoublement de la personnalité.* (1967, p. 80; Bally, 1944, p. 37)

Of course, the transference referred to by Hirsch is not equivalent to the more conventional psychoanalytic use of the word, but the argument being proposed has one interesting implication. It suggests that one of the determinants of a particular transference stance is the need for understanding; that the patient may need to place the analyst in a particular role in order to maximize his sense of being listened to and understood and that many transference distortions are in the service of reading that kind of understanding into what the analyst is saying. Similarly, distortions in the patient's associations are in the service of maximizing the chances of being understood.

The process is circular. Once the patient has made an assumption about what the analyst wants to hear (based on his assumption of "who" he is), he will try to choose content and language which will most favor that choice, and he will read into the analyst's response further clues which will be used to influence subsequent associations. Again we quote from Hirsch: "The speaker knows that his type of meaning must be grounded in a type of usage, since it is only from traits of usage, i.e., vocabulary range, syntactical patterns, formulaic invariants, and so on that the interpreter can expect the speaker's type of meaning" (p. 80). If a particular way of expressing an early memory, for example, seemed to evoke from the analyst a response that seemed well suited to his assumed role, the patient might well continue to present his past in that particular form. On the other hand, if an early memory was met with only a neutral response or one which seemed out of character (i.e., incompatible with the analyst's presumed role), then the patient might shift his approach in order to win more understanding; he might use more explicit language, for example, in recalling an early memory or perhaps generate four memories where before there was only one.

We are now in a position to understand how one set of unwitting interpretations, assumed by the patient, can interact with the second set, assumed by the analyst, to produce even greater overall confusion. Misunderstanding is generated, first, by the fact that the specific genre chosen by patient and analyst is never made explicit; and second, by the fact that the choices are made from two different sets of possibilities: the patient chooses from the significant figures in his life, whereas the analyst chooses from among the different conventions of listening. The chances of both patient and analyst choosing the same genre are, therefore, quite small; even if the analyst chooses a transference stance most of the time, he may not always be accurate in deducing exactly what role the patient expects him to play. Much more likely is the possibility that different genres will be adopted by patient and analyst, thus maximizing the chances that each will misread the other. Here is another reason for challenging the assumption that the analyst's stance of "evenly hovering attention" is "the necessary counterpart of the demand made on the patient that he should communicate everything that occurs to him without criticism or selection" (Freud, 1912, p. 112). We are suggesting that there may be a critical asymmetry between patient and analyst in the choice of interpretative assumptions, an asymmetry that is apt to potentiate misunderstanding. One role is not the complement of the other; rather, patient and analyst have different agendas and, in their attempts to interpret one another, may actually add to the overall confusion.

We have, again, the potential for something similar to dramatic irony—an action or a statement will be interpreted in different ways by different actors in the play if they are each possessed by different sets of assumptions. Suppose the patient, for reasons based on his early upbringing in a large family, needs to feel that in the analysis he is really an only child. This need, we will further assume, is expressed by a need for constant reassurance and a need to appear as a model patient. He remembers incessantly, and with unbelievable detail, remarkable scenes from early childhood. Suppose the memories are, in fact, true. But suppose, in addition, that the analyst makes the assumption that memories of this kind suggest the failure of early repressive defenses; he, therefore, chooses not to respond. The patient, feeling slighted and perhaps misunderstood, tries to better his position by increasing the number of memories and perhaps adding details that he knows are false but that he hopes will elicit a more favorable response. The analyst, for his part, hears the change as proof of his early diagnostic impression and decides to test the issue by querying the patient at length about one of the fabricated memories. When it turns out that the fabrications were consciously supplied by the patient, the analyst becomes even more convinced that the patient is untreatable and decides to cut short the analysis.

The impasse just described is not the typical kind of countertransference complication caused by the acting out of unanalyzed impulses; rather, the analyst believes he is behaving properly by not giving too much reassurance too soon. But the meaning of this forbearance is perceived differently by the patient, and in his determination to win more approval, he ends up by losing the analyst's trust. Also worth noting is the fact that the impasse was caused by a series of unwitting interpretations, and the very fact that the assumptions were unverbalized helped to increase the mischief they caused. Once again we have something similar to dramatic irony. Othello does not voice his suspicions until too many clues have appeared to show his wife is unfaithful; and many of these clues, it turns out, were actions caused by his wife's love for him.

Unwitting interpretations are pernicious because they carry extreme conviction. In contrast to the hypothetical flavor of many formal interpretations, often prefaced with such tentative phrases as "It looks as if" or "I wonder if it has occurred to you . . . ," unwitting interpretations are often sensed as matters of fact which leave no room for discussion. The latent conviction which can be discovered in the minds of many analysts may be one of the unfortunate consequences of the popular model of "evenly-hovering attention" with its implication that if the analyst simply suspends critical judgment, the correct formulation will appear in due time. Suspending critical judgment usually means giving way to associations, and very often an analyst will use his association to the patient's response as a kind of unwitting interpretation. Because it occurs to him in this intuitive manner, he reads into it a kind of creative truth; it becomes a heuristic that is used to search for further clues. As these appear, his conviction grows that this particular heuristic must be correct and he may lose sight of the fact that any number of other formulations are equally correct.

What is the risk of being wrong? The danger of making the wrong interpretation, as Freud noted in his paper (1937) on construction and reconstruction, is rather small; the patient may simply listen with incredulity and proceed to his next association. But the danger of mis-hearing is more pernicious. If the analyst chooses to use an incorrect heuristic, he will continually try to hear meaning A and be deaf to meanings B, C, D, and so forth. A wrong unwitting interpretation fosters the worst kind of selective inattention, and it makes the analyst next to useless as an evenly-hovering listener. And because of the fact that the wrong interpretation is operating on the fringes of awareness and carries the extreme conviction we noted in the preceding paragraph, it is likely to continue to exert an influence long after its usefulness has come to an end.

Just as it blinds the analyst to other ways of viewing the material, so it blinds him to other strategies that are open to the patient. The chances of flexibly responding to a shift in the transference are considerably reduced when the analyst is rigidly pursuing his own interpretative stance; the more he feels frustrated in his search for confirming clues, the harder he may try to find them and the more inventive become his attempts to construe the data. Engaged in this frenzy of Holmesian detection, he is even less likely to notice subtle changes in the manner and form of the patient's responses, changes that may signal a shift in the transference. Particularly chaotic are those situations in which the analyst's attempts to confirm his hypothesis are misread by the patient as a response to his particular transference wish, which leads him, in turn, to produce associations which further frustrate the analyst. When this happens, each party in the dialogue is secretly responding to the other but, in both cases, for the wrong reasons.

A full discussion of the problem of unwitting interpretation must await a comprehensive annotation of recorded analytic cases (see Chapter VII). By definition, these interpretations do not appear on the surface of the protocol; they must be provided by the treating analyst as he goes over the transcript and tries to supply the organizing assumptions that determined his choice of responses (see Farrell, Wisdom and Turquet, 1962, for a rare exception). As recorded cases become more extensively annotated, we will have a greater opportunity to study these unofficial interpretations and understand in greater detail how they affect the more official interpretations and, more generally, the course of the analysis. We turn now to a study of the more formal interpretative process.

CHAPTER V

Formal Interpretation

When we make a formal interpretation, we are finding a narrative home for an anomalous happening. We are using language to clothe this event in respectability and take away some of its strangeness and mystery, and by fitting the language into the patient's life story, we are giving it a narrative home. The linguistic and narrative aspects of an interpretation may well have priority over its historical truth, and we are making the somewhat heretical claim that an interpretation is effective because it gives the awkward happening a kind of linguistic and narrative closure, not because it can account for it in a purely causal sense. An interpretation satisfies because we are able to contain an unfinished piece of reality in a meaningful sentence; that is part of what we mean by finding its narrative home. The sentence acquires additional meaning when it meshes with other parts of the patient's life; it acquires narrative force by virtue of these connections, and adds narrative understanding to what is already known and understood. The power of language is such that simply putting something into words gives it a certain kind of authenticity; finding a narrative home for these words amplifies and expands this truth. Although finding a linguistic form is a necessary precursor to finding a narrative home, it is possible to have the first without the second; some interpretations gain their force by simply being put into words.

The fact of language distinguishes the formal interpretation from the unwitting, informal interpretation discussed in the previous chapter. The unwitting interpretation, as we have seen, tends to operate on the margin of awareness, guiding the analyst as he listens and helping him to make sense out of (and sometimes distort) the patient's utterances. He is only rarely aware of these interpretations in any explicit sense. The formal interpretation, by contrast, owes much of its power to its linguistic structure. It is designed to be expressed in language in order that it can be made visible to the patient and produce a response; and in order that it can be eventually tested for narrative fit in the larger story of the patient's life. The formal interpretation is a public event; the unwitting interpretation, by contrast, is essentially private.

Our definition of formal interpretation overlaps with Ricoeur's discussion of what constitutes a fact in psychoanalytic discourse (see Ricoeur, 1977); it agrees with Edelson (1975) and Shapiro (1970) in its emphasis on its linguistic character; and it agrees with Viderman (1979) and Loch (1977) in placing the emphasis on an interpretation as a kind of creative act that is not necessarily true in any historical sense. We will first look at the linguistic nature of the interpretation and show how its verbal form gives it a particular power to persuade; we will then move on to the issue of narrative fit. Let us now turn to some examples.

A SPECIMEN INTERPRETATION

In a paper on the primal scene and its effect on the child's later life and character, Greenacre (1973) presents a brief account of the life of Mondrian, the abstract painter. She draws her information from an autobiographical sketch, published posthumously; from an earlier essay, written when he was forty-seven; and, most important of all, from his life work—a sequence of paintings that moved from early landscapes and portraits to the abstract squares and rectangles we now associate with his name. His writings give us a clue to this shift in subject matter. He was, apparently, made very uncomfortable by motion of any kind—people in action were particularly disturbing—and he ultimately felt that "the only really constant relationship is expressed in the right angle; that the two fundamental forces of nature are expressed in the horizontal and the vertical meeting in the perfect right angle" (p. 35).

Greenacre concludes her account of his life and work with this summarizing interpretation:

> Obviously, this is the story of a talented man who had from childhood struggled against both sexual and aggressive drives. Nor is this strange when one considers that probably from his earliest years he suffered from extreme stimulation. For he was the oldest of five children born to the sternest of Calvinistic fathers, who was a headmaster in the school. The children came in about ten years and there was every chance that this oldest child had multiple primal scene experiences as well as awareness of the birth of the younger siblings, certainly a situation which inevitably would compound oedipal jealousy, and sibling jealousy and envy. His symptoms themselves bespoke the extremest sensitization to movement and noise; his infantile anger was expressed in his wish to keep all objects, whether animate or inanimate, separated from each other. Not even flowers should be seen with intertwined stems. He seemed to have taken into his body the multiple and unorganized as well as rhythmic motion around him, and to have attempted to convert it into a cosmic rhythm

which would be perfect and eternal, and to project this in his painting. His fascination with dancing with his whole body in a state of stiff erectness proclaimed, unknown to him, the displacement of genitality to the total body self. He was ultimately unable to live according to the art form he had created, in which motion and emotion would be walled safely into rectangles. But he had only a brief period of freedom before he died. (p. 38)

In this specimen interpretation, Greenacre attempts to account for Mondrian's lifelong fascination with the straight line and the right angle. Multiple primal scenes, argues Greenacre, must have created the need to wall himself off from people in motion, especially when the motion was unexplained and apparently uncontrolled; the discomfort aroused by these scenes was expressed in a wish to keep all objects always separated. Greenacre further speculates that multiple primal scenes may even have sensitized him to movement, thus explaining his distaste with motion and his need to turn life into static forms.

We can judge this interpretation against two criteria: its historical truth value and its linguistic appeal. Consider its truth value first. If we had clear evidence that Mondrian had been a witness to multiple primal scenes, Greenacre's explanation might strike us as a rather ingenious attempt to build a bridge between an early experience and a later fascination with lines and rectangles. But even under those conditions, there is nothing necessary about the explanation; if we knew only that he witnessed multiple primal scenes, we could still not have predicted that he would become fascinated with straight lines. Evidence for primal scenes (assuming we had some) is neither a necessary nor sufficient condition for his particular line of painting.

The steps in the argument become even less convincing when we confront the fact that the primal scenes are *entirely* suppositional. Greenacre reasons from the large family and the painter's modest upbringing to the conclusion that close quarters must have been the rule and, therefore, he must have been exposed to many primal scenes. But would a stern Calvinist minister not have taken fairly elaborate precautions to protect his privacy? Although the family was large, it could have been larger; does not its moderate size suggest some kind of sexual restraint and, therefore, a somewhat smaller base line of possibilities? And if we assume that Mondrian's sensitivity to motion was indeed greater than average, it would be more parsimonious to attribute this sensitivity to an inborn preference rather than to exposure to multiple primal scenes.

We begin to see that the evidential grounds for Greenacre's interpretation are sketchy at best. But despite its rather dubious reasoning and complete lack of independent evidence, it still has a substantial claim on our attention. What gives it its appeal? What lends credibility to an interpretation that can be so easily questioned?

Part of the appeal of this particular interpretation is a direct result of its linguistic form. We not only put the interpretation into words but we use words which have been used before. By using a familiar concept to account for a series of unfamiliar events, Greenacre has made us feel that we can account for some of the strangeness of Mondrian's career. Part of the appeal of the interpretation lies in the fact that we almost always prefer the known to the unknown.

Not only is the interpretation familiar; it also has a long history within the psychoanalytic tradition. Some of it seems to be relevant once again; we have a kind of confirmation. We are reminded of the Wolf Man case and the fact that Freud had made a similar interpretation in different circumstances. If the same explanation can be used more than once, it acquires added credibility. Even though the evidence in each instance is semihard at best, when the two cases are combined, they acquire an overall respectability that is greater than the sum of the parts. It is as if we had discovered a general law and each new instance of this law somehow adds to its power.

Greenacre's interpretation is further strengthened by the fact that it can never be disproved. Obviously, we will never know what Mondrian experienced as a young boy. Since they lie outside the domain of discovery, the multiple primal scenes can never be falsified. As Loftus and Loftus (1980) have recently suggested, to claim that a particular early experience is real is something like claiming that you lost a coin in your shag rug. There is no conceivable way of *disproving* this assertion because if I search for the coin and fail to find it, you can always say that I have not looked far enough. To find the coin proves you right; not to find it proves nothing.

This kind of logical asymmetry applies with particular force to interpretations of early childhood events. Until you can prove that the Wolf Man did *not* see his parents coupling *a tergo*, it remains a possibility that seems to account for many elements in his dream. And because it can never be disproved, it will always remain a part of the accepted explanation, even though there are probably many other explanations that might be found. As we have seen, very little space in the psychoanalytic literature is taken up with a search for alternative explanations.)

Jacobsen and Steele (1979) have discussed Freud's habit of pushing explanatory events further and further back into the past. "He begins with observations of adult pathology and moves from the adult present via psychoanalytic interpretations to the infantile past. This past is then considered to be real and contain within it causes for the present" (p. 353). He was led to this strategy by the requirements of the genetic point of view, which assumes that the pregenital organization of the child contributes to the symptomatology of the adult. But one of the by-products of this tendency to push critical happenings deep into the past is that they remain inaccessible to proof or disproof. The evidence must be taken on faith; since it is out of reach, it can never be reformulated by the addition of new evidence. Any given interpretation is beyond the reach of any future critic. Once the possibility of revision has been eliminated, we are inclined to be seduced by the explanatory magic of the preferred interpretation and by what might be called its linguistic appeal.

The fact that the infantile experience can never be documented has a further implication. Not only will the explanation never be disconfirmed; its very inaccessibility means that there are very few historical constraints on the form of the presumed triggering event. The final solution need only be plausible, and, in the last analysis, its form will be justified by how much it explains. Suppose we come up with an ingenious interpretation that explains a great deal but seems unlikely. Its unlikelihood will probably be excused because no other single event will explain so much. The unusual explanation has a kind of inverted parsimony because even though it may combine a number of unlikely occurrences (as in Freud's reconstruction of the Wolf Man primal scene), it could, if true, account for such a large number of clinical details that all other explanations seem inadequate. Once we have constructed a hypothetical event which, no matter how unlikely, seems to account for all the important features in the case, then the success of our invention tends to confirm its existence. Its truth value, we might say, is a hostage to its explanatory success. Once again we have exchanged the uncertainty and mystery of the clinical happening for a plausible and compelling explanation—and who would prefer the first to the second?

TRUTH VALUE AND NARRATIVE FIT

The question of whether Greenacre's interpretation was true or false did not exactly loom large in the preceding discussion; indeed, we found that despite its rather inferior evidential base, it carried a great deal of appeal. Much of that appeal seemed to depend on its linguistic familiarity. By linking a known construct with a mysterious series of events, we were able to bring order out of chaos and, in addition, borrow credibility from prior use.

We now need to consider some of the criteria for good interpretations; once again, the issue of historical truth will appear relatively unimportant. If an interpretation meets the criteria listed below, it will have a good chance of surviving whatever its evidential base may happen to be. Each of these criteria contributes to its narrative truth.

There is, first, the rule of clinical parsimony. The preferred explanation for a series of symptoms tends to be cast in terms of single events—the primal scene is the outstanding example—rather than different events on different occasions. The single event may be repeated over time—thus we have Greenacre's presumption that Mondrian was the witness to many primal scenes—but the form of the event tends not to change. Notice that the parsimony takes an unusual form; its simplicity is deceptive. One cause is preferred to many, but the event may be unlikely and even improbable—as in the Wolf Man's viewing of his parents coupling *a tergo*. The two points are related—*because* it was unusual, it probably happened only once; and *because* it was unusual, even though happening only once, it still might have reason to influence subsequent behavior.

In somewhat different terms, we would describe this rule as the "mapping" of many results onto relatively few causes. The constructed (or reconstructed) past is never as complex as the manifest present, and the smaller the ratio of explanatory cause to subsequent effect, the better the interpretation. Here is another analogy with the power of a general law in natural science, and some of the appeal of a wide-ranging interpretation may stem from this congruence. Notice that generality tends to compensate for improbability; if the presumed early event can account for a sufficient number of the patient's symptoms, we will accept it as true even if it seems preposterous or improbable.

Second, there is the rule that similarity of form suggests similarity of content. If the formal structure of a current event—e.g., a symptom—can be mapped onto the formal structure of an early event, we assume that the first is somehow related to the second. The assumption that external form is a clue to inner meaning is an important aspect of analogue reasoning (see Spence, 1973) and figured prominently in medieval theories of the universe, as we will see later in the chapter. Using this rule, we look at clinical behavior with the eye of an archeologist or painter, emphasizing the appearance and reappearance of form and pattern. As we will see below, however, the analogy with archeology and painting is misleading and in many cases actually wrong.

Narrative fit is significantly enhanced by the discovery of a pattern match; by finding a correspondence between an anomalous happening and earlier events in the patient's history, we have increased the chances that the former will be fitted into his overall life story. Language, furthermore, plays a critical role in bringing about this match. Since external form in the clinical setting always depends on a particular verbal description, we see that much depends on how a clinical happening is described by the patient or how the interpretation linking two events is worded by the analyst. Since language is infinitely flexible, a wide range of descriptions is possible.

Third, there is the rule that all pattern matches are indications of cause and effect—and its corollary, that the better the mapping, the stronger the assumed causal link. Discovery of a formal similarity between a symptom and an early event is almost always taken to indicate a meaningful connection. It is almost never argued that such matches could occur by chance, or that they might be the result of a fortunate choice of words; these and other alternatives are almost never considered.

We now look at three clinical examples to see in more detail how these rules apply. We begin with one of Neiderland's cases (1965).

A patient complains of compulsively making strange faces while staring at himself in the mirror. Many months of analysis fail to provide any significant insight into the symptom. Suddenly he is interrupted during an hour by a twelve o'clock whistle, which reminds him of being in London with his mother during the war; the whistle reminds him of an air raid siren, and he experiences some of the same fright he felt as a child. He then has a sudden image of his mother with a strange face, and further association leads to the thought—gas mask. As a child, he was terrified of this strange monster and the compulsive symptom can be understood as an attempt to repeat the experience and thereby master the trauma. The childhood crisis is supposed to reveal itself in the later symptom (rule 1). The close structural correspondence between the current symptom of strange faces and the bizarre appearance of his mother wearing a gas mask provides the link between past and present. It is presumably the formal similarity between symptom and memory that provides the associative bridge and allows the memory to emerge (rule 2). We also assume that correspondence indicates cause and effect—the wartime episode lies at the root of the symptom (rule 3). And we assume that the discovered pattern match is significant (rule 3).

Our second example comes from Greenson (1967).

> A woman patient in her third year of analysis develops a resistance to coming to her analytic hour because she feels there is something ominous about me which frightens her. I persuade the patient to try to clarify this ominous quality she perceives about me. Hesitantly she begins to draw a picture of me as a man who seems kindly on the surface but who is secretly hostile to women. She goes on to depict a man who seems manly and active but who is actually feminine and passive. He is so passive that he would let his women patients slowly bleed to death without

lifting a finger. The moment the patient says "bleed to death," she gasps: "Oh, my God! I know what this is—that's my father. I am mixing you up with my father." The patient is referring to an incident in childhood when, at age four, she discovered she was bleeding from the vagina and ran to her father, in a panic. He tried to comfort her by saying, "It's nothing, it will go away, forget about it." For many complicated reasons this was most disturbing to my patient. (p. 309)

In this example, it is the close correspondence between the metaphor "bleed to death" and the memory of her father, unwilling to treat her bleeding vagina, that gives the patient (and tacitly the analyst) the feeling that she has arrived at a reasonable interpretation.

Our final example comes from a paper by Ramzy (1974) in which he describes a patient who, just prior to the hour, had returned home to leave money for his cleaning lady and was troubled to find her not there. The analyst, somewhat later in the hour, makes the following interpretation: "Your earlier thoughts about the cleaning lady which occurred to you on the way here and your worry over losing her makes me think that they may be connected with my upcoming absence for the next two weeks, starting next Monday" (p. 546).

Once again, it would seem to be the structural parallel between the two events in question that prompts the interpretation. The absence of the cleaning lady (and the patient's associations to the effect that perhaps she will not return) seem to parallel the upcoming absence of the analyst and possible fears that he, too, will not come back. Whether or not the interpretation is correct, it was apparently inspired by the close structural correspondence between the two events. Once again, similarity of form suggests similarity of content; overlap of form suggests cause and effect.

The clinical reasoning illustrated in these three examples represents a particular kind of thinking in which the formal structure of the critical event is assumed to reveal something about its content and, in addition, is used to discover its causal antecedent. The discovery of a similar pattern, somewhere in the past, is assumed to provide us with the cause of the target event. What is striking about this kind of reasoning is the emphasis placed on the outward appearance of the event and on the extent to which language can affect this appearance by controlling description.

FORMAL SIMILARITY

The search for formal similarity—what we have called pattern matching—has been singled out by Loewenstein (1951) as a central element in the interpretation process:

> It happens frequently in the beginning of analysis that a patient describes a number of events which strike the analyst as having certain similarities. The analyst's task is then to show the patient that all these events in his life have some elements in common. The next step is to point out that the patient behaved in a similar way in all these situations. The third step may be to demonstrate that this behavior was manifested in circumstances which all involved competitive elements and where rivalry might have been expected. . . . The interpretation extends in installments throughout the analysis, and only in later stages of treatment does an interpretation become complete, encompassing the origin both of ego elements and id derivatives. (p. 4)

Underlying the search for similarity is the assumption that formal similarity expresses psychical commonality. Unfortunately for the search, it often happens that the pattern does not grow out of the material but is consciously or unconsciously imposed. While it often happens that formal similarity gives a clue to underlying meaning, if the similarity is partly constructed by the analyst's choice of material and his use of language in its description, then the matches he discovers may be more arbitrary than inevitable.

This possibility is usually overlooked in the standard clinical accounts; one source of error goes back to the belief that we always listen with "evenly-hovering attention." Given this passive view of the listening process, it would follow that the meanings we discover simply grow out of the material and the similarities we choose to interpret are naturally forced on us by the specific meanings that emerge. But a moment's thought will show that what is being matched is usually the lexical description and because of the loose match between image and word, there are always a wide range of possible "translations." In Freud's famous screen memory of the meadow and the delicious bread (see Chapter IV), he depends heavily on verbal mediation in two places: by labeling a family position as a "bread and butter" occupation, he finds a link with the bread offered by the older women; and by using the word "deflowering" to describe a later sexual fantasy, he makes a link with the dandelions in the meadow. But these labels are not the only words that could be used; other choices, equally appropriate, could also be found, but they would significantly weaken the pattern match and thus interfere with the interpretation.

To take a more recent example, consider the following case from Browne (1980). The patient, a talented artist, had visited an art exhibition and was acutely disappointed with the collection. The exhibitors, writes Browne, "had mixed the good with the mediocre. . . . [The patient] went on in this vein for a large part of the session until, in describing a fellow artist as being still in the mud, I interrupted her to interpret to her something of how I felt at being pushed into the mud of her incessant talking" (p. 498).

By using the word *mud* to describe his situation, the analyst is constructing a link between the patient and himself. The word is present in her material but less evident in his; it would be more correct to say that the analyst created the correspondence by using one of the patient's words to describe his own predicament. It seems clear that this tactic allows the analyst to establish as many overlaps as he likes because some word can always be found to form the bridge. As a result, we should be careful not to assume that our selected link is either "demanded" by the material or is the only choice available. It is, more precisely, our association to the patient's material which, by virtue of our position, we can raise to the status of an interpretation. And the correspondence we are trying to establish depends, in the majority of cases, on a language link that is being imposed on the clinical material.

Now we can also turn this argument around. To the extent that linking bridges of this kind are used all the time, we have evidence that formal interpretation is more creative (and constructive) than our theory usually assumes. To say that an interpretation, in many cases, does not grow out of the material may not impair its effectiveness because, as we noted in the opening paragraphs of this chapter, its historical truth may be less important than its narrative truth. It should be realized, however, that more often than we like to think, we are using language in rather ad hoc fashion; we often choose a label or a phrase in order to *create* a correspondence (as Freud did in his screen memory) and should not be deceived into thinking that we are merely using the only words available. Whereas Loewenstein would argue that our job as analysts is simply to report whatever pattern matches we discover and that these form the basis of our interpretations, we are making the claim that our reporting is often largely creative in the service of finding similarity. The creative aspect of our interpretative stance is developed with particular emphasis by Viderman, but before we turn to his arguments, let us take a closer look at the nature of pattern matching.

PATTERN MATCHING

We have suggested in the previous chapter how listening with free-floating attention is hard to carry out and apt to be observed mainly in the breach because informed listening is an active rather than a passive process that requires the making and breaking of countless hypotheses as the material unfolds. Many of these hypotheses take the form of looking for the structural similarity between a single event and a complex of other events. In the example from Ramzy, described in the previous section, the analyst seemed to be searching for a pattern in the patient's associations which would correspond to his upcoming vacation; in the first example, Neiderland was able to find a pattern match between the bizarre facial contortions that so tortured his patient and the appearance of his mother with the gas mask. In the case of the Wolf Man, Freud was trying to show a close correspondence between the position of the mother in the presumed primal scene (on all fours) and the position of the maid Grusha while she was scrubbing the floor.

In each of these examples, the pattern being matched is an external, often superficial attribute of the scene in question. It is the outside appearance that is determining rather than the intentions of the participants. The total meaning, and in particular the inner experience, of scrubbing the floor is completely different from the experience of being sexually stimulated; the differences are so great that one would be tempted to put the two events in separate categories. But looking with purely an artist's eye, we could argue that the two events belong together because they share a common external form. Once again, the structural correspondence between the events determines their underlying psychical commonality.

Let us look more closely at the way in which we go about finding correspondence between forms. Look at Plate B and compare it with Plate C. The first illustration is from an engraving by Raimondi entitled *The Judgment of Paris* (c.

Plate B. Marantonio Raimondi, *The Judgment of Paris* (c. 1515), Engraving.

Plate C. Manet, *Le Dejeuner sur l'herbe* (1863).

1515); the second is a painting by Manet entitled *Le Déjeuner sur l'herbe* (1863). The Raimondi engraving shows three figures in the same position as the picnicking group in the Manet painting. We not only have a good pattern match; we also have a causal link because there is general agreement among art historians that the Raimondi engraving apparently inspired the Manet painting (see Chapter III, p. 75). In this instance, then, the structural correspondence can be reliably used as an indicator of causality, and it is this kind of pattern match that serves as the model for psychoanalytic reasoning. If, goes the argument, we can find a certain degree of formal correspondence between two images, then we have reason to assume that they have something in common and, furthermore, that the first is somehow causally related to the second.

The trouble with this kind of reasoning is that the vast majority of clinical pattern matches come from a different domain. Once we get beyond the exact correspondence of the two forms shown in Plates B and C, we have entered the vast, uncharted region of approximate matches. The size of this domain is almost always being understimated; rather than assume that a discovered match is merely a preliminary indication that a relationship may exist, the clinician tends to conclude that a pattern match is the final, definitive indicator of some underlying relation. Once we find a match, even a partial correspondence, we rarely stop to think that such a match probably happens by chance much more often than we would assume. Because we underestimate the number of approximate matches, we underestimate the probable number of chance matches that have no significance at all. As a result of these errors, we take the correspondence as much more informative than it actually is; finding a match leads directly, as we have seen in the preceding examples, to a conclusion about causation. It is precisely this line of reasoning that leads to rule 3—all pattern matches are meaningful.

Why is the base line so high? Because of the richness of the visual world. In an earlier paper (1976), I described a patient's dream of a dog charging across the lawn and hurling himself at the screen door. "Missing the door, he hit the side of the house and fell down, stunned. Later that day the patient, while driving to work, narrowly avoids being hit by a car from the side" (p. 369). If we focus on the pattern of dog-hitting-house and car-hitting-car, we might agree that we have found a kind of analogue correspondence; and further, that this correspondence allows us to view the dream as a kind of precognition which anticipated the narrow escape. But if we focus on the dog and car alone, we find less overlap, and if we asked the patient to draw images of the dream and the narrow escape, we might find no evidence at all. "We are always dealing," I stated,

> with essentially ambiguous pieces of behavior, rich in meaning, the meanings often overlapping and not hierarchically arranged. By that I mean that no meaning is clearly foremost in importance—until indicated by us or by the patient. The hierarchy does not reside in the material. We approach these ambiguous specimens with our own framework of beliefs and ideas, in the context of our own immediate experience [as we have seen in Chapter IV], and from our private perspective of recent and distant happenings. Just as the boy with the new hammer sees the world as a collection of nails, waiting to be pounded, so we cannot help being sensitized to the themes which resonate with our own concerns, and tend to resolve the ambiguity of the dream specimen in terms of our favorite set of categories. (p. 369)

Looking for matches, the analyst is almost sure to find them. We have seen in Chapter IV how he may often impose his own categories onto the patient's associations. One way of doing this is to adjust the clinical material to fit his favorite template. In the excitement of discovery, each new match comes to resemble the correspondence between Raimondi and Manet, and we lose sight of the fact that if there is a resemblance, it probably accounts for only a "corner" of the "painting" and might easily not be noticed by anyone else. In contrast to the striking similarity found between Plates B and C, the usual kind of clinical pattern matching owes at least as much to what is being contributed by the onlookers (analyst and patient) as to what is contained in the material.

Even in cases of striking similarity among paintings, degree of pattern match is not necessarily an indication of cause and effect; we always need to go to other sources to confirm an explanation. The correspondence between Plates B and C did not prove that the first painting inspired the second; it only suggested the possibility. When the match is less than perfect, the causal significance is even more suspect. But if the similarity is sufficiently striking, these qualifications may be overlooked. In all three of the clinical vignettes cited earlier, it seems clear that finding the match was treated as discovering the cause. Because Ramzy found the structural correspondence between the unexplained absence of the cleaning lady and the analyst's vacation, he was led to believe that he had discovered the reason for the patient's concern. Because Neiderland found a correspondence between the appearance of the mother in her gas mask and the bizarre faces in the mirror, he assumed that one must be the cause of the other. But finding a match is not the same thing as discovering a cause; and, furthermore, the degree of correspondence says very little about the strength of the relationship. A successful pattern match speaks more to the ingenuity of the observer than to the historical truth of the match. In somewhat different language, the success of the pattern match speaks to the context of discovery; finding the causal connection between two events speaks to the context of justification. The two should not be confused.

Finding a match not only depends on the ingenuity of the observer; it also depends on what might be called the size of the search space. If we keep searching for an event that will correspond to a particular dream image, we are bound to come up with a plausible match if we continue to look long enough; and yet the time taken up in the search or the size of the search space are rarely mentioned in a report of the match. One of Freud's associations to his dream about Otto, the family doctor, led to a summer holiday that had taken place *six years before* (1900). Other associations may go back to childhood. Considering the possible number of incidents covered in the patient's lifetime and the multiple ways in which they can be structured, we begin to see the near-infinite range of possibilities. If the search space begins to approach infinity, the significance of any particular pattern match becomes almost negligible.

Finding a match also depends heavily, as we have seen, on the phrasing of the event. We have seen in Chapter III how language can only approximate visual images; hence it follows that our sense of an image can be significantly influenced by the way it is described, and as we have seen, in Freud's screen memory and the more recent case by Browne, by how the language is imposed on the material. To base a pattern match on such a verbal description is to build on sand; to base a causal explanation on a verbal pattern match is to compound the error.

On several grounds, then, the analogy with painting and art history is misleading. In the case of painting we are dealing with a specific art object, open to multiple interpretations but quite singular with respect to form and content. We might classify the Manet-Raimondi correspondence as a *hard* pattern match. But the "paintings" we are comparing in the course of our work with patients are intangible, changeable, and imperfectly described, and the chances for analogue similarity are correspondingly much greater. In the case of painting, we are dealing with a finite set of objects; in the case of memories and symptoms, we are dealing with a near-infinite universe. In the case of painting, we are dealing with bounded perceptual units; in the case of memories and symptoms, we are dealing with a particular linguistic representation that can be changed to suit our requirements. As a result, the significance of a clinical pattern match is usually inflated. In clinical work, we are usually dealing with *soft* pattern matches.

In only rare cases, then, are we finding meaningful matches; in only rare cases does the analogy with art history or archeology have any direct application. Instead of finding a true instance of structural correspondence, we are often generating a similarity by a clever application of language to a pair of random events; given the flexibility of language, we can almost always succeed. Once we begin to see, on the other hand, that pattern matches are inclined to be arbitrary, we can begin to understand why discovering a match says very little about possible cause and effect. Finding the similarity may be, as Loewenstein suggests, the first step toward making an interpretation, but it does not necessarily follow, as he claims, that similar events necessarily have something in common. Finding a similarity may narrow the search space, but it does not follow that we have necessarily discovered a psychological connection.

To carry this line of thinking very far, the analyst is in danger of repeating an earlier mistake in the history of ideas. Before a particular phenomenon was fully understood, it was tempting to use external similarity as a clue to understanding. We can find many examples of this principle in the history of medicine—the cure for baldness was supposed to be the fat from a bear (an obviously hairy animal); the cure for consumption was supposed to be the lung of a fox, a long-winded animal (see Shapiro and Morris, 1978). The analogue correspondence between the cure and the disease presumes a causal link; we look for a medicine that resembles the illness. But obviously a fox is not *only* long-winded; it can also be described in many other ways. Thus there is nothing in the argument that draws us necessarily to the fox as the remedy for consumption, and we can find other attributes that might argue against its use. As a general rule, the choice of a particular analogue match depends heavily on which feature of the event we choose to emphasize.

This is only one example of an all-pervading trend in the history of ideas. Up to the beginning of the seventeenth century, the search for resemblance was considered to be a primary path to knowledge. "It was resemblance that largely guided exegesis and the interpretation of texts; it was resemblance that organized the play of symbols, made possible knowledge of things visible and invisible, and controlled the art of representing them" (Foucault, 1973, p. 17). Four types of similitude were identified: *convenientia*—the assumption that forms that appear in close proximity have something in common; *aemulatio*—the assumption that similarity of form, even at a distance, corresponds to similarity of function; *analogy*—the assumption that similarity of function explains underlying process, as a tempest is analogous to an attack of apoplexy; and *sympathies*—the assumption that all parts of the universe share the same set of ingredients and are, therefore, all variations on the same thing. Sympathy, writes Foucault, "attracts what is heavy to the heaviness of the earth, what is light up towards the weightless ether [for this reason, the flames in a fire tend to rise toward the sky]; it drives the root towards the water and it makes the great yellow disk of the sunflower turn to follow the curving path of the sun" (p. 23). The lung of a fox will cure consumption because of the play of sympathies; since the lung and the diseased organ are both lungs, they will be attracted to each other and a cure will take place.

In conclusion, writes Foucault, "because of the movement and the dispersion created by its laws, the sovereignty of the sympathy-antipathy pair [antipathy being the tendency of similar things to remain apart] gives rise to all the forms of resemblance. The first three similitudes are thus all . . . explained by it. The whole volume of the world, all the adjacencies of 'convenience,' all the echoes of emulation, all the linkages of analogy, are supported, maintained, and doubled by this space governed by sympathy and antipathy, which are ceaselessly drawing things together and holding them apart. By means of this interplay, the world remains identical; resemblances continue to be what they are, and to resemble one another. The same remains the same, riveted onto itself" (p. 25).

The practice of detecting similarities consisted in looking for the presence of a *signature*. The signature was the outward sign of a buried similarity; its presence revealed a resemblance and, therefore, opened the way to an explanation. The signature, however, is not a direct copy of the thing in question but some kind of transformation, governed by the four types of similitude we have just discussed: thus a certain amount of knowledge is required to identify the signature and detect its significance.

For an example of how the system was used in practice, take the discovery that aconite (monkshood) was a cure for diseases of the eye. The critical signature reveals itself in the appearance of the seeds: "They are tiny dark globes set in white skinlike coverings whose appearance is much like that of eyelids covering an eye" (Foucault, 1973, p. 27). From the resemblance revealed by the signature, we can make the further assumption that aconite has a particular sympathy for the eye and, therefore, can be used in its treatment (compare Ehrlich's "magic bullet"). Armed with this argument, the medieval philosopher looked upon the world as a system of resemblances expressed in a network of signs. If he could decode the transforming signatures, he could discover the critical signs and, in this way, learn the key to the universe. The problems with this approach are obvious; the similarities to certain forms of psychoanalytic reasoning are troublesome.

As medicine became more sophisticated and the underlying biology of disease better understood, it became clear that cause and effect might be superficially quite different; we see nothing unusual nowadays in prescribing a drug whose appearance has nothing in common with the illness being treated. As we learn more about biological causality, we pay less attention to external appearance. By the nineteenth century, the rules of resemblance became an intellectual curiosity. Why, then, does the principle of analogue correspondence loom so large in psychoanalytic reasoning?

We come back once again to Freud's life-long fondness for archeology. It would seem to assume critical importance in his style of thinking. In a number of places in his writing, he compared analytic work to uncovering ruins. Not only did he try to take current fragments and use them to reconstruct earlier happenings, but he saw a parallel between the age of a fragment and its state of preservation, with early memories likely to be more fragmentary than more recent experiences. One of the earliest expressions of this metaphor appears in his paper "Fragment of an Analysis" (1905):

> In face of the incompleteness of my analytic results, I had no choice but to follow the example of those discoverers whose good fortune it is to bring to the light of day after their long burial the priceless though mutilated relics of antiquity. I have restored what is missing, taking the best models known to me from other analyses; but, like a conscientious archaeologist, I have not omitted to mention in each case where the authentic parts end and my constructions begin. (p. 12)

And again, toward the end of his life:

> But just as the archaeologist builds up the walls of the building from the foundations that have remained standing, determines the number and position of the columns from depressions in the floor and reconstructs the mural decorations and paintings from the remains found in the debris, so does the analyst proceed when he draws his inferences from the fragments of memories, from the associations and from the behavior of the subject of the analysis. (1937, p. 259)

Not only does he use the same model; he "works under more favorable conditions than the archaeologist" because the latter may be faced with the destruction of significant objects whereas for the analyst, "all of the essentials are preserved; even things that seem completely forgotten are present somehow and somewhere, and have merely been buried and made inaccessible to the subject" (1937, p. 260). Even by the end of his career, he was firmly convinced of the truth of this metaphor.

Seeing himself as an archeologist, Freud was tempted to use external form as a clue to meaning; to use analogue reasoning as a guide to psychical significance; and to draw conclusions about cause and effect from examples of structural correspondence. If we are dealing entirely with concrete fragments, then form is conclusive because they have no "inner life." And if the form is exhaustively described, it becomes a good indicator of causation—similar forms found in widely distant regions are a good indicator of cultural contact; broken fragments may suggest an accident or a fight; and the layering of fragments may tell us something about the history of a community. But memories, images, and associations are far more than mute fragments, and to emphasize their external form at the expense of their inner meaning is to make a serious category mistake. It confuses what philosophers would call appearances with essences and does not make sufficient allowance for the changeable nature of the world and the mediating role of language in influencing our perceptions.

CREATIVE INTERPRETATION AND NARRATIVE TRUTH

"Nothing perhaps is more surprising in this world of ours," writes Hannah Arendt, "than the almost infinite diversity of its appearances, the sheer entertainment value of its views, sounds, and smells, something that is hardly ever mentioned by the thinkers and philosophers" (1977, p. 20). Far from being made up of the "concrete observables" so dear to the heart of the behaviorists, the world seems far richer than any one theory. It is because of this near-infinite diversity that appearances are deceiving; any description is at best only a partial truth. And in addition to their overwhelming diversity, appearances are also mute with respect to meaning. As Arendt describes the problem, "no experience yields any meaning or even coherence without undergoing the operations of imagining and thinking. Seen from the perspective of thinking, life in its sheer thereness is meaningless" (p. 87).

But if description is partial, it is also formative. I must choose in order to speak, and choice implies inclusion and exclusion; at the same time, my description is bound to influence your view. As we noted in an earlier chapter, the meaning of things is not exactly lying around, waiting to be picked up; it is always waiting for the right interpreter to come along. And the interpretation, when it comes, is almost always more compelling than the "sheer thereness" of the relevant facts; thus it is no surprise that any commentary, no matter how false, can have a significant influence on subsequent views of the same set of facts.

These observations apply with particular force to the role of formal interpretation in the analytic situation. We not only try to arrive at an understanding of the world of the senses; we also try to put into words a completely separate domain which is, because it is unconscious, not accessible to awareness. If interpretation is compelling with regard to our view of reality—and Loftus's research on eyewitness testimony is relevant here—it has probably even greater force when applied to events that lie outside the patient's immediate experience. Any psychological event that belongs to the domain of the unconscious is, by definition, not available to the patient's immediate observation and any construction that the analyst chooses to place on it takes on an additional priority. Not only is the phenomenon expressed in language but it is more than likely worded in a form that fits the context of the patient's life.

In the previous section on pattern matches, we noted how many discoveries of similarity were probably more a comment on the ingenuity of the analyst than on the truth of the finding. Now we can be more specific. The limitless possibilities of finding a match are a consequence, first, of the "infinite diversity" of the real world and, second, of the fact that language, with all of its potential flexibility, is always mediating between the external event and its representation in the analytic "space." Because language is flexible, it can impose different meanings on the same event; it can discover equivalent meanings in different events; and, in general, significantly multiply the ways in which we can "discover" a pattern match.

A formal interpretation takes advantage of this flexibility. It chooses which of several linguistic formulations to emphasize. We saw in an earlier example how the patient's dream could be described as the pattern of dog-hitting-house; given this formulation, we could then find a similar pattern in the near accident of car-hitting-car. We could, however, with equal fidelity to the dream have described it as an instance of frustrated aggression; given that formulation, it would not have seemed similar to the car accident but might have been seen as the precursor of some other, different event. We are always creating our particular reality through language and through our various formal interpretations, which are always couched in language.

Yet interpretations work—and perhaps that is the greatest puzzle. As we have seen with respect to Greenacre's formulation, they have a certain compelling quality in the face of obvious errors of reasoning and judgment. There is satisfaction in seeing a tangled life reduced to a relatively small number of organizing principles; satisfaction in seeing a previous explanation (e.g., the primal scene) come to life again in new circumstances; and finally, satisfaction in finding correspondence between events that are separated in time and space. There is no doubting the aesthetic value of these different satisfactions. Even though they should not be confused with the historical truth of the resulting interpretations, they should not be dismissed as having no significance in their own right. And we may come to find that it is the excitement of the discovery, in finding an explanation or in participating in its unfolding, that accounts for its therapeutic effect much more than the substantive nature of the reasoning. In other words, it is the interpretation as a creative act—as a piece of narrative truth—that takes precedence.

We now come to Viderman and his belief that the analyst functions much more as a poet than as a historian. Viderman has argued for the proposition that an interpretation need have no necessary connection with the patient's past to be therapeutic; rather than representing some kind of newly discovered historical truth, such an interpretation acquires narrative truth in the process of being created. By choosing the right word or metaphor or quotation to illustrate his point, the analyst, if he is lucky, may set in motion a train of associations that leads to new discoveries.

A similar position has been expressed by Loch (1977). He makes a distinction between truth as the historical fact which only discovery will bring to the surface, and truth "as the emergent, the construction of something that makes sense" (p. 221). The second meaning parallels Goethe's statement that only what is fruitful is true—*Was fruchtbar ist, allein ist wahr.* Psychoanalysis concerns itself more with the second meaning of truth than the first; it "does not discover truth understood as a correspondence between facts of the past and propositions in the form of interpretations concerning this past. Rather, it constructs truth in the service of self-coherence for the present and for the future, on the basis of mutual agreement [between patient and analyst]. . . . On the whole . . . analytic material does not give a veridical picture of the past and therefore does not contain 'scientific truth values' " (Loch, 1977, p. 238).

As we have seen earlier in this chapter, the construction of "truth in the service of self-coherence" can be separated into two stages: first, finding a verbal expression for the anomalous event, and, second, finding a narrative home for the verbal expression. Viderman chooses to emphasize the first stage ("only interpretative speech can shape [the archaic experiences] and endow them with a new representation . . ." [1979, p. 262]), whereas Loch chooses to emphasize the second by placing the emphasis on coherence. But even though a fully detailed narrative is undoubtedly more persuasive than a highly schematic, discontinuous account, it should not be forgotten that merely finding a verbal expression for a vague memory immediately puts it in contact with our symbol system, with all of its implicit and explicit associations; as a result, even an isolated interpretation acquires a distant connection with the rest of the patient's contents of consciousness. Thus the idea of narrative truth can be seen to have two forms: a weak form, defined as finding a verbal expression for the anomalous event, and a strong form, defined as fitting the expression into the patient's life story.

The difference between narrative and historical truth parallels the difference between *construction* and *reconstruction* in the interpretative process. In one of his final papers, Freud made his position plain: *construction* was the word to be preferred. Viderman apparently agrees with Freud. But Freud never quite abandoned the archeological model, with its emphasis on reconstruction. Even in his final paper on the subject, a construction was defined as putting before the patient "a piece of his early history [*sic*] that he has forgotten." He proceeded to give the following example: "Up to your nth year you regarded yourself as the sole and unlimited possessor of your mother; then came another baby and brought you grave disillusionment. Your mother left you for some time, and even after her reappearance she was never again devoted to you exclusively. Your feelings towards your mother became ambivalent, your father gained a new importance for you" (1937, p. 261). It seems clear that he was still under the influence of his archeological metaphor and believed that the proper interpretation comes about by making contact with the past and bringing it into the presence of the patient. And somewhat later, he emphasized the same point: "our construction is only effective because it recovers a fragment of lost experience" (p. 268).

Viderman, on the other hand, makes a clean break with the archeological tradition and takes the position that the interpretation is always a creative act whose historical truth is indeterminate. All interpretations are constructions with varying amounts of foundation in historical fact; they are created by the analyst in much the same way as he creates the transference or the larger treatment situation—what Viderman calls the "analytic space." And he emphasizes the factors of choice and selection. After describing an interpretation by Melanie Klein, he comments that "this is a perfectly likely interpretation but . . . it conforms to a model that is only one among other possible interpretations, a model chosen according to the Kleinian system of interpretation for tactical reasons; and it cannot lay claim to any other truth than the one created for it in the analytic space by the speech which formulates it" (1979, p. 263).

ASPECTS OF NARRATIVE TRUTH

How do interpretations acquire narrative truth? First, it would appear that putting the formulation into words helps the patient "see" in a new way and gives reality to what was previously unknown or misunderstood. We have seen in Chapter IV how specific questions after an accident can lead the witness to change his memory of the event; he begins to "see" it in a different way, and the new memory tends to displace the earlier memory. In similar fashion, the analyst's construction of a childhood event can lead the patient to remember it differently if he remembered it at all; and if he had no access to the event, to form a new memory for the first time. Within his private domain, the newly remembered event acts and feels like any other memory; thus it becomes true. Once this kind of memory has been created, its roots in the patient's historical past become almost irrelevant, and even if it were objectively disconfirmed (by, for example, discovering an old letter or hearing from a long-lost neighbor), its subjective truth value would probably continue.

If the new construction fails to produce a new memory, it may often provide something almost as useful—a reason why. Finding a single event to explain a train of bewildering and apparently happenstance occurrences can, as we pointed out earlier, be enormously satisfying and provide great psychological support. (Loch [1977] argues similarly with respect to the importance of providing the patient with a *coherent* account of his life.) Such a reason often becomes true by virtue of necessity. It may be doubtful; it may be improbable; but if it supplies the missing link in a complex pattern of events, it tends to be held in place by the pattern, and, vice versa, to hold the pattern in place. If propositions are accepted for a sufficiently long time period, they come to be treated as true because they gain confirmation from repeated use.

A third reason why a construction may become true, in the narrative sense, is related to the issue of responsibility. Many interpretations about the patient's early childhood speak of actions or feelings about which he has no direct recollection. In a significant way, he is not responsible for them. Early constructions of this order would seem to fall into the category of what Schafer (1976) calls "disclaimed actions," and to be told that his present behavior is a consequence of some earlier event about which he has no recollection can be, for some patients, a great relief. The fault, as it were, is taken out of his hands. The psychological benefits of such an account may produce the belief that it *must* have happened that way; thus it becomes true. Schafer has criticized such locutions as "Tell me everything that comes to mind" because they allow the patient to disclaim responsibility for his actions during the analysis, and a similar criticism might be leveled at too many constructions about the patient's early past. (The recent interest in pregenital experiences would tend to augment this tendency.) But aside from this and other technical considerations, it would seem that such interpretations fit particularly well into Viderman's category; they cannot fail to become true because they serve a useful need for the patient.

Fourth, many interpretations become true because there is simply no disconfirming evidence to be used against them. Quite apart from the issue of being needed (our first point), a construction rooted in a presumed early childhood experience will survive—no matter how thin the evidence—simply because there are no competitors. It fills what had previously been an empty niche in the patient's inner world; he may have no particular vested interest in the explanation, but he may find it "true" simply because it exists.

For an illustration of how an interpretation asserts a claim to truth simply by coming into being, we can take an example from contemporary literature. A recent book entitled *Flaubert and an English Governess* (Oliver, 1980) makes the claim that the French author carried on a twenty-year affair with a woman who was the tutor of his niece. What is the evidence? He continued his relationship with the governess long after she stopped tutoring his niece; his dog was called Julie, the name of the governess; in his notebook, he mentioned a time when she met him at Victoria Station; and there are occasional references to dining at her home. What evidence we have is largely circumstantial; most damaging to the claim, there is

no existing correspondence between Flaubert and the governess. But if we assume that both parties in such a relationship
would, during the Victorian era, have taken every possible pre-
caution not to leave any clues, there is some reason to assume
that possibly an affair did take place.

What is of interest here is not the evidence for or against the
affair but rather, how the assertion that there may have been
an affair brings about a significant change in our view of the
events. Once the possibility has been raised, it can be enter-
tained with various degrees of frivolity; to a nontrivial degree,
it becomes true. Furthermore, its truth status will continue to
exist for us (perhaps forever) because it can never be disconfirmed; like the coin in the shag rug, there is always the possibility that the governess *was* his mistress and that many
ambiguous references in his notebook may, in fact, have
referred to this liaison. Also, the assertion fits with the well-
documented fact that Flaubert had many other liaisons and
was known to be in London on a number of visits during the
period in question. The fit with these more widely accepted
facts of his life gives an additional legitimacy to the claim; we
might say that its narrative truth is enhanced by its good fit
with other pieces of the past.

The claim does something more. Once the possibility of a
secret liaison has been brought to our attention, it is difficult
to see the relationship between Flaubert and the governess in
any other way. Here is another way in which the interpretation becomes true. Whether we need to see Flaubert's life as a
succession of *amours;* whether we are intrigued by his ability
to have a secret affair with a woman who lived with her mother
and sisters in a small house; or whether we have other reasons
for being interested in the suggestion, its claim on our imagi-
nation is clearly stronger than the idea of a mere friendship.
To make the claim touches on our interest in mystery, sex,
and intrigue, and these issues, in turn, help keep it alive.

But how exactly does it become true? What seems to happen is that our need to draw certain kinds of conclusions takes precedence over the idea that, in fact, nothing is known; our need for closure and continuity enables us to jump over the absence of facts. Once the conclusion is established, it can co-exist comfortably with other beliefs that come into being in more established fashion. Much as a leading question to the eyewitness in Loftus's research produced a change in his memory of the accident, so the suggestion of a liaison can change our conception of Flaubert and his relationship with the governess. We continue to think about them in a significantly new way without always being aware of why we changed our beliefs; as analysts know very well, we may believe many things without knowing the source of these beliefs or remembering exactly how we came to know them. And each time we reflect on a certain belief, we do not automatically stop and check its truth value.

We begin to see that truth is now being used in quite a different way from what is customary. Once the claim has been raised that perhaps Flaubert had an English mistress, we recognize the possibility as plausible; it fits the pattern of his life, and thus is *true* to his character. We are now back to the issue of narrative fit, and as we have seen earlier, this fit lends a compelling kind of truth to the pieces of the pattern. If someone else has read Oliver's book and tells us of the argument, we recognize the claim as *familiar* because we have encountered it before, and familiarity is another aspect of what is true. And if, in a short space of time, we encounter the argument once or twice a day, we have a new sense of it being true because *frequency* is highly correlated with likelihood. Notice that during this time nothing has happened to change the historical basis of the claim—no new evidence has been uncovered—and yet its subjective truth has undoubtedly been enhanced.

Because truth in a narrative sense seems partially independent of historical or objective truth, it is easily brought into being by claims of the kind we have been discussing. If they are plausible, familiar, and occur with sufficient frequency, they establish their own kind of truth, and their truth status, as we mentioned earlier, may remain secure for a long period. Because we are not constantly checking the source of each new piece of our contents of consciousness, we are usually unaware of which pieces to view with suspicion and which are perfectly credible. After a time, the more doubtful arrivals lose their trial status and become as fully accredited as our more established beliefs.

We begin to see how an undocumented assertion begins to acquire a life of its own, a life that is significantly unrelated to the status of the evidence. In similar fashion, an entirely imaginary interpretation may achieve a certain truth status in the analytic space. It becomes true because it is plausible, because it fits with other parts of the patient's past; over time, if repeated sufficiently often, it becomes familiar, which adds a further sense of truth; and its very frequency, as noted above, can be reassuring. It becomes true, furthermore, because it becomes useful; a particular construction may "enable the patient to discover and construct new meanings . . . either by destroying an attachment to an object . . . or by releasing him from a permanent and unnecessarily restricting commitment to a fixed moral system" (Loch, 1977, pp. 245–46). And there is the additional impact, in the analytic situation, of the transference that surrounds statements by the analyst with a particular significance. Viderman makes it clear that the process of becoming true depends on a number of factors, all acting together; if a given interpretation is delayed, for example, or expressed in slightly different language or a different tone of voice, its effects may be quite different. "Scattered at the wrong time [the interpretation] will disappear without a trace . . . the interpretation is valid and capable of being integrated only if a whole complex of conditions is present; otherwise it will come to nothing and leave no trace . . . its truth was founded solely on a specific and fugitive moment in the treatment" (1979, p. 266).

CREATIVE AND INEXACT INTERPRETATIONS

In a well-known paper on the differences between psychoanalysis and suggestion (1931), Glover posed a distinction between *inexact* and *apparently exact* interpretations and began to explore some of the clinical consequences of the former. An inexact interpretation, he reasoned, might provide the patient with a new fantasy in place of the true explanation; because it was inexact, the fantasy would not correspond to the actual circumstances surrounding the event in question; as a result, it would provide the patient with a defensive substitute and might do more harm than good. Just as an undocumented assertion acquires a life of its own, so an inexact interpretation, because it meshes with a set of beliefs that the patient may find less disturbing than the more complete formulation, may acquire subjective significance for the patient and become difficult to dislodge.

But all formal interpretations, as we have argued earlier in this chapter, depend more for their power to persuade on their linguistic characteristics than on whether or not they represent historical truth. Almost no interpretation can be exact in the sense that it corresponds to a particular time and place in the patient's past; almost every interpretation is a linguistic creation. By emphasizing the creative underpinning of every interpretation, Viderman is making us aware, once again, that psychoanalysis is not archeology and that putting things into words is much more than mere description. We interpret, as we have seen, in order to understand.

To the extent that our interpretations are more creative than otherwise, Glover's famous distinction loses some of its force.

The focus has shifted from historical truth to narrative truth. An interpretation may be inexact in the sense that it does not correspond to a piece of the past, but to the extent that it is creative and allows a new theme to emerge, it becomes a positive factor in the treatment and not necessarily a resistance (as Glover would have us believe). Glover may have been unduly optimistic about the chances of finding *exact* interpretations; as we emphasize construction over reconstruction and begin to see how the analyst, in his choice of themes and his use of language, is always putting his own stamp on the material, we begin to realize that all interpretations are inexact to a greater or lesser extent.

From the perspective of Viderman and Loch and by means of the concept of creative interpretation, we come to see Glover in a new light. Inexact interpretation should not be dismissed; rather, it may be our stock in trade. But its lack of historical fit may be less important because we have loosened our dependence on the past. A formal interpretation allows us to make certain kinds of experience accessible to the patient; once expressed in words, they can be integrated into other parts of the patient's life story and linked up with other parts of our theory. Its fit with the present may be more relevant for the treatment than its correspondence with the past; indeed, once we have expressed in words an early childhood memory or vaguely sensed dream, that translation becomes the new reality, for better or worse. We never see the clinical data in the same way again; there is no going back.

In making a formal interpretation, we exchange one kind of truth—historical truth—for the truth of being coherent and sayable—narrative truth. Language gives us this power. "The archaic experiences," writes Viderman, "have no structure, no figurable shape. Only interpretative speech can shape them and endow them with a new representation of what no longer exists except in a splintered, fragmented, unrecognizable form.

Speech provides a denomination that unifies and concretizes them in a totally original way and in a form that exists nowhere in the unconscious of the patient, or anywhere else but in the analytic space through the language that provides it with form" (1979, p. 262).

CHAPTER VI

Narrative Fit
and Becoming True

The idea that something may become true simply by being put
into words now needs to be taken up in more detail. It represents a clear break with the archeological tradition, which has
been, as we have seen, one of the principal organizing themes
of psychoanalytic theory and practice. Not only does it mark a
new departure; more to the point, the notion of becoming true
may even preclude an archeological approach. For once we
have chosen a particular construction, we have fixed, in language, the form of the event we are seeking; the words define
the object (and frequently the outcome) of our search. The
evidence from the past that emerges in the course of our clinical work may be used to confirm our search, but it has fallen
under the shadow of our construction, whatever it happens to
be. Once we have decided on a particular construction, we see
the past in a particular manner. The construction not only
shapes the past—it *becomes* the past in many cases because
many critical early experiences are preverbal and, therefore,
have no proper designation until we put them into words.

Freud could never bring himself to give up the archeological model. Even in his last major paper on the use of construction in the clinical setting, he blurred, as we have seen, the distinction between construction and reconstruction. The same ambivalence is evident throughout his case histories. The construction, initially hypothetical, gradually changes into a piece of reality in the clinical situation; in almost every instance, his initial guess about an infantile event is assumed to be correct. There seems to be no obvious difference between construction and reconstruction; the change in terminology does not alter Freud's persistent faith in the possibility of uncovering the past, a faith in the idea that psychoanalysis is an archeology of memories.

The emphasis on the past as the determining factor, the belief that he was mainly restoring to consciousness what had been repressed or forgotten, remained a significant part of his theory—in part because it protected Freud from the charge that suggestion played a critical role in treatment. So long as the analyst devoted himself to *uncovering* or *reconstructing* what had happened in the patient's early life, he could not be accused of influencing the treatment with his own fantasies and preconceptions. The word *reconstruction* suggested authenticity, making contact with what had actually happened; the word *construction,* on the other hand, carried implications of creating something new and opened the door to influence and suggestion.

The same concern is in evidence in Freud's use of the concepts of fantasy and reality. Fantasy suggests something made up, something contrived; reality represents what is given, the proper subject matter of science. Suppose, however, that fantasy is redefined as a particular kind of reality—then we are on firmer ground. The need for such a redefinition may have inspired Freud's concept of psychical reality. "The phantasies possess psychical as contrasted with material reality, and we gradually learn to understand that in the world of the neuroses it is psychical reality which is the decisive kind" (1917a, p. 368). The concept of psychical reality makes it possible to take seriously the content of a patient's fantasy by treating it as a tangible given and thus conform to the archeological model. Psychical reality is clearly not the same as material reality, but by making it a piece of something real, Freud makes it a legitimate subject for investigation. It, too, can be uncovered, reconstructed, and brought to light; it is not a subject for guesswork and supposition but is only waiting to be discovered in the course of treatment.

In the archeological model, the past is prologue, and discovery is the key. Truth is waiting for us, hidden in the patient's life; it simply remains to be uncovered. The role of the interpretation is to assist in the process of discovery. Once we shift to the idea that we can create truth by statement—the concept of becoming true—we have left the domain of archeology and opened up new and dangerous doors. Now the concept of construction takes on new significance because it represents a shift from discovery to creation. The interpretation, as we have seen in Chapter V, can bring an idea into being for the first time. Once stated, it becomes partially true; as it is repeated and extended, it becomes familiar; and as its familiarity adds to its plausibility, it becomes completely true.

Along with the shift from discovery to creation, we also have a shift in our approach to time. Working within the archeological model, Freud reasoned that the past had priority and represented the proper subject matter of psychoanalysis. Reconstructions were devoted to rearranging fragments of the patient's early life; symptoms were supposed to have their source in infantile conflict; dreams were assumed to require an infantile wish simply to come into being. But if we assume, with Viderman, that interpretation is creative and that something may become true simply as a consequence of being stated, then we necessarily shift our focus from past to present.

The change in focus becomes clear in what is perhaps Viderman's most famous clinical example. One of his patients reported the following dream: "My father and I are in a garden. I pick some flowers and offer him a bouquet of six roses." Viderman, in an attempt to bring out the patient's ambivalent feelings toward his father, tried to combine the positive connotations of the gift with the negative feelings he may have had about the fact that the father had died of alcoholism. He took advantage of the phonetic similarity between the six roses of the dream and the father's fatal illness—cirrhosis of the liver (the similarity in sound connecting *six roses* and *cirrhosis* is particularly evident in French)—and made the following reply: "Six roses or cirrhosis?" Here are his explanatory comments:

> After it was uttered, several possible perspectives were opened up, according to the variable and mobile aspects of the transference-countertransference relationship. If, on the one hand, the appraisal of the unconscious proximity of negative feelings was correct and if, on the other hand, the quality of the transference cathexis allowed the interpretation to be accepted and integrated, it became true through a dynamic process which created it. . . . The interpretation has brought forth a new representation. (1979, p. 265)

The focus, as this quotation clearly shows, has now turned to what lies ahead, toward the changes brought about by this particular construction in the clinical situation (Viderman's "analytic space"). The interpretation is designed to open up new possibilities, to bring separate ideas together in a new and potentially evocative combination. Its fate will be determined by how the patient responds and by what new associations come to mind. The analyst has not attempted to reconstruct a specific piece of the past by listening to the patient's associations; rather, he has attempted to create a new cluster of ideas, a cluster that has probably never been expressed in exactly that way, in an attempt to make the patient aware of both positive and negative feelings toward his father.

By putting his interpretation in that particular concise form, Viderman has created a mnemonic that is likely to persist; in the process he has defined the dream in a particular way that the patient is likely to remember. From its initial manifest sense—a gift of roses to the father—the dream has become a representation of ambivalent feelings (the patient is making him a gift of the disease which killed him), and by taking advantage of a convenient similarity of sounds, Viderman has made it into a useful bench mark in the treatment, which can be brought into the analytic space at some future time.

We now begin to see the creative possibilities of this kind of interpretation. The analyst can, in effect, introduce new evidence, remind the patient of old themes, add or take away emphasis, and otherwise extend the clinical material in almost any direction. His ultimate aim, in Ricoeur's classic statement, is to raise the "case history to the sort of narrative intelligibility we ordinarily expect from a story" (1977, p. 869). This goal, seemingly simple, now deserves more extended consideration, and we will see as we analyze the concept of narrative fit how much of a deviation it represents from the traditional archeological model.

NARRATIVE FIT

"Psychoanalytic reports," Ricoeur tells us, "are kinds of biographies and autobiographies whose literary history is a part of the long tradition emerging from the oral epic tradition of the Greeks, the Celts and the Germans. It is this whole tradition of storytelling that provides a relative autonomy to the criterion of narrative intelligibility." "We interpolate explanation," he suggests, "when the narrative process is blocked and in order to 'follow-further.' These explanations are acceptable to the extent that they may be grafted upon the archetypes of storytelling which have been culturally developed and which rule our actual competence to follow new stories" (1977, p. 869).

Exactly how do we "follow-further"? Gaps must be filled; explanations must be supplied; puzzles must be clarified. What we are after, it seems, is a narrative account that provides a coherent picture of the events in question. Atkinson, in his philosophy of history, defines coherence as "comprehensiveness with unity, nothing relevant omitted, everything irrelevant excluded" (1978, p. 131). Putting the events in chronological order is a beginning but by itself, he argues, is not sufficient because it is no guarantee that all relevant events have been included; in the same fashion, evidence as to the truth of each event is not sufficient because truth alone says nothing about chronology.

Sherwood (1969) in his discussion of the requirements for a satisfactory psychoanalytic narrative, takes a similar position. The psychoanalytic narrative, he argues, must meet the criteria of *adequacy* and *accuracy*. Criteria of *adequacy* include self-consistency, coherence, and comprehensiveness and serve to define what we have called narrative truth; criteria of *accuracy* cover the truth value of the individual assertions and the degree to which they correspond to what is actually uncovered in the course of the analysis—what we have called historical truth. Again we see that historical truth, by itself, is not sufficient because the pieces must be fitted into an understandable Gestalt (narrative truth); and, of course, narrative truth could not be maintained if all pieces of the narrative were fabricated (zero historical truth).

Both Atkinson and Sherwood agree that a satisfactory narrative must be comprehensive and coherent, and this emphasis brings us back to the tradition of storytelling described by Ricoeur. But as we begin to consider this requirement in more detail, we see that the need to make a good story may often be at odds with the need to be historically truthful: what is plausible may not be proven, for example, and what is required by the story in terms of satisfying an aesthetic requirement may be outside the scope of the analysis. We begin to see an inherent contradiction between Sherwood's two sets of criteria. Not only is there a contradiction; on occasion, the need for narrative fit may be controlling and the constructions that are needed to make the narrative coherent and comprehensive may later be accepted as true.

We now come to understand another aspect of what is meant by being true. A particular clinical event—an association, for example, or a partly recovered memory—may seem to clarify the unfolding account of the patient's life history so precisely that both patient and analyst come to the conclusion that it *must* be true. As we have seen, under these conditions narrative fit is usually taken to be conclusive, and if a piece of the past completes the unfinished clinical picture in just the right way—and we will come back to the criteria of adequacy at a later point—then it acquires its own truth value and no further checking is necessary. Many of Freud's constructions seem to have followed this path. What was originally hypothetical and problematic, possessing no known truth value, turns out to bring together pieces of the patient's life story which, up to that point, had seemed disconnected and even contradictory. The construction that began as a contribution to the coherence of the narrative (Sherwood's first set of criteria) gradually comes to acquire truth value in its own right and is assumed to satisfy the criteria of accuracy (Sherwood's second set). As soon as that step is taken, the *construction* becomes a *reconstruction*—a piece of the past that is taken to be as real as the name of the patient's father or the date of his birth.

This kind of clinical reasoning, in which we use the coherence of the narrative to establish the truth of the separate parts, depends heavily, it would, seem, on our definition of coherence. If we are putting together a jigsaw puzzle in which each piece has one and only one final resting place, we can use what might be called the narrative fit to establish the correct position of each of the pieces. But coherence in a psychoanalytic case history would seem to depend on much looser criteria, and as soon as we admit that, for example, a given account might have a number of different endings, all equally satisfying, we begin to see that establishing narrative fit may be a less definitive outcome than we might have wished and, as a consequence, a rather shaky basis for making claims about truth value.

Part of the difficulty stems from the familiar problem of pattern match. It seems much easier to find items that would clarify or extend a narrative than to find items that would not fit or that might even invalidate major portions of the narrative. A narrative, in short, is almost infinitely elastic, accommodating almost any new evidence that happens to come along. One reason for this almost embarrassing flexibility stems from the fact that narratives depend, as we have seen, rather heavily on chronology. The syntax of the narrative can be represented in the form "and then . . . and then . . . and then . . ." (see Atkinson, 1978, p. 129). Given this loose syntax, it becomes easy to insert a wide range of happenings at any particular point in the story. Freud made such an addition in his construction of the Grusha episode. According to the Wolf Man's initial memory of the event, Grusha was kneeling on the floor, alongside a pail and a short broom made out of twigs, and he was being teased or scolded. Freud inserted the hypothetical urination to help account for the teasing. Because early memories tend to be vague and fragmentary, clearly not exhausting all of the events that may have taken place in "real time," there is always room to insert new happenings that can add to the coherence and clarity of the narrative. But just as it is easy to embellish a narrative in this manner, it is much more difficult to use the narrative to exclude certain possibilities and to argue that, given this memory, such and such could *not* have happened. We are confronted, once again, with an embarrassing asymmetry in the logic of events—narrative fit is far easier to establish than narrative failure.

So far as story tellers or myth makers are concerned, this narrative flexibility simply provides them with more opportunities to practice their craft and add embellishment to what has gone before. But for the psychoanalyst, we see that narrative flexibility can become a serious problem. For if narrative suitability is used to justify the truth value of a particular construction, then we begin to see that the criteria of adequacy (narrative truth) may sometimes be a poor substitute for the criteria of accuracy (historical truth) because an almost infinite number of items can be accommodated in any particular chronology.

Chronology is not our only guide to relevance; we also depend heavily on repetition of theme and convergence of similar patterns. Arlow (1979) has provided a more extended account of how we go about establishing the truth of an interpretation:

> Most important is the context in which the specific material appears. Contiguity usually suggests dynamic relevance. The configuration of the material, the form and sequence in which the associations appear, represent substantive and interpretable connections. Other criteria are to be seen in the repetition and the convergence of certain themes within the organized body of associations. The repetition of similarities or opposites is always striking and suggestive. Material in context appearing in related sequence, multiple representations of the same theme, repetition in similarity, and a convergence of the data into one comprehensible hypothesis constitute the specific methodological approach in psychoanalysis used to validate insights obtained in an immediate, intuitive fashion in the analytic interchange. (p. 203)

Let us look in more detail at each of these items. Contiguity, first of all, is a somewhat unreliable guide to relevance because, as we have seen in another context, a great deal depends on the size of the search space. An association that follows immediately after a given interpretation and that seems to continue its theme is reasonably impressive as confirmation; one that appears after ten minutes of unrelated associations is somewhat less convincing. In our eagerness to search for confirmation, we may overlook the first ten minutes altogether or collapse it, retrospectively, into a much shorter time period. Contiguity, in the last analysis, is always a function of the time interval in question, and we rarely have information about it.

Assume for the moment that the relevant association came immediately after the interpretation; would that be sufficient validation? Not necessarily—because of the familiar problem of pattern match. On what grounds do we decide that association A1 is relevant to interpretation A? A moment's thought will show that similarity of meaning is remarkably easy to establish because of the fact that we can almost always find a mediating link. Interpretation A and association A1 may both remind us of B; given a link in common, they naturally seem to be related. In the famous Grusha episode in the Wolf Man case, Grusha is remembered kneeling on the floor beside a broom of twigs. The patient associates to the story of John Huss being burned at the stake—*twigs* are the stimulus for *fire* and *stake*. Freud happens to believe that people who suffer from enuresis are often admirers of Huss; thus the idea of urination is brought into the formulation. Both the twig broom and urination have links with the story of Huss; it provides the mediating concept by which Freud is able to introduce the idea of urination into the Grusha memory. Notice that the twig broom and the idea of urination have nothing in common aside from this mediating link, and notice, further, that the link is not made explicit in the reconstruction.

Given the proper mediating links, there is almost no limit to the pairs of associations that can be found to be similar. Just as we are not aware of (and almost never document) the size of the search space in an instance of contiguity, so we are equally unaware of the number of mediating associations that provide the link between interpretation and association. Because the links are almost never included in the documentation, the reader is usually at a loss to know how similarity was established; he can only assume that the treating analyst had good reasons for deciding that a given association was relevant. But a moment's thought will show that the proper mediating idea is more often the product of the analyst's private store of associations than specific to the material in question; thus it opens up the possibility of a subtle kind of countertransference, to which we will return in a later section. For the moment, we need only emphasize the fact that the criterion of similarity is much looser than we might like to admit.

Finally, let us look at the use of thematic convergence as a way of validating an interpretation. Similarity of theme can be established by the use of mediating links and by the proper selection of subthemes. In the Grusha episode, Freud chose to focus on Huss as a kind of emblem for urination; he could just as easily have decided to focus on his helplessness in being tied to the stake, his pain at being burned to death, his standing as a heroic figure, or any number of other aspects of the scene. Complex themes, by definition, are always composed of multiple parts; two complex themes can almost always be found to share something in common. Once again, we see that the criterion of thematic convergence is looser than we might wish.

But surely, goes the reply, chronology, contiguity, and repetition are not all we use to establish the truth of an interpretation. Case histories also rely heavily on general laws, which form the backbone of psychoanalytic theory. But in the past two decades we have witnessed a growing skepticism about metapsychology. Holt (1975) has mounted a series of attacks on such basic concepts as psychic energy and primary process. Klein (1973) has argued for a renewed emphasis on the clinical theory in favor of the metatheory—an argument, in our terminology, in favor of narrative truth over historical truth.

And Schafer (1976) has criticized metapsychology on more operational grounds, claiming that many of its referents are metaphorical and that we must focus instead on the more concrete objectivity of actions and action language. Because many of the general laws are metaphors, he claims, they must be set aside in favor of more observable formulations. As metapsychology has tended to come under attack, clinical reasoning, as represented in clinical reports, tends to depend more and more on narrative fit. The aesthetic quality of the case history has tended, as a result, to pre-empt the use of general law. Narrative truth has tended to supplant historical truth.

Now we are in a position to identify one of the current problems in psychoanalytic thought. As general laws, particularly those contained in traditional metapsychology, become less persuasive, we are tempted to turn to narrative fit as the guiding criterion for what is true. A focus on narrative fit brings with it a shift toward the present, the "here and now," and the state of the transference (see Gray [1973] and Gill [1979]). From the standpoint of evidence alone, we seem on firmer ground when we base our interpretations on what happens in the hour "in plain sight" as compared to what is reported by the patient, often unsupported by other witnesses. Further uneasiness about the past as a source of data has been reinforced by the gradual awareness that the archeological model, of which Freud was so fond, may not apply so clearly to the analytic situation; as we noted in Chapter V, memories are changeable, form does not always lead to insight about content, and—perhaps most important—the memories themselves are not always real. As we made clear in Chapter IV, a memory can sometimes be altered by an interpretation.

Turning away from the past and setting aside the archeological model, we focus on the present and rely more and more heavily on narrative explanation as the final criterion. And the initial experience seems promising; the remembered account, as given by the patient, is sufficiently elastic so that any number of additions seems possible. We may be further reassured when many of these constructions are gratefully accepted by the patient; they give him explanation in place of uncertainty, and they sometimes lead to further recall. Putting a construction in the proper context often gives it a reality that is so compelling that we quickly assume, along with Freud, that we have uncovered a piece of the past.

But that is precisely the trouble. The unfolding narrative, in all of its embarrassing elasticity, can embrace almost any piece of information, and once caught up in its folds, the piece in question becomes, ipso facto, genuine. The truth test is instantly passed; forever after, the piece in question is legitimate. No matter how tentative the construction or its trigger, once embedded in the unfolding narrative, it takes on a special kind of grace and is automatically granted a kind of privileged status. By virtue of becoming true, by taking on some piece of psychical reality, the construction becomes a bone fide piece of the patient's life story.

Two cautions seem important to keep in mind. First, the particular satisfaction that comes from good narrative fit should not be confused with the excitement of making a historical discovery; constructions should not be shaded into reconstructions, and the difference between the two kinds of truth statements should always be kept in mind. That is not to say that good narrative fit should be discounted; on the contrary, it would appear to be an important part of what brings about change. Creative interpretation—finding the right words at the right time—is a clinical gift that we all value highly, and we know from experience in supervision how a badly worded or badly timed interpretation falls on deaf ears.

At the same time, the fact that we (as analysts) are dealing with narrative truth places a certain restriction on how we use our findings. Just as the context of discovery is not equivalent to the context of justification (see Reichenbach, 1951), so a truth that emerges in the context of a particular analytic interchange may not support a general law. In moving from the particular to the general, we may lose the specific mixture of ingredients that made the formulation effective at the time it was uttered. What convinces patient and analyst in a particular piece of analytic space may appear groundless to the outside observer. Some of the power to persuade may be restored by careful unpacking of the interchange (we discuss this possibility in the next chapter), but there are probably many interpretations that will not "travel well," even when fully glossed.

The most serious mistake, of course, is to confuse the two kinds of truth statements—to assume that good narrative fit indicates a bona fide historical discovery. Freud was fond of speaking of the "kernel of truth" in every construction (see Freud, 1937, p. 268), but as yet, we have no sure way of isolating these pieces as a foundation for a more general theory. We will return to some implications of this problem in the last chapter; now we turn to the problem of countertransference and its contribution to clinical understanding.

COUNTERTRANSFERENCE AND NARRATIVE FIT

We have seen how mediating associations, known only to the analyst, can be used to form links between two pieces of clinical material and, in the process, help to facilitate the understanding of the patient's utterances. We will now argue that many of these mediating links are very likely triggered by memories or fantasies that are specific to the analyst and that properly come under the heading of countertransference. We will use the formulation proposed by Annie Reich and define countertransference as "the effects of the analyst's own unconscious needs and conflicts on his understanding or technique" (Reich, 1973, p. 138). Consider now the following example: A student in supervision "suddenly visualized, in connection with a dream of the patient, the inscrutable smile of the Mona Lisa. When this was transmitted to the patient, a great deal of relevant, new material came to light. The image thus served like an interpretation that confirms its correctness by stimulation of new material" (Reich, 1973, p. 350).

To what extent has correctness been confirmed by narrative fit? Placing the emphasis on narrative truth over historical truth, we would tend to place less stress on whether or not the intervention was correct, and more stress on what it produced in the way of new material. In other words, what seems important in this example is that the Mona Lisa smile, when communicated to the patient, happened to produce new associations; it had a facilitating effect on the treatment. But since narrative fit is a rather loose criterion, the fact that relevant material emerged says very little about either the correctness of the intervention or about the historical validity of the associations. Narrative fit speaks to narrative truth; it says relatively little about historical truth.

A rather famous example of how the two kinds of truth may be confused may be found in the familiar case of the Wolf Man; this time we will consider it from a somewhat broader perspective. One of Freud's reasons for writing the case was to show that an early childhood event, in specific and concrete detail, could be reconstructed from the patient's associations and dreams many years later. He was determined to show that psychoanalysis was, in fact, a procedure that could bring back to awareness events that had long since been repressed. Equally important, he wanted evidence for his belief that early sexual experiences exerted a critical influence on later development. "The primary significance of the case history in Freud's eyes at the time of its publication [writes Strachey in his introduction] was clearly the support it provided for his criticisms of Adler and more especially of Jung. Here was conclusive evidence to refute any denial of infantile sexuality" (Freud, 1918, p. 5; editor's note). By reconstructing the famous primal scene in which the Wolf Man is witness to his parents' copulation *a tergo* and by showing how derivatives of this scene can be found in subsequent dreams and screen memories, Freud was making the attempt to show that a sexual experience, with all of its ramifications, could be the primary cause of a neurosis.

We have seen how the Grusha episode, a privotal link in Freud's chain of reasoning, was changed from an initial memory of being teased by a servant girl to a scene in which the young Wolf Man had urinated at the sight of the girl scrubbing on her hands and knees; the girl teased him in response and (Freud assumed) threatened him with castration. Changing the episode from one of teasing into a scene incorporating urination and threats of castration helps to increase the similarity between the Grusha memory and the presumed primal scene; we may assume that the need to show that Jung was wrong and his own theory correct may have prompted Freud to improve the pattern match. But now we can be more specific about the source of the urination construction; we have good reason to believe that Freud himself was troubled by bedwetting as a child. Two pieces of relevant evidence appear in *The Interpretation of Dreams,* where Freud is describing his associations to the Count Thun dream. In the first, he reports occasionally wetting his bed and, around the age of two, being reproached by his father; in the second, Freud remembers urinating in his parents' bedroom and hearing his father say, "The boy will come to nothing." "This must have been a frightful blow to my ambition," Freud writes, "for references to this scene are still constantly recurring in my dreams and are always linked with an enumeration of my achievements and successes" (1900; both references can be found on p. 216). We see that loss of control over urination was a significant issue in Freud's development; even more important, we can interpret the second scene, where he was told he would come to nothing, as a rather thinly veiled castration threat. We can thus claim a fairly good pattern match between this early memory of being confronted by the father and the reconstruction of the Wolf Man scene that turns it into a castration threat in response to urination. The many similarities between the two scenes suggest that Freud's reconstruction had its roots in his own experience and, therefore, can be classified as a piece of countertransference.

COUNTERTRANSFERENCE AND CONSTRUCTIVE LISTENING

Signs of the influence of countertransference are usually searched out in the wording and timing of formal interpretations. But as we have seen in Chapter IV, listening by itself is necessarily subjective and constructive; we are always shaping material in order to understand it, and we might assume that the analyst's needs and wishes, his unconscious hopes and fears might be constantly at work in shaping what he hears and how he hears it. One way, then, by which the analyst's unconscious needs can affect his understanding (to return to Reich's definition) is in the way he chooses to hear his patients' productions. In other words, countertransference plays a critical role in shaping the analyst's unwitting, informal interpretations of what the patient is saying and would seem to enter the scene long before the analyst arrives at a particular interpretation.

Clues to this preliminary influence are significantly hard to find. The impact of the analyst's needs and wishes on his initial hearing of the material is rarely documented because we almost never have access to *both* the raw material of the session—the literal words of the patient and the analyst—and exactly how the analyst understood this material. Part of the problem stems from the traditional need of the analyst to remain silent; thus we only rarely have an explicit response to the patient's utterance. Process notes are usually of no help because these concern the dynamic implications of the material and are rarely devoted to the more primary questions of understanding. (It is here, by the way, that we see one consequence of the traditional view of free-floating attention. In teaching us that all the analyst need do is listen to the material with "evenly-hovering attention," Freud created the impression that listening is a relatively uncomplicated activity and, therefore, needs no particular comment in the day-to-day notes of the practicing analyst.)

Nor have tape recordings helped the matter to any considerable extent. Even though we may have the verbatim text of many sessions, in only exceptional cases do we have a gloss on this text that was contributed by the analyst within moments or hours of the hour in question and that would give us an understanding of how he heard each particular statement. As we make clear in the next chapter, it is usually too late to ask the analyst to provide this gloss after the case is concluded, or even several weeks after the hour has actually taken place; private understandings are too fleeting to last long in their original form, and the object of the exercise—the analyst's unconscious hopes and fears—are too easily repressed to expect much clarity long after the fact. Thus the gloss must be generated immediately after the session; if it is not created then, we will probably never again have the opportunity to understand exactly how the material was understood.

Verbatim texts are also deficient for another reason. Just as listening with free-floating attention is not as uncomplicated as Freud would have us believe, so the transcribing of a tape-recorded session is far more complex than most people realize. Some passages must be played a dozen times or more before their meaning is clear; other passages, perhaps because they are spoken through a sob, muttered, or whispered, will never become clear, no matter how often they are played. Some passages mean one thing to one listener and something else to another—and we might assume, something still different to the treating analyst, who does not usually transcribe the tape.

Even if the session were transcribed to a level of 99.9 percent accuracy, however, we are still left without the most crucial part of the data—the treating analyst's understanding of what was said. Only by seeing both the initial utterance and how it is construed (even when nothing is spoken) are we in a position to understand how the analyst brings his own needs and wishes to bear on what he hears. What is spoken of in case histories and theoretical papers as "the material" is probably some indeterminate mixture of what was said and how it was construed. Thus the basic data of our literature are probably a mixture of construction and fact. To make matters worse, this mixture is usually referred to indirectly; when it is quoted verbatim, it is almost never broken down into (a) the patient's actual statement and (b) the analyst's conception of what he said. Before the advent of tape recording, of course, this kind of breakdown would have been impossible because all the analyst had to work with was (b); the content of (a) was lost as soon as it was spoken. But even now, with tape recordings more and more in fashion, we rarely see both parts of the construction made explicit because of the problems just mentioned—and because the issue is usually not conceptualized in exactly this fashion.

As a consequence of the general tendency to equate what the patient says and what the analyst hears, we are short of material to discuss. But we do have certain clues that what was said was sometimes different from what was heard, allowing us to make a beginning on the problem of how countertransference may influence the very early stages of listening.

Our first example has already been cited in an earlier chapter. The analyst who turned off the tape recorder at the *patient's* request was discovered, on listening to the recording itself, to have misremembered the incident and turned it off for reasons of his own; these reasons were then projected onto the patient. Our second example comes from the case recorded by Dewald (1972); it occurred during the third month of treatment. We

begin with a question by the analyst, which occurred shortly
after the beginning of the hour:

A: What comes to your mind about having feelings for me, and
that I don't respond in the same way to you?

P: (90-second silence). I feel it now and I felt it earlier this
morning, and it was in the dream also, that I'm feminine
and soft and cuddly and warm and loving. I was never
accepted by my father this way as a child, but now I feel as
if you might accept me. In the dream, we were in the playpen and it was in Evanston and all of us girls were there.
We were dressed up kind of frilly and there were people
looking in on us, and the men were in tuxedos. I was lying
on the floor and I had no pants on and I kept wondering
what the men would think. Before this, when I used to dream
that I'm naked, I'd feel embarrassed because I was missing
a penis, and I would want to run and hide away. I wasn't
last night, although I was unsure, but I thought I wanted to
take the chance.

A: What comes to mind about this feeling that I might accept
you as feminine and soft and loving?

P: That's just the way you are. You are capable of loving me
and of not caring what I look like, and for you it wouldn't
make any difference about the— (60-second silence).

A: You cut something short there.

P: The surface things.

A: I think you mean the presence or absence of a penis.

P: I'm suddenly getting very nervous and hostile. I had a wonderful feeling until I came but now you are making me feel
that I had a penis. I don't want one. (p. 175)

Did the last statement by the analyst complete the patient's
thought? We can think of alternative possibilities—the "surface things" might have referred to frilly clothes, to the fact
that the patient was lying in a playpen, perhaps even to the
fact that she was wearing no pants. Each of these thoughts
might have led, through association, to the fact that she felt

castrated, but this thought may not have been in awareness at that time.

Dewald admits, in a later discussion of the hour, that the intervention was a poor one, but he is critical more for reasons of timing than anything else ("This turns out to be a poor intervention since I did not anticipate that the transference reaction would cause her to experience my remark as depreciating and would thus cause her to withdraw"—p. 178). Its truth value is never discussed. His comment gives us the feeling that he sees the material as very clearly pointing to a castration theme; reading through the sequence, we suspect that he imposed a standard interpretation onto material that may have been leading in a different direction. Despite his statement that he supplied "the obvious association to the penis," we have reason to question whether or not it was all that obvious.

The intervention, furthermore, seems to shift the direction of the hour. In the section just quoted, the patient said about the analyst that "You are capable of loving me and of not caring what I look like"; shortly after the intervention, she negates this by saying, "You'll *never* say 'I'm so glad that you don't have one and it's wonderful just the way you are ' " (italics added). It could be argued, in fact, that the analyst's intervention about the penis made it clear that he was very much aware of what the patient looked like—quite the opposite from not caring.

By making this particular interpretation, the analyst imposes a certain shape and direction on the material. We suspect that completing her thought in that particular manner allowed him to better understand the material and partly reduce its ambiguity—the ambiguity that would have been left standing had he said nothing and allowed the silence to continue. Thus his intervention can be described as stemming directly from an unwitting interpretation designed to facilitate constructive listening. Although the example is far from conclusive, it suggests that by giving the material this particular construction, the analyst was better able to organize its different features into a coherent whole. The castration theme becomes a convenient heuristic by which he can make sense out of a collection of unorganized details.

Not only is the interpretation not accepted—by imposing this particular construction on the material, the analyst has prevented the patient from developing her own sense of the underlying theme. For purposes of our argument, however, the point to be stressed is the failure of the analyst to separate fact from interpretation. He seems to have no doubt that his construction is exactly what the patient had in mind. Far from supplying one of many equally plausible alternatives, he is simply giving the only correct answer.

Now we can return to the issue of countertransference. If we allow for the moment that the analyst's unconscious needs and wishes may play a part in the preliminary understanding of the patient's utterances, then we must draw the further conclusion that countertransference is much more a part of the treatment situation than we usually like to assume. If an interpretation represents a creative decision, one choice among many, then the analyst's own hopes and fears must inevitably contribute to choosing a particular intervention. In this particular instance, we cannot specify the reasons for this particular response; they belong to Dewald's privileged competence (a concept that will be defined more precisely in the next chapter). The point we are making is that the intervention should not be seen as flowing inevitably from the material and that a comprehensive account of the session needs a listing of the reasons that persuaded the analyst to make this particular statement. It becomes a question of how this particular session combined with his specific assumptions to produce this particular response. Dewald has already glossed the hour; we are suggesting that he expand his gloss even further and raise questions about issues that he seems to take for granted.

Not only is countertransference always present; it can probably never be removed. For if listening is necessarily subjective and if we are always shaping the material by our own hopes and fears simply in order to understand it, then the result of "analyzing away the countertransference" would lead to a serious loss of understanding. Let us examine this paradox in more detail.

"The act of understanding the patient's productions in analysis," writes Annie Reich (1973), "and the ability to respond to them skillfully is not based solely on logical conclusions. Frequently the analyst can observe that insight into the material comes suddenly as if from somewhere within his own mind. Suddenly the confusing, incomprehensible presentation makes sense; suddenly the disconnected elements become a *Gestalt*. Equally suddenly, the analyst gets inner evidence as to what his interpretation should be and how it should be given" (p. 136).

Reich is clear in her distinction between understanding and interpretation; the first must precede the second and, it could be argued, may even take place without leading to an interpretation. She is discussing the way in which *dynamic* understanding takes place; we are suggesting that something similar may accompany what might be called *semantic* understanding. Because the insight and comprehension is often instantaneous, because the analyst usually feels clear as to what the patient is talking about (as distinct from what he means), he is usually unaware of the extent to which he has taken a hand in shaping the material. He may, for example, add emphasis; supply a missing phrase; think of a recent example; or simply choose to hear a homonym in a particular way. Each of these decisions is made without awareness; the analyst is only conscious that he understands the semantic content and is not aware that this act of understanding is the outcome of a complicated series of maneuvers that have inevitably added something to the raw material of what was being said.

Not only is he unaware of making these alterations in the text; he is almost certainly unaware of the unconscious grounds for many of these decisions. If the patient's statement reminds him of a particular example, we might assume that what example is chosen will depend on just how the analyst's hopes and wishes are aroused by what the patient is saying. If the utterance is incomplete and the analyst supplies (if only for himself) the missing phrase, the choice of this phrase will almost certainly depend on some mixture of private feelings and patient needs. In each of these examples, his unconscious needs have affected his understanding of the material; each example, therefore, satisfies Reich's example of countertransference. Neither example, furthermore, is likely to be accessible to self-analysis because of the fact that, first, the analyst will almost never be aware of what was actually said (the exceptional cases being those where a tape recorder was also present); the second, because the rearrangement of the material is almost always instantaneous. This speed, it should be noted, is almost a requirement of fluid understanding; without the immediate rearrangement of patient utterance into a meaningful response, the analyst could hardly hope to maintain an attentive listening posture over long periods of time.

When the analyst unwittingly translates the patient's partial utterance into something that makes conceptual sense, he not only creates a construction composed of a mixture of the patient's thoughts and his own hopes and fears, but he also, unwittingly, makes the assumption that this construction corresponds to the complete utterance; that what he created, in other words, is what the patient actually thought. In contrast to the self-consciously crafted constructions we discussed in the chapter on formal interpretations, this kind of construction may even take place outside of awareness. Nevertheless, it still conforms to the same rule of being true; once created in a particular form, it becomes persuasive in its own right. The rule of becoming true may even apply with added force to this kind of unwitting construction because the analyst is usually unaware of making a choice. Its truth value is so well established that it probably comes as a surprise to most analysts to be told that other rearrangements might have been possible.

A close inspection of most case reports in the analytic literature shows that the reasoning usually takes up far more space than the evidence and that the evidence, when presented, is usually more *about* something the patient said than a presentation of his actual statement. But unless it is produced by tape recorder, we now have reason to be suspicious of even the actual utterance; if it relies on process notes or merely on memory at the time of writing the paper, it may well represent more of a construction than a raw fact. Verified patient utterances in their raw form are very difficult to come by, and this may be one clue to the interminable nature of psychoanalytic debates. As we will see in more detail in the next section, the proof of a new concept usually depends more on narrative fit than on evidence. Claims are usually supported by private data, and the evidence, if introduced at all, tends to be second-order, *about* something the patient said, rather than first-order, the actual statement.

But to return to the problem of countertransference; what position should be taken? We have seen that it very likely plays a role in determining what the analyst believes is being said by the patient; we have also seen that the impact of a possible countertransference interference is usually judged by looking at the consequences. But in the case of unwitting interpretations, the outcome rule can never be applied because neither the analyst nor his severest critic is likely to be aware that an issue of interpretation is at stake. Far from being held in abeyance until the outcome can be studied, the construction is immediately redefined as a fact.

NARRATIVE FIT AND CONCEPTUAL CHANGE

At the close of a paper summarizing his position on the significance of the transference, Gill (1979) reminds the reader that similar arguments have appeared many times before in the history of psychoanalytic thought. "But like so many other aspects of psychoanalytic theory and practice they fade in and out of prominence and are rediscovered again and again, possibly occasionally with some modest conceptual advance, but often with a newness attributable only to ignorance of past contributions. There are doubtless many reasons for this phenomenon. But not the least, in my opinion, is the almost total absence of systematic and controlled research in the psychoanalytic situation" (p. 296).

Gill is pointing to one of the more worrisome characteristics of psychoanalytic thought. It tends to be cyclical rather than cumulative; old concepts may give way to new ideas, but their disappearance is more temporary than otherwise, suggesting that the change in focus is a matter more of fad and fashion than the outcome of a new conceptual advance. Lack of research may be one reason for the cyclical nature of psychoanalytic thought, but a more fundamental cause lies in the nature of the evidence used to support the concepts in question. As we will try to show in this section, justification of a new concept tends to depend more on giving it a name and finding it a narrative home than on any appeal to evidence; and the evidence, when presented, tends to be second-order or worse. In other words, as we will try to argue, the acceptance and validation of new beliefs in the development of psychoanalytic thought follows much the same pattern as the acceptance and validation of interpretations during a clinical session. New concepts behave much like constructions because they fill a missing link in the chain of reasoning without necessarily bring with them much in the way of supporting data.

To study this process in more detail, we will look closely at the development of one concept in particular—the concept of therapeutic alliance. This analysis will provide us with a case history of conceptual change, and we will be able to see what kind of evidence was used to formulate the concept in the first stages of development; how it came to be validated and eventually accepted; and how it survived subsequent attack. But first, before going to the case history, we need to identify some general principles that bear on the issue of conceptual change.

In his discussion of the question of proof in psychoanalysis, Ricoeur (1977) sets forth four criteria for what constitute *facts* in the clinical situation. To qualify as a psychoanalytic fact, an item, Ricoeur argues, must first be "capable of being said"; second, it must be said to another person; third, it must represent a piece of psychic reality; and fourth, it must be "capable of entering into a story or narrative" (pp. 836–43). The same set of criteria could be used to identify a new concept in psychoanalytic theory. First, the concept under consideration must be given a name, and as we will see, the act of naming is by itself a kind of validation and contributes significantly to its truth value. Once named, it is well on the way to being true regardless of its subsequent validation. Corresponding to Ricoeur's second criterion, we would say that the new concept needs to be introduced into the literature. (And here, it helps to be backed by someone with a certain amount of professional authority.) Third, it must supply a felt need in our collective clinical experience; and fourth, it must conform to our notion of narrative fit. We will argue that if a new concept complies with these four criteria, it will have a fair chance of surviving the test of time—and that subsequent validation, based on the conventional rules of evidence, is more or less irrelevant.

Before we try out this line of argument on the concept of therapeutic alliance, consider for a moment the implications for the problem of conceptual change. If a new concept relies more on naming and narrative fit and less on validating evidence, then the dismissal of a concept comes about more by neglect than by disproof; if it is not mentioned sufficiently often, it will tend to disappear. Thus the currency of an idea depends more on the number of its adherents and how frequently they publish than on whether or not it matches the evidence. Second, the fact that evidence is not used for purposes of justification or validation allows the reader to supply his own conception of what exactly is being proposed. Third, we can now clarify the role of research. If a concept is justified by being named and by fitting in with prevailing theory, then the presence of research data may have no immediate bearing on its life span. Since data are not germane to validation, having more data would not, despite Gill's hopes to the contrary, have much impact on the shifting fashion of ideas.

Now we can take up the concept of therapeutic alliance. It received its first full presentation in a paper by Zetzel (1966) on the analytic situation. She based her definition of therapeutic alliance on the model of the early mother-child relationship and argued that the early stages of the analysis parallel, in many ways, the early months of infantile development. Since, she claimed, any interference with the mother-infant bond can often lead to lasting disturbances in the growing child, making it difficult for the child to respond properly to subsequent developmental challenges, so an early disturbance in the analytic relationship can lead to difficulties in the course of treatment.

To offset this danger, she encouraged the analyst, particularly in the early stages of treatment, to shape his behavior along the lines of the good mother. He must "continue throughout to respond intuitively to affect, indicating the patient's basic need to feel accepted and understood as a real person" (p. 103). He must constantly keep in mind the mother-child parallel and remind himself that an intuitive response to the patient's needs is the prerequisite to the establishment of basic trust and positive identification.

To support her claim, Zetzel presented material from the

early hours of a supervised case and showed how its character changed after the analyst became less distant and more "human." (Note the quality of the data—the fact of supervision means that the evidence used to support Zetzel's position is at least once removed from the clinical interchange.) Soon after lying down in the first hour, the patient began to present her feelings of loneliness, coupled with the idea that the analysis was a luxury. She thought of herself as one of Erich Fromm's receptive characters (i.e., someone who wants and wants and can never get enough; presumably nothing could assuage her loneliness). She then thought of her mother and thought that she was probably similar—or more exactly, a "hoarder."

Zetzel wondered whether the analyst, at this point, should not have done something or said something to convey the idea that *he* was not a hoarder. Such a move would, presumably, have strengthened the therapeutic alliance, increased the patient's initial sense of trust, and "fostered the development of a secure working relationship" (p. 96). But it might also have (1) represented a denial of a possible transference wish, long before the wish had been properly analyzed; (2) placed the emphasis on reality as opposed to fantasy; (3) shown the analyst in a defensive light; and (4) made it more difficult to develop similar transference themes in the future because if the analyst claims that he is not a hoarder, it reduces the chances that the patient will subsequently project onto him similar fantasies.

Zetzel apparently felt that these risks would be outweighed by the advantage of getting the relationship off to a good start. Further in the same hour, the patient talks about her surprise that the fee per hour had been set higher than she had expected. She associates to a job she had just concluded with a printer who ended up charging more than three times his initial estimate. The link to the analysis and the theme of its being a luxury seemed clear, and her final remark to the printer—"I told him I didn't think much of his way of doing business"—could just as easily have been applied to the analyst. This material is related to point 4 in the preceding paragraph, for to reply, as Zetzel suggests, that the analyst was not a hoarder might easily have prevented the story about the printer from being expressed because of its implicit criticism of the analyst.

Subsequent hours convinced Zetzel that the analyst was seen as an unreal and omnipotent figure; he also became aware of his rigidity and discussed the problem with Zetzel. At this point, her analogy with the mother-child relationship becomes significant. If she chose to see the analytic relationship as an extension of the early mother-child bond, then the complaints of loneliness and the implied criticism of the analyst as greedy and ungiving could be heard as the complaints of an abandoned child, at the mercy of a selfish mother. Something must be done to reassure the child/patient that care was forthcoming, and this line of thinking would have (1) prompted Zetzel to encourage a more supportive relationship, and (2) been particularly responsive to the concerns of the analyst. But if, on the other hand, she were to hear the complaints of loneliness and hoarding as transference projections, then there was less cause for alarm; the transference would seem to be developing nicely, even from the first hour, and no special precautionary measures need to be taken.

Zetzel chose the first course and apparently encouraged the analyst to be more supportive. And now comes the crucial test of the formulation—did the change make a difference? At this point we are left somewhat in doubt. We are told that the analyst "adopted a slightly more active and human attitude, indicating to the patient his recognition of her anxiety. As a result, the patient reported that until yesterday she had thought of the analyst as a distant, Olympian, somewhat magical figure. . . . Now she realized that this picture had been fantastic. He was, after all, an ordinary man" (p. 97).

Three points are worth discussing at this time. First, we have no way of knowing exactly what Zetzel said to the analyst and exactly how he responded to her suggestion; thus we have no explicit description of exactly how he tried to foster the therapeutic alliance. Admirable in many ways, her vignette is critically defective as an illustration of the precise nature of therapeutic alliance. This lack of information is important because it allows each reader to interpret the concept in his own fashion, and, as we will see later in more detail, some of these interpretations are unrelated to Zetzel's original formulation.

Second, we have no way of knowing whether the change in the patient's behavior and, in particular, her statement that now she realized that the analyst was an ordinary man was a consequence of the change in the analyst, a result of something unrelated to this change, or a mixture of the two. Despite Zetzel's claim that the two events are causally related, we have no sure way of knowing whether the first triggered the second.

Third, is it good or bad that the analyst has now descended from his "Olympian" throne? Zetzel claims the change is for the better because the new evaluation represents a more realistic appraisal. But if we wish to encourage the expression of unrealistic hopes and fears, then the shift toward reality might be seen as something of a setback, and perhaps even as a sign of resistance.

Despite the fragmentary nature of this incident, it was taken seriously by subsequent critics, and it effectively launched the concept of the therapeutic alliance into the analytic literature. Some writers were not even troubled by the sketchiness of the evidence; thus Kanzer (1975) makes the surprising statement that "Zetzel's constructs are bolstered by ample and fascinating clinical material which permit the reader to apply his own experience and draw independent conclusions" (p. 58). That is exactly what the anecdote does not allow; because we do not have access to the specific intervention, we cannot make an independent evaluation. Others, like Brenner (1977), are more skeptical of the quality of the evidence—"The reader will note that we have not been told just what it was that the analyst did after the supervisory hour that he had not done before" (p. 142)—but he seems inclined to accept Zetzel's claim that change in the analyst brought about a change in the patient ("what Zetzel recommended worked in the case she reported"—p. 143).

As a result of the fact that we are given neither a full account of the intervention nor an account of the patient's specific response, each reader can form his own impression of what was done or said and how the patient did or did not react. The way is now open for a wide range of creative elaborations on Zetzel's original concept. If we like the formulation, we can imagine a scenario in which the analyst makes some supportive remarks and the patient brings forth a set of new associations; if we are critical, we can imagine the patient falling silent, becoming less productive, and perhaps less cooperative, and within that framework, her remark that now she sees the analyst as an ordinary man can be heard in a much more critical light.

We now turn to subsequent formulations of the therapeutic alliance. To appreciate the range of possible transformations, consider this definition by Friedman (1969):

> The therapeutic alliance thus postulates a congruence between patient and analyst on the analyst's terms. . . . By virtue of the therapeutic alliance the patient was implicitly endowed with another set of needs . . . which were happily the same as the analyst's. The patient was in effect thought to share the analyst's professional aims. (p. 151)

The reference to the mother-child relationship has been dropped; instead, the therapeutic alliance has come to describe the analyst's need to see himself in the patient. He wants to turn the patient into a mirror of his hopes and fears. To strengthen the alliance, therefore, he has projected onto the patient his own needs and tries to behave in such a way that the patient will begin to act like him. The relationship has moved from the imbalance of the early months of infancy to a pairing of equals. Does this represent the concept as proposed by Zetzel, or has it become an original formulation of Friedman's, shaped by his own hopes and fears?

Zetzel's concept becomes extended even further when taken up by Langs (1975). He defines the therapeutic alliance as "the conscious and unconscious agreement—and subsequent actual work—on the part of both the patient and the analyst to join forces in effecting symptom alleviation and characterological changes through insight and inner structural change within the patient" (p. 78). The mother-child model has disappeared; the patient contributes to the alliance as much as does the analyst; the concept now covers both conscious and unconscious activity; and in its sweep and overall aim, it would seem to be almost identical to the analytic process. Nor does Langs consider the optional nature of moves to support the alliance and the question of under what conditions it should be reinforced. Rather, it is taken as a treatment given, the norm against which mistakes in technique (what Langs calls the "therapeutic misalliance") should be judged.

From the examples just presented, we can see that substantial changes have taken place in Zetzel's original concept. From its initial formulation as a treatment option, something that represented an exception to the rules of abstinence and interpretation, it has now become (at least for Langs) a definition of proper treatment and the standard against which defective treatment should be compared. From the original parallel with the mother-child alliance in the early stages of infancy, it has come to represent (at least for Friedman) a relationship of equals, a kind of mirror countertransference (to paraphrase

Kohut [1977]) in which the patient becomes invested with qualities of the analyst. It is particularly worth noting that the change in conception came about for reasons that seem to have nothing to do with the original evidence, such as it is, or the subsequent history of the concept. Langs's paper, for example, makes no mention of Zetzel's formulation or her clinical vignette, nor does it take into account Friedman's revised definition; rather, it begins with a somewhat a priori definition, which is presented without comment. Friedman, as well, makes no mention of Zetzel in general or of her vignette in particular. It is not as if Langs or Friedman found reason to quarrel with Zetzel's evaluation of the anecdote and, reaching a different explanation of the case material, proceeded to develop their own formulations; on the contrary, the original clinical material has apparently ceased to exist. Unencumbered by history, they are free to develop the concept on their own terms.

The more critical readers of Zetzel—Brenner and Kanzer, in particular—are more faithful to the early history of the concept and to Zetzel's originating illustration. Both Brenner and Kanzer give proper credit to the earlier papers and to Zetzel's central concern with the mother-child relationship; they do not, however, make reference to the more sweeping formulations of either Langs or Friedman. After a critical review of Zetzel's original illustration and its implications, Brenner concludes that the therapeutic alliance does not "deserve a special name nor require special treatment" (p. 156), despite the fact that he admits (p. 143) that her intervention worked in the illustration we have described. Why, then, his negative stance? In part because the illustration is not convincing (p. 143); in part because problems of the kind Zetzel is describing are more properly discussed under the heading of transference; and in part because of what might be called reasons of taste. "I do not believe," he writes, "that therapeutic alliance or working alliance [a variation proposed by Greenson] are useful concepts. I do not agree with Zetzel that an alliance is distinct from the remainder of a patient's transference. . . . These are conclusions I have reached pragmatically, though I believe them to be consonant with psychoanalytic theory as well. . . . I believe that the distinction they propose is a specious one and that its consequences for analytic practice are, generally speaking, undesirable" (p. 155). Once again, we see the low priority assigned to evidence. While Brenner alludes to data that might support his claim, he presents no new findings, and thus the reader is not in a position to independently make up his own mind. He must either accept the recommendation as an appeal to authority and experience or wait until more evidence is mustered.

In both the elaboration and (with Brenner) the attempted eradication of the concept of therapeutic alliance, clinical evidence seems secondary to issues of naming and narrative fit. As we noted earlier, giving the concept a name brings it into being; from this point of view, it is significant that Brenner concludes his discussion with an argument for giving up the name ("neither deserve a special name nor require special treatment"—p. 156). Take away its name and it will drop out of circulation. It has not been proved false; rather, it was declared invisible and, for that reason, will cease to exist. There is something magical in this line of thinking—and something disturbing as well. Creating something by giving it a name brings us back to Viderman and his discussion of being true. As with a creative interpretation, a concept acquires significance and validity by being given a name; once created, it becomes true and acquires its own meaning for each user. We have seen how Langs and Friedman have endowed the concept with their individual private formulations; creative elaboration is all the more likely in this instance because of the fact that Zetzel failed to provide us with either a clear formulation or a well-documented illustration. Brenner as well, we might assume, has his own conception of what Zetzel has in mind; a clue to this conception is given on page 142, where he speculates that "perhaps he [the analyst] smiled at her as he greeted her or dismissed her," and we might wonder how much this particular scenario (which may have nothing to do with the facts of the case) may have influenced Brenner's final disapproval of the concept. Be that as it may, the important point here is that the concept seems to have acquired multiple meanings, with each author reading into it what he wanted to find, unaware in many cases that his reading may differ from the others and unconcerned that his reading may have nothing to do with the original formulation or the supporting clinical findings.

This may be a good time to return to Ricoeur's four criteria and ask to what extent they apply to the concept of therapeutic alliance and to its acceptance by the psychoanalytic community. We have just seen testimony to the importance of being given a name (Ricoeur's first point); not only could the concept not exist without it, but having a name seems to give it respectability. Second, we find it has been named in innumerable publications; thus it satisfies the second criterion. Does it represent a piece of psychic reality? Presumably so, because many authors (although not all) seem to find it a useful concept and one that corresponds to their clinical experience. And the stress on *psychic* reality may be significant because supporting data, by definition, are somewhat more subjective than we might prefer. Psychic reality tends to be private and not open to public encounter, and perhaps for that reason there is less concern with the lack of clinical evidence than we might expect.

Finally, we come to the question of narrative fit. In this case, the narrative does not refer to the story of the patient that is being developed during the course of treatment but, rather, to the unfolding, constantly developing conception of psychoanalytic theory that is being constructed by each member of the psychoanalytic community. Does the concept in question fit this narrative? If it does, it will tend to be cited; if it does not, it will tend to disappear.

In concluding his critique of the concept of therapeutic alliance, Brenner ends with the hope that the concept will drop out of circulation. This seems unlikely—for a number of reasons. First, it tends to be used synonymously with the similar concept of "working alliance" formulated by Greenson (1967); as long as one concept is active, it will tend to support the other. Second, it is contrasted, since Langs, with the concept of therapeutic misalliance; interest in the latter will tend to keep alive interest in its opposite and vice versa. And finally (and perhaps most important), therapeutic alliance seems to fill a need to see our patients as replicas of ourselves. This view is best expressed in the definition proposed by Friedman, and if this definition is shared by a significant number of other analysts, the concept will tend to stay in circulation. Here is a case where the fantasy is sufficient—no supporting evidence is needed. If only the patient could be a replica of the analyst, how smoothly the analysis would proceed, and how enjoyable, even blissful, the experience. Our understanding would be perfect and our progress flawless.

NARRATIVE TRUTH AND CONCEPTUAL CHANGE

We can begin to see how a concept in psychoanalytic theory may operate as an interpretation—and, in particular, as a construction. We have a clue as to why the definition shifted from one proposed by Zetzel to one proposed by Friedman. And we begin to see why clinical evidence tends to be disregarded. If a concept is supported by a prevailing fantasy, then its evidential grounds become less important than the need it serves in each analyst's psychic economy. Against this need, Brenner's recommendation (that it be dropped) will not have much effect.

If the concept meshes with a prevailing fantasy, it gives it legitimacy by providing it with a name. It fills a gap in the unfolding narrative of psychoanalytic theory that each analyst is trying to construct for himself; it is held in place by other pieces of this narrative. To the extent that each new concept contains a piece of the truth, it will tend to be supported by one or more portions of clinical material; thus the concept is held in place by each analyst's private experience. And because private experience is always more compelling than published evidence, we begin to see why the latter is conspicuous by its absence. Each analyst has his own private data base, immediate and persuasive, which informs him of the truth value of any particular concept.

Each analyst develops his own private narrative of the clinical theory by combining his clinical experience with his interpretation of theoretical concepts. Much of this narrative is loosely formulated; therefore, it can assimilate contradictory pieces of experience. We have seen in an earlier section how a narrative, because of its loose syntax, can accommodate a near-infinite universe of new information, and the private, unfolding narrative of the practicing analyst follows many of the same rules. Much of the narrative is never made explicit; as a result, many of the inherent contradictions are never made visible. And furthermore, disagreements between analysts never become apparent. The private formulation of each analyst is projected onto the analytic community in such a way that we all come to believe that each of us understands the theory in the same way and is practicing by the same set of rules. (In the next chapter we will provide a more explicit definition of this phenomenon—the "projective fallacy.")

If a new concept seems compatible with the analyst's private narrative, nothing more is required in the way of evidence or proof to make it seem a useful addition to clinical theory. Evidence, in the form of clinical illustration or anecdote, may be seen as informative but rarely countervailing because for every published negative instance, the believing analyst can think of a host of positive confirmations. Many of these may not fit a strict definition of the concept in question because once the concept has been found to be useful, its formulation will become subjectively rearranged to conform to the user's particular clinical experiences. We see instances of this kind of rearrangement in the varying definitions presented earlier in this section, and we can assume that similar kinds of rearrangements are taking place in the private world of each practicing analyst. But so long as the name remains constant, the subtler changes in formulation do not become visible.

We now see why research may not change the situation to any significant extent—despite Gill's hopes to the contrary. Someone else's research, no matter how careful the study and how significant the outcome, is not likely to be as persuasive as the day-to-day experience of the practicing analyst. He may not be aware of how he has adapted the concept to suit his own particular needs, nor is he aware of the number of negative instances he has experienced and forgotten that could easily countermand his favorite positive illustrations. What stands out first and foremost is a positive instance. If the concept in question has received support—even if only once—at the moment when he reads the research, his private experience is likely to carry the day, no matter how pessimistic the research. A recent, positive instance would be probably more persuasive, but this is not critical because, as we have seen in Chapter V, the size of the search space is rarely taken into account. Because positive instances stand out, they come readily to mind; we probably do not keep careful track of when or how frequently they occurred, but their subjective truth value is overwhelming and able to stand up against any number of published negative findings.

In the final analysis, a piece of narrative truth has been prematurely elevated to the status of a general concept ("therapeutic alliance"). What happened to work for Zetzel's student in a particular clinical encounter has never been properly documented nor fully explained; nevertheless, it was given a name and somewhat hastily established in the literature. There it became part of another kind of narrative, the private narrative of each analyst. But the truth of this narrative is equally wanting as a basis for theory. The private context generated by each analyst in his attempt to understand the literature may be subjectively persuasive, but because it is not based on public data, it can hardly be used to support a general concept. To argue from private reasons carries only a faint chance of convincing the nonbeliever; what is sufficient for the individual analyst and loosely sufficient for the community at large can hardly be convincing in general, much less earn a place in the accepted theory. It becomes clear that just as a general theory should not be founded on narrative truths developed within the session, so it should not rest entirely on the private convictions of individual analysts. How these convictions come to be understood (and misunderstood) by the analytic community will be discussed in more detail in the next chapter.

CHAPTER VII

Psychoanalytic Competence

We can define psychoanalytic competence as the knowledge and background necessary and sufficient to understand a therapeutic utterance or interaction. Formed by clinical training and experience, didactic analysis and self-analysis, it is the "analyzing instrument" that we routinely apply to utterances (from either analyst or patient) in order to go beyond their surface structure to reach an integrated understanding of the manifest content, and that we routinely apply to manifest content in our search for latent content. Although psychoanalytic competence has traditionally been invoked to construe latent meanings from manifest content, it is often required simply to construe the manifest content, as we shall see in some of the examples to follow.

NORMATIVE AND PRIVILEGED COMPETENCE

It seems important to distinguish between what we will call *normative* competence and *privileged* competence. *Norma-*

tive competence belongs to all members of the psychoanalytic community; it is the competence we share at discussion groups, scientific meetings, editorial-board conferences, and similar gatherings. *Privileged* competence belongs to the analyst at a specific time and place in a particular analysis. (His ability to understand sections of this analysis more removed in time shades into normative competence.) Privileged competence will always be more complete than normative competence; for any given psychoanalytic interchange, the outside observer, no matter how fully trained and/or dynamically sensitive, can never be more than sympathetic to the dialogue. We see here a contrast with literary competence that is presumed to be sufficient for the understanding of literary texts; no privileged information about the author is assumed to be necessary except in certain special cases. By contrast, normative psychoanalytic competence, although necessary, is probably never sufficient for even a moderate degree of clinical understanding; not even privileged competence always suffices!

We need the private commentaries of the analyst in part because the spoken interchange is only a small part of any clinical episode. Without the full context, the meaning of any interchange is indeterminate and can never be fully reconstructed. The point applies not only to latent meanings; even the most superficial manifest content may be opaque to normative competence. Many of the sentences spoken by either analyst or patient employ an agreed-upon set of referents— shorthand terms for significant childhood events, important people, important places, milestones, and the like. As the shared understanding develops over time, the shared references are likely to become more and more elliptical and fragmentary. Other sentences are ambiguous because of faulty syntax (see Dahl, Teller, Moss, and Trujillo, 1978) or because the vital paralinguistic cues are missing. But these are specific issues. Most significant, all spoken utterances are significantly impoverished because we lack the historical and experiential context that is only available to the treating analyst—the main ingredients of his privileged competence.

Some of the context necessary for understanding the text can be gleaned from a study of the previous sessions. But this added knowledge will never be more than a crude approximation of the privileged competence possessed by the treating analyst at the particular time and place when the patient made a specific statement, because much of the privileged context does not become part of the record. Suppose the analyst sees his patient on Friday and is planning to start his vacation on the following day. We would expect him to be acutely sensitized to references to his upcoming departure, and this sensitivity will color the way he "hears" the material and the way he responds. Suppose, further, that we learn of this upcoming vacation in one of the earlier hours; it still seems unlikely that this information will enable us to experience the session in exactly the same way as does the treating analyst. He might, for example, feel guilty about leaving because he feels the patient is particularly vulnerable to loss; this feeling of guilt might further sensitize him to references to separation or trigger a defensive denial of these referents. However it turns out, it seems unlikely that we could do more than identify this sense of guilt in an abstract sense; unless we feel correspondingly guilty, for reasons of our own, it seems unlikely that we would read the material in exactly the same way. Part of the difference between normative and privileged competence in this example stems from the difference between knowing and experiencing. No matter how complete our knowledge of the treating analyst, it will never transform us into the same "analyzing instrument," and there are many aspects of the analyst's privileged competence that, unless they are added to the text, we will never learn about in the first place.

NATURALIZING A TEXT

We can define the process of adding private commentaries to the psychoanalytic transcript as the process of *naturalizing* the text. This step provides the link between privileged and normative competence. Once a session has been naturalized by the treating analyst with all (or most all) of its implicit meanings painstakingly unpacked, it then becomes accessible to someone with normative competence.

"To naturalize a text," writes Culler (1975), "is to bring it into relation with a type of discourse or model which is already, in some sense, natural and legible. . . . To naturalize . . . is to make the text intelligible by relating it to various models of coherence." To naturalize a psychoanalytic dialogue is to bring the analyst's privileged competence to bear on each of the utterances in order to make them intelligible to the reader with normative competence. Whenever possible, this task must be carried out soon after the utterances were spoken because privileged competence is, to some extent, time-limited; what is transparent to the treating analyst immediately after the hour may not be clear after weeks or even hours have passed. It is for this reason that privileged competence refers primarily to the current moment of an ongoing analysis and shades off into normative competence when that moment becomes part of the past.

Naturalization can be described as an optional feature of literary understanding. It may, for example, be clearly needed to make an ancient text fully accessible to the modern reader but may not be necessary in the case of a contemporary text. But naturalization is probably an essential step in the understanding of a psychoanalytic protocol because of the particular nature of psychoanalytic explanation. We have seen in Chapter VI (see Sherwood, 1969, for a more developed argument) that the essence of explanation in psychoanalysis is narrative rather than hypothetical-deductive. This conclusion leads to some important consequences. A narrative explanation becomes convincing by virtue of how many details of the case it includes and the way in which these details are presented. The more comprehensive, coherent, and self-consistent the narrative, the more adequate the explanation (here again we are borrowing heavily from Sherwood, 1969). Hence, it follows that the more complete the record, the more it will convince an outsider. Ergo, only when the treating analyst has fully naturalized the text will it become equally understandable and convincing to the reader with normative competence. Naturalization becomes an essential step in filling out the record and in providing the necessary context by which the seemingly random bits and pieces of the patient's behavior begin to make sense. Naturalization is a necessary consequence of the fact that we depend heavily on a narrative form of explanation and that parts of this narrative can be supplied only by the treating analyst.

Suppose that the facts were otherwise and that an analytic case could be fully explained by a finite subset of hypotheses. If a hypothetical-deductive model were sufficient to account for the multiple details of the case, then it would be possible simply to list the hypotheses and assume complete understanding. Normative competence would be sufficient to evaluate the critical hypotheses, and the understanding of the treating analyst, because it could be in principle reduced to the same set of hypotheses, would be no greater than the understanding of the outside reader. Naturalization would not be necessary, and our understanding of each other's cases would be as great as the physicists' understanding of each other's experiments. But as Sherwood (1969) has made clear, the hypothetical-deductive model cannot be applied to clinical material. Because we need a narrative mode of explanation, we have a critical need for near-complete naturalization.

How do we go about systematically unpacking the text of an hour and extracting the greatest number of implied meanings? We can distinguish between (a) contextual information that is implicit in the transcript but not explicitly brought into the hour in question, and (b) information that is completely private and never becomes part of the transcript. Both kinds of information are unmarked, but whereas the first is accessible from the record, the second can be provided only by the treating analyst.

We can begin by studying several ways in which unmarked context, known to the treating analyst but not to the outside reader, can significantly influence the latter's understanding of the material. Our examples are intentionally simple in order to demonstrate the point.

In our first case, suppose that the patient is depressed, that his depression has become a chronic condition in the analysis, and that because of its chronicity, neither patient nor analyst feels the need for comment. Largely for this reason, the depression goes unmarked in the hour. Suppose that the patient says, "I guess I am happy." Knowing his mood, the analyst may hear that statement as a heavy form of irony, and perhaps hear it, in addition, as an invitation to him to contradict, interpret, question, or make some other comment. Suppose he chooses to say, "Once again, you are saying less than you feel." How will that be interpreted?

Suppose the outside reader sees only this hour; it follows that he will be ignorant of the patient's depression. Given this ignorance, he has no choice but to take the patient's statement at face value. In this particular setting, he might assume that the significant word in that statement was "guess" and that the analyst is calling attention to the patient's distance from his feelings ("I *guess* I am happy"). The ironical message completely escapes him. Focused on the word "guess," he might see the interpretation as a comment on the patient's access to his feelings and, perhaps more generally, as a comment on his obsessive style. The outside reader might well wonder about the need for such a comment at this time, and he might think the timing could be improved, that more examples could be given, and so forth.

Already we have a serious misreading of the patient's condition and cognitive style, and of the analyst's tactics. The misreading is bound to influence the way in which he responds to the remainder of the session, and in particular, to further comments that allude to the patient's prevailing mood. Moreover, we can assume that once a particular set has been established (for example, that the analyst is impatient and inexperienced and that the patient is an obsessive who is not in touch with his feelings), further examples will be used to confirm this hypothesis, on the assumption that it is much easier to hold on to an established paradigm than to search for a new paradigm more in tune with the facts.

Now it may be true that other clues to the patient's mood are scattered throughout the hour that, in theory, would allow the outside reader the opportunity to reconstruct his mood and begin to understand the irony. But sessions are not usually read in that kind of clue-hunting spirit; and even if the patient's depression were partly reconstructed, it could not compare with the day-in, day-out sense of this depression experienced by the treating analyst. Under these conditions, naturalization of the dialogue by the treating analyst is critically necessary in order to allow the underlying mood to assume its proper significance in the material.

For our second example we look at the significance of certain kinds of allusions. Suppose that the patient begins the hour by saying, "I am tired of the analysis, hour after hour; it's like measuring out my life in coffee spoons." The outside reader may recognize the allusion to T. S. Eliot, but if he sees only this hour, he will not know that three days before, the patient had taken his qualifying exam for the Ph.D. and that T. S. Eliot was one of his special topics. Thus the allusion to Eliot could well be the first reference to the ordeal. Suppose that turns out to be the case. Then this and further references to Eliot qualify as significant derivatives to the exam, and we would not be surprised to find that the treating analyst hears them in this light. He might make one or more interpretations along these lines, but if the outside reader is not familiar with the code, he would see these interpretations as unnecessary and might see the treating analyst as someone who is "side-tracked" by irrelevancies.

Once again, we have the potential for serious misunderstanding. Without knowing the private meaning of the Eliot material, the outside reader runs the risk of treating the references in a purely conventional manner and his assumption about interpretative technique follows accordingly. And, again, it may be possible to find scattered allusions to the exam and to Eliot throughout the hour, but they would probably not be clearly identified unless we knew where to look for them. The treating analyst must bring these allusions to the foreground by naturalizing the text; only then can someone with only normative competence hear the material in the appropriate fashion.

There is a paradox in both of these examples. What is obvious to the analyst and patient is not accessible to anyone else. Here, in a nutshell, is the root need for naturalization and the reason why naturalization must take place soon after the hour has passed. The largest number of glosses are probably needed to explain the obvious, and it is the very fact of their obviousness that makes the analyst feel that the work is unnecessary and that "everyone" can understand the material. (This is another statement of the "projective fallacy," which we discuss in more detail in a later section.)

There are other kinds of private information that are not available, even from a complete transcript. Suppose the patient is recovering from a minor operation, and a member of the analyst's family has just died from the same operation. It would be unlikely that this piece of highly personal information would ever become part of the record, and yet it might easily influence the analyst's sensitivity to the event and his willingness and his ability to analyze it. His own personal tragedy might make him acutely responsive to scattered allusions to the event; he might become better able to interpret certain dream fragments or to understand the course of the patient's associations. On the other hand, his tragedy might mobilize his anxiety and make him, for defensive reasons, less sensitive to the material; he might miss an obvious interpretation, for example, or make an unnecessary comment in an effort to change the subject. Viewed by someone with only normative competence, both the oversensitive and the insensitive interpretations might be seen as "errors"; the first because the evidence (when viewed with only normative competence) seems insufficient, and the second because outstanding clues were allowed to go begging. Thus an accurate evaluation of the analyst's performance is highly dependent on naturalizing the text.

To avoid these and other kinds of misreadings, the private feelings of the treating analyst (and his reflections on them) must be added to the record—and they must be added before too much time has passed, before they are no longer available. With this added information, the text is partially naturalized and someone with normative competence stands a better chance to "read" it with its crucial meanings intact—that is, to read it in the same way as the treating analyst—and as a result, be better able to judge the quality of his performance.

Privileged commentary is particularly needed at points of transition between speakers—analyst and patient, and patient and analyst. Normal conversation, as we have seen in Chapter IV, is always disjunctive because each speaker must decode the other's intentions before making his own contribution, and these intentions are often deeply buried. But in normal conversation there is a natural feedback mechanism which takes over when either speaker departs too far from the shared goal of the dialogue. The analytic interchange is not only a very special case of the general class of conversations but it purposely chooses not to invoke corrective feedback, because to do so would violate the convention of free association. As a result, the two threads of the dialogue tend to be rather loosely woven and the outside reader is put to a particular disadvantage in trying to understand the sequence of statements. Privileged competence, as noted above, is particularly necessary in order to properly interpret the transition from one speaker to another. It is here that some of the most interesting events— e.g., interpretations—are likely to occur. Interpretations can be classified according to how successfully they maintain the continuity of the patient's associations. What seem to be abrupt transitions (such as the interpretations, quoted above, to the chronically depressed patient) may, given the necessary additional information, turn out to be appropriate and continuous with the earlier material. Here, again, a fully naturalized text may be necessary before we can properly evaluate the quality of the analyst's performance.

Mayer raises the interesting question of whether some transition points may be, in principle, closed to unpacking.* Suppose the analyst who had just experienced the personal loss (see above, p. 223) becomes, by virtue of this loss, exquisitely sensitized to this theme in the patient's dream; without knowing exactly why, he makes a series of interpretations that lead to further, richer associations from the patient. When the time comes to unpack this transition, he may be in a somewhat different state of consciousness and not have access to the full extent of his personal feelings; hence he could not supply us with much in the way of an informed gloss. This example also highlights the importance of prompt unpacking; even when delays are kept to a minimum, some conflicting material may likely be lost.

In normal conversation we share the "conversational pos-

---

* I am indebted to Dr. David Mayer for raising this possibility.

tulate" (see Grice, 1967) that assumes that what I say is relevant to what you just said. Grice has pointed out how this postulate makes it possible to understand irony: If I say "I haven't seen John recently" and you reply "Have you heard of any bank robberies hereabouts?" I will assume that your reply is relevant (even though superficially disjunctive) and that you are making a comment about John. (Notice that the postulate in question is not stated in the text but comes into play because it forms part of what might be called our competence as conversationalists.) A similar convention allows us to understand metaphor and other figures of speech; once we realize that the surface structure of an expression is not relevant to its immediate context, we "hear" it in a new way.

Now turn to a transition between patient and analyst. Suppose the patient reports a dream in a department store in which she steps off the escalator. After a few brief associations, she falls silent. Suppose the analyst responds with the question, "I wonder if you have been doing some more thinking about termination?" Coming to this material with only normative competence, we might assume that there was some link between getting off the escalator and getting out of treatment—that the analyst had understood the escalator to be a symbol for the analysis and had responded accordingly. We might find the response somewhat abrupt, but not completely disjunctive.

But using only normative competence, we run the risk of making a serious error. It may be the case that the equation getting off equals termination did not in fact apply to this incident. Suppose that the patient had been planning to take a job in the same department store pictured in the dream; that she had decided to put off the job until she had finished the analysis; and that the dream was the first reference to the store in several months. Given this sequence, it would be reasonable to conclude that the link between dream and interpretation had nothing to do with the escalator per se but with the references to the department store and to its role in the patient's life. Only the treating analyst would be likely to hear the material in exactly that way; even though references to this sequence might be scattered over other hours, only the treating analyst who has followed the material as it emerged is likely to understand fully this particular sequence. Hence it follows that privileged commentary on this interchange is the *sine qua non* for the proper reading of the material; without this gloss, we might delude ourselves with a clever but essentially incorrect interpretation.

The proper gloss in this example would provide the context necessary to understand the transition between the dream and the interpretation. It would trace the changing role of the department store in the patient's life, the interplay between job and analysis, and show how a decision on one affected a decision on the other. A fully developed gloss might even rule out the superficial link between escalator and analysis.

In this particular example the reader with normative competence is misled by an apparently meaningful connection between dream and interpretation, a connection that tempts him to apply his everyday clinical wisdom and that seems to yield to it. But this line of reasoning leads to a false solution. This example illustrates the risk assumed whenever we try to understand someone else's material without a comprehensive gloss. The majority of patient-analyst transitions probably hides an ambiguity that we fail to recognize. Attempting to explain the transition with only our normative competence, we are likely to make wrong interpretations without knowing it (see the previous examples of the depressed patient and the Ph. D. candidate).

Consider next an unmarked transition. Suppose the patient has come late and begins the hour with a ten-minute description of his difficulty in getting to the office. He ends by wondering, out loud, whether a later time might be arranged. Suppose the analyst remains silent. His lack of reply is, of course, a particular kind of response that might have, as its aim, the goal of urging the patient to reflect on his request and perhaps on the feeling of not being answered. Reading the transcript, we might easily miss the "reply" because it goes unmarked in the text. Suppose the patient (after failing to get a response) begins to talk about feelings of loneliness and rejection. Without some kind of privileged commentary we would be unaware of the analyst's decision not to speak and, therefore, unaware of the probable reason for the patient's feelings. Even worse, we might search for some link between the old topic—the difficulty in getting to the office—and the new theme—loneliness and rejection—applying our convention that events in sequence tend to continue a single theme. We might easily conclude that his inability to come to the office has triggered his feelings of loneliness and rejection—in short, a piece of positive transference. Unless we realize that the change in topic was motivated by the analyst's silence and the feelings triggered by silence, our search for linkage is apt to be misleading.

Now, one could reply that this problem could be solved if the analyst called attention to the silence and to the patient's feelings about it. But the analyst may have a different agenda, and if he chooses to pursue a different topic, the transcript goes unmarked with respect to these particular features. Here is an example of the perils of treating clinical material as public data and making conventional assumptions about it based on normative competence. Without a privileged commentary, we end up being just as wrong (although for different reasons) as the rankest layman. We are tempted to treat the text as potentially decipherable whereas, in actuality, we should treat it as one treats a manifest dream—essentially opaque without associations.

It remains for future investigation to provide us with a listing of the kind of information that must be routinely supplied by the treating analyst. As a start, it would be useful to study a sample of transcribed hours in consultation with the treating analyst and determine what kinds of data normally go unmarked. From this survey, one could make up a check list to apply to each hour. Glosses are particularly needed to explain the transitions between speakers; all interpretations fall into this category. A complete gloss should include the evidence and motivation for a particular intervention; how the analyst's understanding of a specific utterance prompted his reply; his reasons for making the reply rather than remaining silent; and his reasons for choosing one theme and ignoring others. Glosses are also needed to explain a silence; not only is the decision not to speak a kind of reply, but it is a reply that usually goes unmarked. To carry out this kind of annotation, the treating analyst would ideally add a comment to every pause over a certain minimal length. Finally, glosses are needed to explicate all ambiguities, to supply the missing paralinguistic cues, and where necessary, the missing syntax (see Dahl et al., 1978). Once again, the treating analyst must supply all necessary information; the more complete the gloss, the closer we come to naturalizing the text.

PRIVATE AND PUBLIC TEXTS

Because it was never meant to be published (certain patients' fantasies to the contrary), the psychoanalytic transcript does not carry the ritualized form of an established genre. Any attempt to treat the dialogue with only normative competence assumes it to be more or less of a public text, a text that can be naturalized with no further knowledge on the part of the reader. Any attempt to treat the dialogue as a public text leads the reader to impose arbitrary meanings on much of the material. These meanings may be different from the intentions of patient and/or analyst. Partly because of our training as analysts, we may be prone to read meanings into clinical material, and our training leads us to impose specific structures on the data (see Spence, 1976). We assume, unthinkingly, that our normative competence is sufficient to decide which structure is appropriate.

As analysts, we may be particularly challenged by discontinuity. Part of our stock in trade—an important ingredient of normative competence—consists, as we have seen, in the ability to make sense out of apparently discontinuous themes—in being able to discover the links between two pieces of unrelated content. Thus we are apt to be challenged by an apparently chaotic hour, and the more continuity we find lacking, the more we may rise to the test of supplying the underlying meanings. But just as *any* two pieces of information can be linked by means of a third association common to both, so it follows that there is no check on the truth value of whatever connection we may happen to discover. Thus we are susceptible to overinterpreting the material and to reading meaning into elliptical and ambiguous material. If we apply this skill to seriously incomplete material—to texts that have not been sufficiently naturalized—then we are taking the risk of "discovering" only what we contribute.

What is operating here is something that we have called the projective fallacy. When we assume this fallacy, we assume that everyone (or at least everyone with our level of training) will read the psychoanalytic dialogue in the same way we do. This fallacy neutralizes the distinction between normative and privileged competence and assumes that the proper reading of the material is simply a matter of thought and reflection; that, given our normative competence, all meanings are potentially decodable. The projective fallacy is exposed by the failure, after almost one hundred years of analytic practice, to find a specimen hour that all of us will agree represents a good sample of analytic work. No agreement is reached because the text is always ambiguous without the gloss—the privileged commentaries of the analyst. Lacking this gloss, the text in question is subject to the private interpretation of each reader, and depending on one's private context, some call it brilliant, some unfortunate, and only a few will agree. In exercises of this kind the failure to agree often comes as a surprise—which can be read as a testimonial to the strength of the projective fallacy. It is worth noting that probably the most frequently cited specimen hour is the one presented by Kris (1956b), an hour which he describes only very sketchily. It is tempting to conclude that it is this very sketchiness that allows it to maintain its reputation.

PROSPECTS FOR RESEARCH

Research on the psychoanalytic process has been widely criticized (see Luborsky and Spence, 1978) because it has so little to contribute to clinical wisdom. One reason for this judgment may lie in the fact that it studies only a fragment of any clinical happening. Until the research community has access to the private commentaries of the analyst—until, in other words, it substitutes privileged competence for normative competence—it is probably doomed to junior partnership in the analytic enterprise. We are not discussing here the enormous problems raised by this requirement but only pointing out the importance of privileged competence for any understanding of the analytic process.

So long as clinical research deals with incomplete data, its conclusions will never carry conviction, because the clinician can always say, with justification, that if all the facts were known, the conclusions would be different. Clinical research can never be binding on clinical practice so long as one approach uses normative competence and the other uses privileged competence. (Note that the problem is not solved by providing researchers with full analytic training, because this experience provides them with only normative competence.)

Because clinical research must necessarily study incomplete data, it can never take what may be its most important step—that of *disproving* a clinical hypothesis. Here, again, an apparent disproof can be set aside by the rejoinder that all facts were not considered. Without the possibility of disproof somewhere in the offing, the research enterprise is never going to attract serious attention from clinicians or from interested laymen in other fields. And because it has only partial access to clinical happenings, even the so-called confirmations of Freudian hypotheses are cause for suspicion. Without complete data in any given area, all findings will necessarily be tentative, and both proof and disproof are out of the question.

If normative competence is judged to be inconclusive and possibly misleading, it follows that so-called data banks should be viewed with extreme caution. The complete recording of an analytical case cannot be fully understood until it is fully naturalized by the treating analyst. He should bring his privileged competence to bear on all critical utterances and, wherever possible, do this at the time they were uttered or soon thereafter. Not only must he provide process notes; he must take the trouble of painstakingly unpacking the majority of the statements he made during the hour to provide the reader with a complete gloss of their meaning. Only when a data bank has been unpacked in this way should it be made available to other researchers; to make it public before this step is taken is to invite the kinds of misreadings we have been discussing. Without attempting a systematic naturalization of each hour, the research-analyst is simply maintaining the projective fallacy that his view of the material will be shared by everyone who possesses normative competence. There is reason—as we have seen—to question this assumption.

Speed is of the essence because the information loss probably increases exponentially with time; a delay of two days in naturalizing a transcript probably destroys four times as much information as a delay of one. This fact suggests that current data banks should be naturalized as quickly as possible by the treating analyst, for otherwise we are in danger of ending up with archives signifying almost nothing. The tapes may be intact but they will be inaccessible to normative competence, and, if we wait too long, perhaps even to privileged competence as well.

NARRATIVE SYNTHESIS AND NATURALIZATION

In an earlier chapter we quoted Ricoeur's statement that "a good psychoanalytic explanation must raise a particular case history to the sort of narrative intelligibility we ordinarily expect from a story. . . . A story has to be 'followable,' and in this sense 'self-explanatory.' We interpolate explanation whenever the narrative process is blocked and in order to 'follow-further' " (Ricoeur, 1977, p. 869). What is being described by Ricoeur can be defined as the necessary preamble to naturalization, carried out by the treating analyst when he transforms symptoms, fantasies, and other seemingly random aspects of the patient's behavior into a story with a central theme, a recognizable structure, and an overall sense of coherence. This synthetic product is the essence of analytic work; it is on making sense of a chaotic life that everything else depends. As Ricoeur has noted, to explain is "to reorganize facts into a meaningful whole which constitutes a single and continuous history" (p. 861); this is what Sherwood (1969) has called the "narrative commitment of psychoanalytic explanation."

It should be clear from the preceding discussion that turning the patient's life into a coherent text does not make it available to normative competence. We must distinguish between two kinds of synthetic activity. The first, the analytic process, carried out by the treating analyst in the process of doing analytic work, operates on the productions of the patient during the hour and leads to his decision to speak or remain silent—and, if he speaks, to his choice of words. The second, the process of naturalization, also carried out by the treating analyst, operates on the *text* of the hour (already more coherent than the patient's productions) and is intended to transform the text into what might be called a public document, accessible to normative competence.

The two levels of synthetic activity are frequently confused, and another version of the projective fallacy stems from this confusion. The treating analyst can easily persuade himself that what is clear to him is clear to all; that making sense out of a particular piece of clinical material in a way that satisfied him and/or the patient—perhaps in a way that leads to new memories, further material, or to other signs of promising analytic work—will also convince an outside observer. Much of the ambiguity in published case histories stems from this confusion, and it follows from the fact that the case history—even though clearly more comprehensible than the raw clinical material—does not yet have the status of a public text. The additional step of naturalization must be taken before the material becomes generally accessible. In a recently published case history, picked at random, we find such expressions as "the patient's personality had an *uncanny resemblance* to her mother's"; "we eventually succeeded in *determining* that . . ."; and "with persistent effort, it became possible to *demonstrate* that . . ."(italics added). The evidence for these rather extreme assertions is only sketchily presented; thus the reader has no chance to draw his own conclusions from the data and match his convictions against those of the author. This oversight may come about because the author is, in fact, sincerely convinced of the rightness of his conclusion and sees no need to add redundant details. He may be right; but the details being withheld are part of his privileged competence and are necessary for a proper reading of the material. The case history, as presented, is not yet a public document and needs the second step of naturalization in order to be understood by the psychoanalytic community.

The issue at stake is congruent with the familiar difference between the context of discovery and the context of justification. The treating analyst makes a certain interpretation or construction of the material; this may be confirmed by the patient and qualifies as a piece of narrative truth. But for this discovery to be justified and for others to be convinced of its truth value, it must be presented in a more general context. Raising the clinical material to the level of coherent narrative is usually sufficient for the initial discovery to take place because the insight occurs in a clinical setting and the standards for truth in that setting are somewhat different from those in the scientific community (see Ricoeur, 1977, and his distinction between "saying-true" and "being-true"; the first applies to new insights on the part of the patient, and the second to truth values in modern physics). But whereas a narrative (case history) is usually sufficient to illuminate the context of discovery, it is not sufficient to persuade and convince the skeptical reader (even with normative competence) that the conclusion necessarily follows from the evidence. It is at this point that a fully annotated transcript is required.

We can begin to see that the significant achievements of psychoanalysis—the day-to-day application of privileged competence in the exercise of analytic work—are just as concealed from the interested consumer as they were one hundred years ago. Each analyst carries within him the memory of a recent hour in which the material developed in classical fashion, in which an interpretation led to a new memory, in which a resistance was suddenly clarified in the transference—but these are private experiences that can be only partially shared. Because they are never fully documented in print, they can never belong to the future. The exciting heritage of psychoanalysis is more of a shared ideal than an encounterable fact. What does appear in print is only a pale reflection of the analytic process. The special excitement of the analytic process has not been captured, and all that is left are a small number of highly condensed clinical vignettes that lead to some partial conclusions—a product that does a substantial injustice to what is being described.

We are largely unaware of the incomplete nature of our literature because we automatically invest it with clinical richness. A published case fragment is more than sufficient to set in motion a train of associations, and the reader may immediately experience a fully developed clinical history; we may even project onto the published text our own set of private meanings and associations and read into it a significance that is probably not there. We are, in effect, applying our normative competence to the literature and—somewhat haphazardly— enriching each paper with our own store of clinical wisdom. We read a published paper much as we listen to a patient's productions, adding associations to correct gaps in the narrative, supplying theoretical assumptions to get around awkward transitions in the reasoning, and making all the other corrections necessary to "naturalize" the text. But because each of us comes to the task with his own set of associations, each of us experiences a slightly different paper, with the differences depending on the particular vicissitudes of our clinical experience. These readings are not true naturalizations; therefore, they can never be identical to the naturalization of the treating analyst because of the fact that normative competence is not the same as privileged competence.

What, then, is our literature? With only a few prominent exceptions, it does not contain the true essence of the analytic event because the treating analyst, as author, does not see the need to supply confirming evidence and, therefore, does not naturalize the material sufficiently to make it available to his colleagues. Because it is not sufficiently naturalized, each reader, in applying his normative competence to the incomplete material, enriches it with his own set of associations and fantasies. Instead of making a particular analytic event available for discussion and comment, the author runs the risk of setting in motion a universe of different "texts" that are all more or less irrelevant to the event in question.

Both the transcripts of recorded sessions and the more usual case histories are vulnerable to misreadings: the transcript because it lacks the private commentary of the treating analyst, and the case study because it lacks the context of the complete case. Both of these products are insufficiently naturalized by the treating analyst; as a result, they are largely inaccessible to normative competence and, therefore, to public consumption. But because of their public status (when published), they are assumed to be public documents and seem to be generally accessible. In fact, however, they are accessible only to those with privileged competence, and attempts to read them with only normative competence run the risk of drawing unjustified conclusions from fragmentary evidence.

There is a further problem. Because each reader constructs his own "text" from a mixture of public anecdote and private fantasy, no single set of "facts" is ever seen by more than one analyst. As a result, the chances for theoretical growth through discussion, disagreement, and compromise are greatly diminished. Occasional papers may bring a momentary flash of recognition, but because any given set of data has never been fully unpacked, it can have little cumulative impact on the theory. Just as we have no specimen hour, so we have no specimen interpretation of specimen resistance. Each new theoretical construct brings with it a new set of examples; each of these examples, because it is only a fragment from a more extended case, invites ad hoc reader elaboration. As a result of just these two sources of variation, we have no systematic way of comparing concepts because we almost never apply more than one concept to more than one set of data.

In conclusion, it seems clear that we are doing a great disservice to both our data and our theory by our habits of piecemeal reporting. Conviction, as Sherwood makes clear, comes only from knowing the full context; the explanation of any clinical sequence can only be persuasive when we have available as much as possible of its complete experiential surround. We have seen how, as believing analysts, we treat fragmentary

context by preconsciously filling in the evidential gaps, glossing over the ambiguities, and adding our own details so that
we may end up more or less convinced but at the cost of con-
founding the original incident with our own experience. But
what of the nonbeliever? Here the danger of piecemeal reporting is much greater. He responds to partial evidence with more
or less complete disbelief because almost any interpretation,
shorn of its necessary surround, seems ambiguous and reduc-
tionistic and another example of analysts' fuzzy-minded thinking. By failing to provide the complete context for a clinical
happening, we jeopardize or in some cases abandon our hopes
of extending our influence. Our best evidence is a well-kept
secret; it may not survive its privileged status.

CHAPTER VIII

From Normative to Privileged Competence

We come back to the hypothesis that members of the psychoanalytic community read their literature much as they listen to their patients. We have seen in Chapter IV how the analyst is continuously filling in gaps and supplying meanings as he listens to the stream of associations from the patient and how, indeed, he must take an active stance in order to make sense out of what he hears. In much the same way, readers of the psychoanalytic literature must go beyond the text and supply their own clinical examples for abstract theoretical terms, imagine linking associations that will connect two apparently disconnected anecdotes and, in general, find their own preferred ways of giving substance to the author's claims. The raw data are usually in short supply and to no one's apparent concern, as we have seen in our analysis of the concept of therapeutic alliance (Chapter VI) where fragmentary evidence was accepted as the norm by all but a small minority of readers. There is no reason to think that this case is in any way unusual.

Filling gaps, supplying private examples of abstract concepts, and otherwise making the published fragment more of a continuous narrative all illustrate and follow from one of the critical aspects of psychoanalytic competence. We have seen in Chapter IV how we listen with the assumption that a unifying theme always remains to be discovered and that the apparent chaos of the surface can often be transformed, given the proper application of our analyzing "instrument," into the latent unity that lies beneath. Given this assumption, heavily emphasized in training and practiced daily in our clinical work, we come to the published case report and, unmindful of our own creative participation, transform it into a public document that we assume is accessible to anyone with normative competence. Because of the particular bias in our profession toward making sense out of nonsense, each member of the analytic community is apt to feel more challenged than frustrated when confronted by a fragmentary clinical report; rather than complain about the lack of evidence and the impossible task of clarifying each and every ambiguity, he may feel fortunate at having yet another opportunity to try out his skill and arrive at the ultimate underlying clinical message accessible only to the fortunate few. The challenge of the hidden message and the subsequent satisfaction derived from solving the puzzle may easily compensate for his initial feelings of confusion and frustration with the incomplete report.

And the outcome, of course, is always successful. Just as we can always find a linking association that will join any other two associations, so we can always find, from either our private clinical experience or what we know of others', some anecdote that will make sense of a seemingly abrupt interpretation or some moderating circumstance that could explain an otherwise vague description. As we read, we preconsciously construct our own mixture of public anecdote and private fantasy and continue to collaborate with the author until we have reached what seems, for us, to be some threshold of narrative perfection. We have seen earlier how each reader is necessarily constructing his own "text" with its own idiosyncratic mixture of public and private ingredients. Given the near invisibility of clinical evidence, the mix must always be weighted toward the reader's subjective clinical experience, and we now begin to see why discussion and disagreement over theoretical issues must inevitably be sensed as a personal attack. Each reader's understanding is partly based on highly personal material; disagreements over theoretical concepts are, at bottom, disagreements over private interpretations. Feelings are easily hurt, and perhaps more important, the argument can probably never be settled because the data, by definition, are never made public and, therefore, never made accessible to third-party review.

This process of creating our own finished narrative from each piece of the literature can be classified as another example of unwitting interpretation. It happens automatically, outside our awareness, and seems so natural (and so satisfying) that we can find no fault with our literature and its standards of evidence or reasoning. And just as we are blinded to its real condition, so we are puzzled or possibly bemused by the cries of critics who never tire of pointing to the serious dearth of evidence, to the confusion of observation with interpretation, and to the many other errors of reasoning and logic that can be found in our clinical papers. Trained—perhaps overtrained—to find harmony in chaos, we can simply no longer read our literature with the eye of a stranger. Because we automatically project onto abstract definitions or fragmentary clinical anecdotes our own favorite, understandable scenarios, we assume that the scenario is visible to all; if the outsider fails to see it, he is not looking carefully, "lacks clinical understanding," or is probably flawed in some other, more serious way. As with all projections, we are convinced by their "obvious" truth, and we may even feel indignant when they are called into question. We are simply not aware of the fact that we automatically surround the clinical report with a fringe of compensating and ameliorating associations that the outside critic fails to see. As a result, psychoanalysis and its critics are usually arguing about different "texts."

The construction of finished narratives from fragmentary case reports is, of course, a kind of naturalization. But it is important to note that it represents a kind of *unintended* naturalization. We have commented on the fact that it happens automatically, outside of awareness; we have also seen how each reader creates his own mix of public fact and private fantasy, with each published paper setting in motion a universe of partially naturalized "texts." Because they are never made public, we can think of them as a universe of underground "texts" that are implicitly invoked in any psychoanalytic discussion but that are never accessible to all participants.

Not only is this kind of naturalization unintended; we must also call it unsystematic. Consider how any given reader may respond to a published case report. Certain scenes may seem intuitively clear and cause him no difficulty, and here we can assume that he is preconsciously supplying the necessary linking associations. Other transitions may cause him more trouble; some concepts he may find unfamiliar or even contradictory. At these points he may find himself actively scanning his recent clinical experience; perhaps he needs to enlarge the search space to discover an appropriate clinical example. There are likely to be important differences among readers with respect to the ease of understanding a particular passage, the awareness of making a search, and the size of the search space, and each of these differences will contribute to a unique naturalization. If we had a chance to compare a sample of these attempts, we would see that some accept what others challenge and vice versa; we can be sure that there is no particular uniformity in the universe of "texts."

By contrast, consider what we will call the intended or official naturalization. It must be carried out by the treating analyst within minutes of the completion of the session (as opposed to being carried out by the frustrated reader months or years after the case is finished). It must, as we noted in the preceding chapter, explain the transitions between speakers; provide the evidence and motivation for each intervention; the analyst's understanding for each utterance made by the patient; his associations to each utterance; his understanding of each silence, with perhaps a comment on its quality—and much, much more. We would want to include an explication of all ambiguities; we would like to see all missing syntax completed. Going beyond the actual text of the hour, we would like to see a full account of all missing paralinguistic cues. The list, we begin to see, is almost endless.

Is it possible? Can a transcript be "unpacked" in such a systematic fashion that it can be made accessible to readers with only normative competence? In other words, can we substitute a single, official naturalization for the hosts of unofficial, unintended, and unsystematic naturalizations that are presently occupying the psychoanalytic underground? The two types of naturalization are linked because until we can provide readers with an official gloss, they will always fall back on their own private readings, adding what seems necessary to pass some threshold of narrative fit. And they are linked because, up to now, the fact that each of us could supply his own, unintended naturalization effectively prevented us from seeing the need for something more official. Our literature suffers, we might say, from our analytic competence. The analyst is his own worst enemy—his training works so well that he never sees the seams in his data.

Can the trend be reversed? This question, it would seem, is much more important than the question of whether psychoanalysis is a science or a pseudo science or whether the treatment is real or placebo. Is it possible to make the case record self-sufficient, accountable only to itself, and, therefore, accessible to any reader with only normative competence? If yes, then we have the beginnings of a shared discipline; if no, we are doomed to a perpetual underground of private "texts" and individual understandings.

PARADIGMS AND WORLD VIEWS

To gain perspective on this question, let us turn to the problem of evidence in physics. At first sight, questions of what and where and why seem ridiculously easy to answer when we turn to problems of falling bodies and bouncing balls. But even here, as Kuhn is at some pains to point out, the data do not speak for themselves; the organizing theory of the observer—what Kuhn has called his paradigm—is always being brought to bear on the observable data and in a variety of subtle and not so subtle ways, affecting what he thinks he can "see." Start with the simple case of the pendulum.

"Since remote antiquity," writes Kuhn,

> most people have seen one or another heavy body swinging back and forth on a string or chain until it finally comes to rest. To the Aristotelians, who believed that a heavy body is moved by its own nature from a higher position to a state of natural rest at a lower one, the swinging body was simply falling with difficulty. Constrained by the chain, it could achieve rest at its low point only after a tortuous motion and a considerable time. Galileo, on the other hand, looking at the swinging body, saw a pendulum, a body that almost succeeded in repeating the same motion over and over again ad infinitum. And having seen that much, Galileo observed other properties of the pendulum as well and constructed many of the most significant and original parts of his new dynamics around them. . . . All these natural phenomena he saw differently from the way they had been seen before. (1962, pp. 117–18)

One might think that the simple pendulum, bounded by time and space, was a clear-cut and explicit piece of the external world, something that we could discuss with no possibility for misunderstanding. But despite its relatively simple appearance, it remained for Galileo to see it as something more than a constrained falling body. Kuhn goes on to point out that what characterized Galileo's observations was not their greater accuracy or objectivity but, rather, their focus on certain aspects of the motion, such as its regularity and (in contrast to the earlier view) its overall simplicity. Note, further, that seeing the stone as a constrained falling body is not "wrong"; seeing it as a pendulum is not "right"; but that seeing it as a pendulum allows certain questions to be asked and certain measurements to be taken, and as it turned out, the questions asked by Galileo had more fruitful consequences than those asked by the Aristotelians.

According to the view developed by Kuhn, we construct our view of pendulum motion much as we unwittingly interpret a patient's flow of associations. Each interpretation is guided, unwittingly, by our favorite paradigm. In reading a case report and supplying our private gloss, we are, in effect, constructing an interpretation that supports our private theory or collection of paradigms.

But we are also doing something more—and here is where the contrast with physics becomes enlightening. The observations and measurements made by Galileo on such things as the weight of the pendulum bob, the distance from the point of support (amplitude), and the number of oscillations per unit time (frequency) were accessible to anyone with scale and ruler. To measure (and thereby name) the weight of the bob requires only the simple operation of putting it on a scale, and the rules for this operation can be precisely specified. But can we find the corresponding measuring and naming operations in psychoanalytic data? Not very likely. Almost every attempt at naming first requires an interpretation; the raw data of the clinical happening are of a different order from stones and supporting strings.

At this point we can return to the issue of naturalization. Its rationale, simply stated, is to put the data of the psychoanalytic session on a par with the data of the observable world. If it were properly carried out, the observations relevant for our theory could become accessible to anyone with normative competence; any outside reader with appropriate training would be in a position to decide whether they support the claims of the treating analyst or whether more evidence is necessary. A proper gloss would make explicit the meaning of every observation, and it would make it possible to name its elements without first assuming an interpretation.

It should be pointed out that the gloss—the formal naturalization—does not necessarily get any closer to the "sheer thereness" of the world; no amount of training will do that because, as Kuhn points out, we simply have no "pure-observation-language," and it seems doubtful if we ever will. And as we have seen in Chapter IV, we need an organizing construction (or paradigm in Kuhn's sense) in order to make sense of any set of routine observations. The gloss would not eliminate this need; quite the opposite, it would make available to all parties the "official" paradigm which, presumably, was organizing all observations. Readers with only normative competence, given access to the official paradigm, would, for the first time, see the material as the treating analyst had seen it and, again for the first time, would be in a position to agree or disagree with his formulations.

BARRIERS TO NATURALIZATION

How did the treating analyst experience the hour? Is it possible for an outsider to step into his shoes and recapture his experience? What we are asking for, in a slightly different context, is an accurate reconstruction of his experience, which will include not only the visible evidence captured by the tape recorder but an exhaustive documentation of the invisible surround that provides context and meaning. We stress the word *reconstruction* because, all too often, attempts to recapture the full experience of the treating analyst frequently turn into attempts at creating merely a *plausible* account. We may supply reasons for an interpretation that were not in awareness when the interpretation was made; we may take effect and turn it into cause; we may reason backward from the *response* to an interpretation to our *intention* in saying it in the first place; and, in general, we find ourselves using the familiar criterion of narrative fit to turn the uneven progress of the session into a finished story.

Once again, we find our taste for coherence and continuity getting in the way. Just as we use our analytic competence to find the themes beneath the surface, so in looking back at a finished session we may easily transform the uneven, interrupted, shifting journey over a range of shifting terrains into a finished episode with one underlying theme. We may remember the beginning and end of an episode and unconsciously fill in the middle, even in cases where there was no middle and either patient or therapist failed to make the transition. Particularly vulnerable are our initial reasons for framing this or that interpretation. If the patient hears in it a message we had not intended and proceeds to develop associations along a new and unexpected theme, the new meaning tends to "wash backwards" onto the original interpretation; we will tend to see it in this new light, and it becomes very hard to keep in mind our original intention. At times we may not insist on our original meaning; our training prepares us for unexpected shifts of this kind, and we learn to follow where the patient leads. Thus our role as free-floating listener gets in the way of our role as historian, and if we train ourselves to follow wherever the patient leads, supplying whatever mediating associations may be necessary to make sense out of his wanderings, we can hardly retrace our journey at the end of the hour and go back to the start with any degree of accuracy. The two roles are so antithetical that one seems to interfere with the other.

To listen as historian, we are bound to emphasize the manifest features of the patient's utterance and stay close to the surface; his associations, wherever they might lead, become the primary data, and we sink back into our own associations only at our peril. At the end of the hour, we may have a clear record of what was said, but we have hardly functioned in an analytic manner. But to take the analyst's role and surrender to the luxury of peripheral associations and supplementary themes, we are bound to lose track, from time to time, of what *exactly* the patient said; hence our history will be incomplete, highly subjective, and hardly the basis for an official gloss of the hour.

The clash of roles is accompanied by interfering states of consciousness. To listen with free-floating attention, amplified from time to time with the kind of constructive additions we described in Chapter IV, requires a certain meditative stance in which we allow ourselves to wander off occasionally into daydream and fantasy. In this altered state of consciousness, we can listen at several levels at the same time; we can shift from what the patient is saying to our interior world of psychic reality and allow this world to supply context—and eventually meaning—to what is being said. At times, we may be more aware of context; at times, more aware of utterance. A full account requires a full presentation of both kinds of material plus—and this is essential—a surrounding organization that allows the reader to experience the events as they were experienced by the treating analyst and to understand what occurred in a way that comes close to his understanding. Up to this moment, this task has not been accomplished anywhere in our psychoanalytic literature; it perhaps has never been attempted.

Part of the difficulty in naturalizing a transcript comes from our erroneous sense of what the reader needs to be told. We tend to underestimate the differences between normative and privileged competence and, as we noted in the previous chapter, assume that he will see and hear the material in the same way as we experience it. This projective fallacy tends to limit the amount of guiding information that is used to create the gloss, and it limits the detail with which we describe the developing associational contexts. We may assume, for example, that most of the features of an hour are familiar and choose to focus only on the bizarre and exotic. As a result, we have critically changed the structure of our description and, in so doing, make it impossible for the outside reader to approximate our experience.

A further problem has to do with how the background information should be presented. We have described (in Chapter VII) how an analyst's personal loss came to influence his reaction to patient utterances about similar themes. His loss is one piece of the background information needed to understand that particular hour, and it must be presented in such a way that the outside reader will experience the patient's utterances as if he, too, has just lost a member of his family. It is probably not enough to make the bare statement at the beginning of the commentary; some way must be found to *dramatize* the event and to allow the reader to share the experience of loss in such a way that he feels it as a burden all the time he is reading the clinical material. Only then will he appreciate its effect on the hour and understand how it colors specific parts of the material.

We are back to the problem of how to put things into words or to what might be called the problem of narrative technique. It is defined by Schorer (1961) as "any selection, structure or distortion, any form or rhythm imposed upon the world of action . . . by means of which . . . our apprehension of the world of action is enriched or renewed" (p. 251). We can make use of the traditional distinction, first proposed by the Russian formalists, between *fabula* and *sujet* (see Sternberg, 1974). *Fabula* refers to the raw material of the narrative—what happens in the story in its original time sequence. *Sujet* refers to the way in which this material is presented in the finished narrative—the order of events as encountered by the reader. The craft of fiction can be defined in part as the way in which the *fabula* are rearranged to form the *sujet,* and the manner and method of rearrangement constitutes the narrative technique. Whether or not a particular piece of writing is effective depends heavily on just how the real sequence of events has been rearranged to form the narrative sequence. It can be seen that certain events can be highlighted by being placed early in the narrative and described in extensive detail; other details, less important for the final story, may be described later in the narrative or in summarized fashion. The final narrative almost never corresponds to the original sequence of events; conversely, the original sequence in almost all cases must be reconstructed from the final narrative. By artful rearrangement of events and shifts in point of view, the accomplished writer is able to enhance certain effects, minimize others, and, in general, control the context against which the content is appreciated.

It may be necessary to make similar adjustments in our clinical material in order to give the outside reader the experience of the treating analyst. The *fabula* of the actual session may no longer be sufficient to convey the necessary background context, and some way must be found to artistically rearrange the material to produce a new account (the *sujet*) that will dramatize the relevant issues and supply the necessary ground against which the actual utterances are heard. The final arrangement must be presented to the outside reader with the critical material in just the right sequence; only the appropriate *sujet* will provide the proper context for each utterance. Only then will the outside reader "hear" each utterance as did the treating analyst and only then will the reader be in a position to understand the analyst's unfolding sense of the hour.

It can be argued that Freud appreciated this problem and tried to present his clinical material in a somewhat novelistic manner. But while he was often dramatic and convincing, he was also incomplete and unsystematic, and the omission of certain details cannot help but change the background context in a significant way. We would argue for a complete presentation that is, in addition, artistically presented.

Consideration of the difficulties in the way of such a dramatization makes us begin to realize why it has never been realized—and perhaps, although here the data are sketchy, has never been attempted. The complete gloss, created along the lines we have been describing, would be quite different from the perfect hour described by Kris (1956b), the partially verbatim transcript published by Dewald (1972), or one of the 1,204 hours recorded by Dahl.* Each of these attempts represents a partial subset of the ingredients of the final gloss; they give us an idea of some of the contents to be covered but very little sense of the final form. The first attempt, by Kris, is something of a poetic construction that seems to be based on a number of different experiences and attempts to capture the feeling of the good hour more than its particular structure. The tape-recorded transcript by Dahl gives us the verbatim utterances; when read together with the analyst's process notes, it gives us a partial gloss of the experience; but no systematic attempt has been made to combine process notes with verbatim transcript in a way that will evoke in the reader the full experience of the treating analyst. Dewald's presentation is open to the same criticism. We must be presented with the critical material in just the right sequence so that the proper context has been created for each new utterance. Only then will we "hear" the patient's statement as did the treating analyst, and only then will we be in a position to understand his unfolding sense of the hour. Too much information will create a misleading context that will have the effect of transforming

---

*See Luborsky and Spence (1978, p. 353) for further details.

any given utterance into something quite different. For this reason we cannot be satisfied with reading first the process notes and then the transcript, or vice versa.

The importance of having the proper context as we listen to each utterance cannot be stressed too much. Anyone would agree that if we took the complete transcript of an hour and alphabetized all words spoken by the patient, the final listing (so many *and*s, so many *but*s, so many *why*s, and so forth) would be a faithful copy of the lexical units used but would tell us very little about the content of the session. A complete transcript, without the surrounding context, is just as much of an approximation. Not only does the written transcript deprive us of tone, pacing, and stress, but it also strips away the fringe of associations that surrounded each utterance at the time it was spoken and that turned it from a spoken sentence into an evocative communication. Ricoeur has stressed the way in which the spoken utterance of the patient can be understood as the "semantic dimension of desire" (1977, p. 837); the utterance is a languagelike expression of a need or instinct. What allows the treating analyst to perceive the motivational dimensions of the utterance depends on the context through which he "hears" the utterance being expressed.

FUTURE PROSPECTS

In the previous chapter, we emphasized the need for careful and exhaustive naturalizations of all analytic sessions; in the early part of this chapter, we have emphasized some of the difficulties that may get in the way. Now we must ask the most critical question of all: Are naturalizations possible?

Many things hinge on the answer. If we decide that no, they are not possible, then we must admit that each analytic hour is essentially unmeasurable and that each analyst's experience is essentially private; as a result, we are left with only minimal correspondence between theory and practice. We must resign ourselves to a literature of fads and fashions, to a cyclical rather than a cumulative development of ideas, and to a field in which opinion looms larger than evidence.

If we decide that, yes, they are possible, then we have the makings of a science—and all the good things that go with it. What are the prospects?

Freud, first of all, was skeptical. Conviction will not come, he concluded, from being exposed to even a full account of an hour, but he was not particularly troubled by this prospect because he was not trying to convince his readers. He failed, however, to appreciate the implications of this state of affairs for the growth of the field. As with all subsequent analysts, he was frequently guilty of the projective fallacy and tended to minimize the distinctions between normative and privileged competence—to assume, in other words, that all readers with analytic training would tend to "read" the material in the same way and would tend to arrive at the same conclusions. And because he emphasized the tentative nature of his theoretical concepts (see Freud, 1914, p. 77), he was less aware of how quickly even a tentative concept may become reified and, in the process, take on as many private meanings as it has users. What was clear to him (or becoming clear) probably had quite a different meaning for each of his followers.

Freud was also skeptical because he disapproved of any attempt to formulate a case while it was still in progress. "It is not a good thing," he wrote, "to work on a case scientifically while treatment is still proceeding—to piece together its structure, to try to foretell its further progress, and to get a picture from time to time of the current state of affairs, as scientific interest would demand. . . . The correct behavior for an analyst lies in . . . avoiding speculation or brooding over cases, while they are still in analysis, and in submitting the material obtained to a synthetic process of thought only after the analysis is concluded" (1912, p. 114). Clearly, such a position would not tolerate any attempt to gloss the session and unpack its implicit meanings.

Interest in the issue was revived during the late sixties, when Gill, Simon, and their colleagues published a series of papers on the possibility of using a tape recorder to transcribe analytic sessions. Implicitly suggested in these papers (see Gill et al., 1968; Simon et al., 1970) was the idea that putting a tape recorder in the consulting room would finally give us access to the complete session—not just the truth but the whole truth. As we have seen, however, words are not to be confused with meanings; the tape recorder may do a good job of capturing the former but can only approximate the latter.

Throughout our literature relatively little attention has been paid to the issue being raised here, and the reason for this oversight may be related to several themes already discussed. First, we have the familiar projective fallacy. We assume that all analysts tend to understand the material in much the same way; we, therefore, see no need to make our assumptions explicit or give background context for a particular association or interpretation. The problem of multiple understandings is never confronted because it is never seen in the first place— and here we have an interesting paradox. Because the issue is never raised, no one has made the attempt to generate independent readings of the same data to see whether they correspond. Such an attempt would probably reveal serious inconsistencies in the interpretations and bring the issue of multiple "texts" into the public eye. But since general agreement as to understanding is more or less assumed, the issue is never raised and the evidence for or against the guiding assumption remains well hidden.

A second reason why so little notice is paid to the issue is related to Freud's model of free-floating attention. His model made it seem *as if* the analyst listens with "evenly-hovering attention" and simply uses his "analyzing instrument" to detect the (unambiguous) underlying theme(s). Any analyst, goes the assumption, if given this model and given the right kind of training, would "hear" the same theme—therefore, the possibility of multiple "texts" never arises. But as soon as we admit that the job of listening is one of actively construing meanings, then we can see how each analyst will be likely to "hear" the material in his own idiosyncratic way. Once we admit that constructive listening is the norm, then we must assume that the spoken text—the tape recording of the session—is not sufficient as evidence, and we realize that we must also gain access to the peripheral contexts through which the analyst listens.

A third reason for disinterest in the issue has to do with the way in which we assess the outcome of an interpretation. As we have seen, a given construction is usually validated by the subsequent material, and the outcome is usually favorable because the material is infinitely accommodating. Many times the reaction to an interpretation may differ from what we had intended, but because, as we have seen, we tend to confuse effect with cause, we may feel that we understand the precipitating reason for some remark when we are merely making a retrospective mistake. What Grünbaum (1979) has called the ravages of *post hoc, ergo propter hoc* may blind us to the need to separate cause and effect and the need to keep one record of the associations that have triggered a particular interpretation and another record of the consequences of the same remark. Once again, we find the same paradox: until we are confronted with the ways in which the actual cause of an interpretation may differ from its apparent cause, we will probably not appreciate the need for more extended documentation.

To return now to the central question—is it possible to generate a contextual fringe for each utterance that can be supplied to the outside analyst as he reads through the transcript and that will allow him to "hear" each statement as it was first heard by the treating analyst and, in that way, turn his normative competence into privileged competence?

THE ROLE OF METAPHOR AND LANGUAGE

In many cases, the contextual fringe can best be represented by a particular metaphor. Weiss et al. (1980) are particularly fond of the metaphor of "testing," and in a high proportion of cases they will tend to "hear" the clinical material against this background. Suppose an analyst makes a positive response to the patient's demand. Weiss et al. might tend to say that he has "failed the test." The decision not to respond might be "heard" as "passing the test." The metaphor is almost never made explicit in the verbatim transcript and may not even be mentioned in the process notes. But it represents a central part of the gloss; and, therefore, even if we do not happen to sympathize with this particular approach, we must assume this position as we read the transcript if we are to "hear" all relevant implications and if we want to fully understand what the analyst is about.

In this particular instance, the metaphor can rather easily be made explicit, but we are faced with the familiar problem of how it should be presented. Should it simply be stated, at the beginning of the hour, as a reminder of the guiding principle, or should it be illustrated in several different ways as the hour proceeds in order that the reader will continually feel its particular emphasis? The question bears on the difference between intellectual understanding and well-analyzed insight. To know the metaphor as a possible guiding principle is to have only a superficial understanding of the rule; we must also experience it as a compelling necessity that forces us to understand each of the patient's demands as a test, accompanied by all the associations that we may bring to the testing situation. These associations might include our private experience of success and failure; our particular struggles with examination anxiety; our need to be competitive, to succeed, and to be in control; and a number of other related themes. If the testing metaphor is properly evoked, it will allow us to bring to bear on the material a cluster of associations which will very likely overlap with those of the treating analyst. If we can succeed in that task, we have successfully naturalized the material because we will now "hear" the patient's utterances through the appropriate context and find them suitably transformed.

We begin to see the requirements for a comprehensive gloss. The reader must be supplied with whatever is necessary in order to transform the visible text of the hour into the experienced text of the treating analyst. We also see the dangers that can result when no context is provided; under those conditions, each reader, as we have made clear, will combine the visible text with his own, half-explicit set of private associations and reach, in silence, his own creative conclusions.

A somewhat different example of how a phrase (not quite a metaphor) can affect the reading of a particular passage comes from a paper by Mahony (1980). In discussing the issue of translation in psychoanalysis and the many ways in which Freud used the term, we find the following passage:

> In the latter half of the seventeenth century there was a gargantuan effort spearheaded by the famous John Wilkins to eliminate ambiguity and hence create a univocal language in which there would be a different word for every conceivable and perceptible entity. . . . Of course this *towering* gesture of folly came *babbling* down, for it would have been necessary to create an infinite language to be adequate to the infinite variety of human experience. (p. 464; my italics)

Only if we are familiar with the phrase "Tower of Babel" does the passage achieve its maximum effect. Knowing that phrase, we can sense the word play in the second sentence

(note the italicized words) and read the sentence as an allusion to a Biblical event as well as a description of the folly of
trying to create a universal language. Now it may be that the
first sentence, through a series of associations, may evoke the
image of the Tower of Babel and, in this way, prepare the reader
for the word play in the second sentence, but this assumption
is far from assured. We conclude that only by coming to the
passage with the phrase more or less readily available—only
when we "hear" the passage against that background—do we
realize its most complete meaning. Put another way, the passage, to be fully understood, requires a reading against an
awareness of the Tower of Babel and the implications of this
symbol; a comprehensive gloss for this passage would include
such an explanation.

For a final example of the way in which context can affect
interpretation, consider the following clinical anecdote from
France. The patient in question had adopted a largely silent
stance in treatment that she characterized as "Je me tais" (I
shut up). Her fear of speaking stemmed in part from her conviction that whatever she said, the analyst would only say
"Non." The analyst, perhaps prompted by the word "non" and
its similarity (in sound) to the word "nom," asked the following question: "De quel nom son père l'appelait?" (What did
her father used to call her?). The patient replied "Maité"—an
affectionate contraction of Marie-Thérèse. The analyst pointed
out that the nickname is an anagram of *t'aime* (I love you) and
also related (partly by sound) to "[Je] me tais"—which brings
us back to the state of the transference (Major, 1980, p. 398).

What context must be brought to bear on this clinical event?
First, the outside reader must know French; only then will he
be able to find the links between "Maité," "t'aime," and "Je me
tais," and the links between "non" and "nom." Only by listening with a French ear, so to speak, can the outside reader find
a connection between the patient's silence and the response
to the analyst's question. Translate the anecdote into English

and the tight cluster of sound and meaning links simply disappears. We might also assume that a knowledge of French and a sensitivity to French sound patterns would reveal still further links which the analyst has not discovered; thus the most enriched "reading" depends on the imposition of a French context.

In the last two examples, the target passage is best read in conjunction with a particular context. Take away the context and we lose certain overlays of meaning. Note further that the passage does not seem to "insist" on the context; in other words, the context is not necessarily an integral part of the passage, which can be discovered by the right detective. Rather, the context is the psychic backdrop against which the passage should be heard. Given this particular context, we seem to have maximal access to the elusive associations; we are in a position to discover more links and detect a greater number of meaningful connections. Listening with some other context— thinking of the last patient as *resistant,* for example, rather than *je me tais*—we will miss many of the important connections and mainly hear a string of words.

Because the context does not usually reside in the passage, there is no necessary reason why the reader with only normative competence is going to read it with maximal understanding. This fact is another consequence of the conclusion, reached in the previous chapter, that the clinical dialogue is not a public document and, therefore, not accessible to the reader with only normative competence. Were it to be made public, the text would be written in such a way that the appropriate context would grow out of the reading: the first chapter in a novel, for example, exists in part to bring the reader to Chapter II in a certain mood and with a certain set of expectations; the playwright sets the stage in a specific way before he lets his characters speak, knowing that only when viewed from this perspective will his dialogue have its maximum effect. But because the case report is not a public document, the necessary background is missing and the treating analyst must add the necessary context.

FINAL QUESTIONS

We can conclude this chapter by listing the more important questions that arise when we try to move from normative to privileged competence.

1. Can we recover the unwitting interpretations of the treating analyst in their original form? We can probably recover some of them, but it seems doubtful whether we can recover them all. We have seen how they occur on the fringes of awareness and are rarely verbalized; to be recovered, however, they must be put into words, and we might wonder whether this attempt would produce partial approximations instead of faithful copies of the original interpretation.

2. Once we were able to uncover the unwitting interpretations, could we integrate them with the other material in such a way that the combined experience unfolds for the outside reader just as it unfolded for the treating analyst? Supposing this step were possible in theory—how would we know when we had achieved it in practice? We are not only attempting to produce a particular artistic effect, but we are hoping to make it resemble the earlier experience of the treating analyst; thus we must go the dramatist one better. *Fabula* must not only be transformed into *sujet,* but the final arrangement of material must be such that, when read by an outside reader, it will reconstruct the *fabula* of the treating analyst.

3. Can we eliminate the private unwitting interpretations of the outside reader as he is exposed to the unfolding case? We have seen how these are naturally triggered by incomplete or ambiguous material; we now suggest that they *must* be eliminated in order that the official gloss achieve its desired effect. For *sujet* to be properly transformed into the original *fabula,* there must be a minimum of interfering formulations.

4. Can we supply the necessary rules by which context transforms content? If we knew more about how content is transformed by context, we might be able to supply the outside reader with the recorded transcript and a set of conventions that would translate the visible utterances into their underlying meanings. Until we have such a set of rules—and it is not even certain whether or not a complete set of rules could be found—we must assume the role of playwright and novelist and learn how to arrange the clinical material in ways that will simulate the experience of the treating analyst.

5. How do we know when enough of the unwitting interpretations have been uncovered to make possible the transition from normative to privileged competence? Given the layers of context within context, it is obvious that naturalization might never stop. Is there, nevertheless, some reasonable standard we can set which will decide when enough clarification has been reached? The answer may turn on our subjective sense of being convinced, and it points up the difference between psychoanalytic argument and other kinds of persuasion. It has been the tradition in psychoanalysis to rely more on assertion than on evidence; conclusions tend to be accepted on faith rather than on independent scrutiny of the facts. The outcome of a particular interpretation, for example, is usually described rather than quoted; the reasons behind a particular clinical formulation tend to be summarized and not documented in detail. Clinical papers achieve various levels of persuasion, but their power to convince would seem to lie more in the author's *literary* style than in the presentation of evidence.

It is against this bleak standard that we can consider the properly naturalized clinical vignette. If we have been successful in bringing to light the necessary and sufficient background assumptions, then we would be able to actually convince the outside reader. Rather than take a particular conclusion on faith (the customary mode of reaction), the reader would have the experience of discovering the new conclusion or formulation along with the treating analyst; he would experience the kind of aesthetic discovery we experience when we see a classic work of art. For the first time, he would be in a position to empathize with the treating analyst (and perhaps with the patient) and recognize the narrative truth of the vignette as well as its more theoretical meaning.

If the outside reader comes to have that kind of empathic experience, then we can conclude that our naturalization has been sufficiently complete, and that no further unpacking is necessary. If, on the other hand, the outside reader shows only an intellectual awareness of the argument without the conviction that such and such *must* have been the reason for a given interpretation, then we would conclude that the unpacking has not been sufficient or that the presentation is flawed and we would have to enlarge our network of clues. Trial and error would decide what kind of additional information needed to be included; in a large majority of cases, we might find that we had made assumptions about certain key parts of the anecdote that were not shared by the reader. Once these assumptions had been clarified, we would expect the appropriate excited understanding to take place.

In the final analysis, the naturalized vignette can be evaluated by the effect it achieves. If it brings to the outside reader the kind of inevitable persuasion that we have learned to associate with a classic philosophical argument or mathematical proof, then we have achieved our goal of making privileged data publicly accessible.

CHAPTER IX

•————————————————————————

The Successor to Archeology

It was one of Freud's major contributions to make us aware of what might be called the ambiguity of everyday life. Every utterance, he showed us, no matter how simple, has many meanings; surface is always deceptive; and the complete truth of any statement may be always out of reach. This position is now being echoed from other traditions. The philosopher Searle, for example, has recently (1979) taken the position that for a "large class of sentences, there is no such thing as the zero or null context for the interpretation of the sentences, and that as far as our semantic competence is concerned, we understand the meaning of such sentences only against a set of background assumptions about the contexts in which the sentence could be appropriately uttered" (p. 117). In a chapter on literal meanings, he shows how even the simple assertion "The cat is on the mat" can take on different meanings depending on different background assumptions. Not only are assumptions critical to understanding; Searle makes the disturbing claim that there are always an indefinite number of such assumptions and, therefore, there is no upper limit to our ability to "hear" different meanings.

The problem of zero context, as discussed by Searle, can be seen as the other side of the principle of multiple function; ambiguity is the rule rather than the exception, and no utterance is simple. No analyst would find this surprising. But, as we have suggested in the last two chapters, this assumption is now coming back to haunt us because it applies to our publications and our findings just as much as it applies to our patients. If we claim that what the patient says must always be heard against the background of his life and can never be fully understood unless we know the complete context, past and present, then we must also agree that protocols, case reports, and even published papers are equally vulnerable to misunderstanding. The notion of zero context applies with equal force to both sides of the couch.

It is by no means clear whether the proper context can be provided to the reader with only normative competence—not only because we are not sure *what* to tell him but, as we made clear in the last chapter, because we are even less certain *how* to tell it. In a discussion of the problems of art appreciation, Aiken makes a similar point: "One does not become a special reader [expert critic]," he writes, "simply by coming to know about the causal conditions which determined the artist to express what he intended to express in the way in which he tried to express it. To understand or 'know about' is one thing; to possess the beliefs and feelings which will transform what one understands into something immediate and actual is something else" (1951, p. 310). We are beginning to appreciate some of the contexts that must be provided for the outside reader, but we are far from clear as to the proper form of presentation. And the difference between intellectual understanding and fully grounded awareness is a difference that is central to the analytic tradition—it corresponds, paraphrasing

Mark Twain, to the difference between lightning and a lightning bug.

If ambiguity is everywhere, then how do we escape? It could be argued that Freud tried to escape through archeology. If we are uncovering actual pieces of the patient's past—early memories, infantile wishes, and the like—and if these pieces, following the archeological model, can be fitted into singular patterns, then we come very close to having created a literal statement that speaks for itself, outside of any context. We have seen how the archeological model, because of its appeal to hard fact, protected him from the charge of suggestion; if he could claim that his method would allow him to make contact with the actual past, he could defend himself against the charge of supplying some of the answers. Suggestion is ruled out: on the contrary, the analyst simply allows the evidence to emerge; as we have seen, "all of the essentials are preserved; even things that seem completely forgotten are present somehow and somewhere, and have merely been buried and made inaccessible to the subject" (Freud, 1937, p. 260).

But the force of the argument rests on the words "essentials" and "things," and, as we have seen, an archeologist and an analyst work with different fragments. We have shown in Chapter III how we can never make contact with the pictorial data of dreams and memories and how the use of language screens us from a true sense of these phenomena. The critical attributes of a pictorial image cannot be expressed in words, and what is expressed may or may not have much in common with what is visually experienced. We have seen how free association is simply not a systematic way of getting back to the original dream or memory and if the method is in doubt, we should be correspondingly skeptical of the emerging fragments and of the guiding model. In the last analysis, we are not dealing with form and fragment but with verbal descriptions of form and fragment, and language is as loosely coupled to form as the title of a painting is to the painting itself. "Each art," writes John Dewey, "speaks an idiom that conveys what cannot be said in another language and yet remain the same" (1934, p. 106). As we have seen, we are still searching for the pure language of observation.

Once we admit that our method is an archeology of verbal descriptions, we realize that the problem of ambiguity is far from solved. Form may be conclusive, as we have seen in Chapter V, and convince us that Manet was inspired by Raimondi, but a verbal description of these two paintings and a pattern match based on such a description only beg the question. Instead of the original image, safe and sound in some clinical archive, we have the patient's interpretation, which, to make matters worse, is further interpreted by the analyst and interpreted again by each new reader. Each of these interpretations is predicated on some kind of mediating context, but since these contexts are usually invisible, we have no way of evaluating the interpretation.

Without the actual fragments, we have no proper archeology. Form is represented only loosely by language, and even the special properties of the analytic situation give us no privileged access to the original "fragments." As we have seen, it would be a mistake to conclude that the method of free association is the simple converse of dream formation. And because the patient must speak his thoughts, he will always be influenced by what we have called the conditions of describability. We can imagine how long art history or archeology would have survived if it depended solely on eyewitness accounts of paintings and diggings. What is sayable is not necessarily the same as what is visually significant, and the conditions of representability, so critical for the process of dream and memory formation, only loosely correspond to the conditions of describability. Using the method of free association, we always run the risk that a dream will be described as a scene of lakes and trees and swans (see Chapter III) simply because these objects have names.

If form, once translated by language, is unreliable, it would follow that form can hardly be used to deduce cause and effect or other kinds of motivational information. As we have seen in Chapter V, the archeological metaphor makes us prone to analogue reasoning and to a kind of primitive thinking that is unhappily reminiscent of medieval philosophy. Appearance, as we have seen, is only vaguely related to essence; and we are further handicapped by the fact that we are dealing with partial descriptions. So long as we have no way of systematically reconstructing the contents of a dream or memory, we are not in a position to draw conclusions from the pictorial data. Here, again, we see the influence of the archeological model; in suggesting terms like *uncovering* or *fragment,* it leads to a kind of misplaced concreteness that does an injustice to the verbal utterance. Rather than representing a piece of the past, the utterance is more likely a creation of the present—a creative act, as Viderman has suggested—that can take on any number of meanings depending on the surrounding context. To take an utterance as a thing (to go back to Freud's usage) is to assume that it has a literal meaning, and, as we have seen, this assumption would seem to apply to only a very small subset of assertions. Thus the archeological model applies, at best, to only the more trivial parts of the analytic conversation; something else is needed to take advantage of its unlimited richness. We must find some other way to cope with ambiguity.

There is an irony here that needs to be expressed. The importance of ambiguity in the analytic *process* has never been properly addressed by the analytic *method.* Once we assume that meanings are multiple, we can hardly assume that the one *we* discover is necessarily the most significant. To discover a meaning is different from discovering a lost fragment.

The ambiguity of the utterance or the symptom still remains after we have put an interpretation on it; if we can claim, with Searle, that there is an unlimited number of contexts that could be supplied for any utterance, we can see that interpretation is endless. Freud would agree with respect to dream fragments or symptomatic acts, but he was unwilling to extend the claim to cover the analyst's understanding. This was somehow exempt—more than that, it was essentially transparent and unambiguous, accessible to anyone with normative competence.

To stay with the archeological model forces us, as we have seen, to concentrate on the trivial. But to give it up opens the way to a number of disagreeable prospects. If we no longer make contact with pieces of the past, what reason do we have to assume that our interpretation is in any way privileged? Not only are we open to the charge of suggestion, but, in addition, we can be accused of making decisions on the basis of insufficient evidence. If our interpretation cannot be validated by a piece of the past and if any utterance is subject to unlimited interpretations, how do we choose? We have seen that we cannot rely on narrative fit because a life story is often so loosely constituted that almost any datum can find a home. What is the alternative?

INTERPRETATION AS AESTHETIC EXPERIENCE

It may be useful to think of an interpretation as being a certain kind of aesthetic experience as opposed to being an utterance that is either (historically) true or false. From this point of view, one can ask what contributes to what might be called the beauty of the experience? Putting the problem this way allows us to make contact with a respected tradition in aesthetics that can be summarized by the question "Is there always truth in beauty?" A significant number of critics have argued that truth, within certain limits, is actually irrelevant to an aesthetic experience. As Isenberg has written, "poetry drugs the dragon of disbelief" (1955). I can disagree with historical fact, for example, and still be impressed by a poem or painting so long as the disagreement is not overwhelming and does not distract me from the more artistic parts of the experience. The conclusion follows from the fact that an aesthetic response includes much more than the simple cognitive appreciation of the message; and furthermore, we can, if we choose, minimize the cognitive contribution and pay more attention to the artistic or structural parts of the experience. This kind of momentary rearrangement is part of what we mean by the "suspension of disbelief," which seems to play an important role in any aesthetic experience.

Applied to an interpretation, this argument would suggest that the historical truth of the interpretation is not necessarily relevant to its clinical impact (read aesthetic experience). It would also suggest that an interpretation must be much more than a simple proposition because in order for an aesthetic experience to occur, we must provide the patient with something in the way of an aesthetic stimulus; the central proposition must be surrounded by something else to which he can redirect his attention. We begin to see, once again, the importance of the rhetorical side of an interpretation; *how* it is said may be just as important as—or more important than—its message. The Viderman interpretation "six roses or cirrhosis" becomes an aesthetic stimulus by virtue of the fact that he has turned a bald statement into a pun; we can appreciate the play on words in addition to its assertions about the father and his alcoholic history, and we can assume that by augmenting its appeal in this way Viderman was making it possible for the patient to respond in an aesthetic manner. Once we have moved into an aesthetic domain, it becomes less important to ask about the historical truth of the interpretation, just as we would hardly think of asking about the historical "truth" of a painting.

But we do, however, ask about another kind of truth when faced with a painting—something we would call its artistic truth. And this response gives us another way of interpreting Viderman. Just as a Constable painting of an English landscape is more than a simple copy but something that possesses a kind of artistic truth, so a good interpretation can possess an artistic truth as a function of its phrasing and timing. The artistic truth has no necessary connection with historical accuracy, but, at the same time, the notion of artistic truth means that not just any painting or interpretation will qualify; it must conform to certain artistic or clinical standards. But so long as these are satisfied, it becomes an object of beauty without regard to how faithfully it represents the scene in question.

The artistic model, then, is one alternative to the archeological approach. We no longer search for historical accuracy but consider the interpretation in terms of its aesthetic appeal. Putting the problem this way allows us to make room for Viderman's notion that interpretations are essentially creative (in the best artistic sense) and for his hypothesis that a number of different interpretations might be provided for any particular clinical event. The notion of artistic truth, furthermore, can be used to amplify and extend our definition of narrative truth. It suggests that not just any narrative will do; that coherence and completeness are necessary but not sufficient; and that an important ingredient of the power to persuade is the aesthetic nature of the narrative. As with any good story, form is as important as content, and insight often emerges when an old memory is told in a new context (consider the remark frequently heard from patients, following an interpretation, that "I knew it all along"). The artistic truth of a narrative may not only contribute to its appeal; it may also maintain its structure over time and enable the patient to better retain what he learned during the analysis.

INTERPRETATION AS PRAGMATIC STATEMENT

A second way to appreciate the peculiar force of an interpretation is to think of it as a claim to the truth that cannot always be verified. We are speaking here of a class of utterances called pragmatic statements that can be defined as follows: "When someone makes a statement, which he wants to induce himself or others to believe, but which he does not at the time know to be true or could not possibly know to be true, *in order to bring about its truth*, I shall say that he is using language pragmatically, and that the statement in question is a pragmatic statement" (Singer, 1971, p. 27). If a politician, for example, says that he is going to win next Tuesday, he may be in no position to know the truth value of his claim because the election is too close to call. He makes the statement, not because he *knows* the outcome, but because he wishes to *influence* the outcome. If he says he will win, he may persuade the voters still in doubt. Thus a pragmatic statement is neither true nor false because we have no grounds for checking its truth value; rather, it is an instrument for bringing about a certain course of action.

Now it seems that an interpretation can be described in the same way. It is, first of all, a means to an end, uttered in the expectation that it will lead to additional, clarifying clinical material. Its truth, as Viderman has made clear, lies more in the present and future than in the past: it may become true for the first time just by being said. As with other pragmatic statements, to speak an interpretation is to lay a claim to its truth, just as when a politician says "I will win," he is making a special kind of assertion. Such statements are usually spoken by authorities.

The truth of such statements is always contingent, never absolute. By that we mean that its truth is a function of other things besides the statement itself; in the case of an interpretation, it depends on such factors as the state of the transference, its relevance to other parts of the conversation, its timing, its phrasing, and other aspects of its persuasive appeal. Because the truth is not absolute, it becomes impossible to look for corroboration in other parts of the clinical record because its historical accuracy would tell us nothing about its pragmatic effectiveness. As a result, we need not worry about the fact that much of our evidence is secondhand and that the patient's verbal statements are only approximations of his experience. Since we are no longer concerned about historical truth, the translation problems described in Chapters II and III are no longer critical.

This line of thinking can be extended somewhat further by asking: From a linguistic point of view, what exactly is the analyst doing when he makes an interpretation? A pragmatic statement is a certain kind of speech act, and it might be argued that the analyst making an interpretation is performing a certain kind of speech act in the analytic situation. A comparison with two other professions may help to clarify the issue. Searle (1979) has claimed that a newspaper reporter, when he writes a factual article, is making three kinds of commitments: First, he commits himself to the truth of any particular proposition in the story; second, he should be able to provide evidence or reasons for the truth of the proposition; and third, he commits himself to a belief in the truth. A novelist, by comparison, is *pretending* to make these claims but actually can perform none of them. He makes certain statements that are not necessarily true, for which he cannot provide the evidence, and about which he may have no particular beliefs. A. Conan Doyle, for example, would hardly claim that Sherlock Holmes *really* injected cocaine, that he believed that Holmes injected it, or that he could provide evidence to prove his assertion. He pretends to make these claims, and the fact that we understand his pretensions and do not require anything more in the way of documentation can be taken as one aspect of our literary competence. It also contributes to the necessary suspension of disbelief.

What about the analyst? In making an interpretation, we are suggesting that he is also pretending to perform certain kinds of speech acts, but in a slightly different manner. We would say that he shares with the reporter a commitment to a belief in the proposition he is putting forward but that he is less committed to its truth—as we will see, the truth may actually be indefinable—and he is often unable to provide supporting evidence. The interpretation, then, can be defined by a claim to a *belief* in the proposition and nothing more, much as the politician believes he will win next week and proudly stands behind this belief but cannot document the truth of this claim or provide supporting evidence. Put another way, we would say that the analyst commits himself to a belief in his formulation but not necessarily to a belief in its referent.

The difference between the two kinds of beliefs would seem to parallel the difference between construction and reconstruction. If we make the claim that a possible past event might have been somehow significant in the patient's early life experience, we are expressing a belief in the proposition or, in more familiar language, formulating a *construction* that is not necessarily tied to a particular time and place. We believe that something of this kind *may* have happened but we do not commit ourselves to producing necessary confirmation. On the other hand, if we commit ourselves to a *reconstruction* of the past, we are making a claim about its historical truth value and are obliged to provide something in the way of historical documentation. The archeological model commits us to the second; the pragmatic model commits us to the first. By the end of his career, Freud was becoming satisfied with the pragmatic model, as shown by the following statement:

> The path that starts from the analyst's construction ought to end in the patient's recollection; but it does not always lead so far.

> Quite often we do not succeed in bringing the patient to recollect what has been repressed. Instead of that, if the analysis is carried out correctly, we produce in him an assured conviction of the truth of the construction which achieves the same therapeutic result as a recaptured memory. (1937, pp. 265–66)

The "assured conviction of the truth" is equivalent to Searle's third kind of commitment—the belief in the proposition—and it is this, we claim, which is central to the effectiveness of an interpretation.

It seems as if a similar claim can be made for the artist. He commits himself to a belief in the truth of his painting—by which we mean its artistic truth—but need say nothing about its truth as a representation of the real world. Nor would we expect him to provide supporting evidence of its truth; art, after all, is only loosely tied to reality.

What have we learned? First, that the historical roots of an interpretation may be less critical than Freud had assumed and that we might be better off if we abandoned the archeological model. Second, that whether we think of an interpretation as an aesthetic creation or a pragmatic statement, they both represent certain kinds of narratives and supply us with additional understandings of narrative truth. And third, that they are to be primarily considered as means to future effects and not the result of past causes.

Let us now turn to some earlier examples. In making her statement that Mondrian suffered from being exposed to multiple primal scenes (see Chapter V), Greenacre was committing herself to a belief in a classic psychoanalytic hypothesis; psychoanalytic theory provided her with the grounds for assuming its impact along the lines discussed, and, as we have shown, similar hypotheses had been put forward in the past. She was, however, as we have noted, unable to provide supporting evidence for the claim, and, therefore, she was unable to commit herself to the truth of the proposition that Mondrian had actually witnessed multiple primal scenes. Once again we must distinguish between belief in a proposition and belief in its historical truth. The analyst, in contrast to the novelist, commits himself to a belief in his hypothesis and is inclined to use it in a pragmatic fashion, as a way of making something happen. He is less committed to a belief in its truth value— either because he has no clear way of knowing whether or not it actually occurred or because he is proposing something that has no clear correspondence with an event in the patient's life. In the same way, the Viderman pun *six roses or cirrhosis* cannot be said to correspond to a particular happening, and thus we can hardly ask questions about its historical truth. The more appropriate question concerns what might be called its artistic truth, its significance as a kind of creative endeavor, a putting-together of known facts about the patient in a new form that carries a high probability of making something happen in the analytic space.

In similar fashion, the proposal by Oliver (1980) that Flaubert might have taken the governess Julie as his mistress can be understood as a commitment to a belief in the possibility more than a commitment to the evidence. It would seem to belong to the category of pragmatic statements, which are more interesting for their effect than for their inherent (historical) truth or falseness.

AESTHETIC AND PRAGMATIC INTERPRETATIONS

By combining our two alternatives, we arrive at the following formulation. By committing himself to a belief in the hypothesis (the pragmatic component), the analyst is expressing the idea that he is interested in the result that certain words will produce in the patient's mind and in the analytic space; that he is presenting these words in the sincere belief that they will facilitate the process of therapy; and that he is arranging them in the best possible combination and at the best possible time (the aesthetic component). As proof of his intention, he will frequently preface his interpretation with such qualifiers as "It seems to me that . . . ," "I wonder if . . . ," "Has it occurred to you that . . . ," and similar expressions. But they are intended to be pragmatic statements, which means that their instrumental function assumes maximal importance.

Thinking about interpretations in this manner, we see that questions about their historical truth are either impossible to answer—as in the case of creative utterances—or relatively unimportant. If we think about them as pragmatic statements, we realize that they are designed to produce results rather than to document the past; they are designed primarily to bring about a change in belief. The more creative they are, the harder to document, because to the extent that they represent truly artistic productions, they have never happened before in just that form (think of *six roses or cirrhosis*) and, therefore, they have no more provable correspondence with reality than a painting or a piece of music. Once we conceive of interpretations as artistic creations that have the potential of producing an aesthetic response, we are, as we have noted, even less interested in the truth of the particular parts.

Thus it would seem as if both approaches bring us to the same conclusion. Whether we think of an interpretation as a special kind of speech act which belongs to the category of pragmatic statements or as an artistic product, to be evaluated according to aesthetic criteria, we are primarily interested in the effect it produces rather than in its past credentials. Once we give up our concern for historical accuracy, we can not only abandon the archeological model but we can also become more comfortable with the flawed nature of the clinical data. We no longer need to be embarrassed by our "archeology of descriptions."

In defining an interpretation as either a pragmatic statement or an artistic creation, we are emphasizing the fact that its truth value is contingent. By definition, therefore, an interpretation can no longer be evaluated in its singular propositional form but must be considered with respect to the conditions under which it was expressed (created) and the outcome it produced. This way of looking at the issue has two important consequences. First, if the truth of an interpretation is always contingent, its evaluation depends heavily on the completeness of the context; we can hardly make an adequate assessment if the data are incomplete. Privileged competence is more than ever a basic requirement for evaluating the clinical data; we simply must be informed of all possible contingencies before we can make a judgment about a particular interpretation.

The second consequence bears on the problem of conceptual change. If truth is contingent and if we can only understand the meaning and significance of an interpretation against the full set of background assumptions that were operating in that particular analytic space, then we should not be surprised at the periodic appearance of theoretical disagreements. What is more, these disagreements may indicate, not a shift in paradigm or some other kind of fundamental re-evaluation, but, rather, the less significant result of drawing conclusions from insufficient data. Supporters of one school, for example, may choose, for a variety of reasons, to take into account only a certain subset of the clinical data, and from within this domain, certain conclusions seem necessarily to follow. Another school, arguing from another subset, reaches different conclusions. Since each group must claim only normative competence (there being no completely naturalized protocols), they are, by definition, less than completely informed, and thus it is no surprise to find that they arrive at significantly different conclusions about the meaning of a particular protocol.

We come back once again to the central problem of privileged competence. Until any particular therapeutic interchange can be made completely accessible to all readers, we have no chance of raising a clinical happening to a higher level of discourse. Until the protocol is fully naturalized, we will always run the risk of mixing private and public mediating assumptions. Since no statement, it would seem, has a completely literal meaning (and the average ambiguity of clinical utterances is probably much higher than the general norm), then it follows that any statement, to be completely understood, must be "heard" against the same background assumed by the treating analyst. Only a slight change in the mix of background assumptions can produce a significant change in assumed meaning.

We have exchanged the problem of finding answers in the past—the archeological model—for the equally difficult problem of naturalizing the present. What Viderman has called the analytic space assumes a new importance because it is only against the background of this space that any particular utterance can be understood. But where Viderman was content to leave the space somewhat mystical and underdefined, we now come to realize that we have no choice but to make it fully explicit. Whether we are referring to the clinical theory or the metatheory of psychoanalysis, we have no choice but to make each interchange completely public and accessible; only when the surrounding space is completely defined can any utterance be understood.

CHAPTER X

Narrative Truth
and Historical Truth

What might be called the immediate appeal of the narrative explanation does not apply only to our formal interpretations; it also plays a significant role in how we try to listen and how the patient tries to associate. We have seen how both free association and "evenly-hovering attention" may be more active and deliberate than we have tended to assume. It now appears that we can understand both of these activities as attempts to enrich the narrative truth of the utterance. Active listening is required because the patient's associations—fragmentary, ambiguous, and allusive—lack the coherence we would find in a fully naturalized text. Because they do not speak for themselves, they must be supplemented with other associations before they can be understood, and often, as we have seen, these additional meanings are projected onto the material. The act of constructive listening is largely in the service of strengthening the narrative voice of the material; we try to give it narrative form in order to better understand.

Free-floating attention, then, could be better characterized as constructive listening in the service of understanding. This understanding is shared between analyst and patient; unwitting interpretations that facilitate the initial listening by the analyst lead directly to formal interpretations that supply continuity for the patient. As we have seen, associations and interpretations, as they are inserted into the developing narrative, become true as they become familiar and lend meaning to otherwise disconnected pieces of the patient's life. The very process that allows the analyst to understand the disconnected pieces of the hour, when extended and amplified, enables the patient gradually to see his life as continuous, coherent, and, therefore, meaningful.

The search for continuity and connection plays a similar role in free association. We have seen how the patient is faced with the difficult task of putting complex thoughts, feelings, and images into words; how language is particularly ill suited to the task of describing visual stimuli; and how often the need to express an idea or scene in words takes precedence over the need to be truthful. What is sayable may pre-empt what is really remembered; the need to assume a coherent part of the analytic conversation may tempt the patient to demonstrate more fluency than is warranted by the data. Rather than appear as a tongue-tied, incoherent bystander, unable to shape a complete sentence, the patient may be lulled by the demand to be verbal in place of being accurate.

As a result of the need to be coherent and conversational, the patient may generate sentences rather than associations and present us with words and descriptions that have little relation to his dreams and memories. The more controlled the patient's productions, the more they resemble a carefully organized narrative that can be understood with only passive attention because both content and context are supplied. On the other hand, the more fragmented and disorganized the associations, the more actively the analyst must listen in order to supply linking associations, to select one from a multitude of possible meanings, and, in general, to arrange the material in such a way that it can be meaningfully registered. Free-floating attention alternates with free association; it does not complement it, as Freud's model would have it. Only when the patient is assuming an active stance and presenting him with a coherent narrative can the analyst afford to be passive; at all other times—and these would include hours when the patient was coming close to the ideal of free association—the analyst must listen constructively.

If active listening is the rule much of the time, requiring the analyst to always apply a context to make sense out of what he hears, we see that what is known as free-floating attention is not—as tradition would have it—the automatic decoder of free association. Instead of working our way back to the latent dream, the original memory, or the "gist" of the hour, we are likely to introduce our own agenda, made up of unwitting interpretations. As we have seen, these interpretations only rarely become part of the record. Thus we have no way of knowing which unwitting interpretations were necessary to make sense out of the material. Even if we did, we have no systematic way of presenting what we know in a format that will provide the outside reader with a similar context. We have a sense that *fabula* must somehow be transformed into *sujet,* but the rules for making this transformation are still unknown. As a result, we have no way of transforming normative into privileged competence because we have no systematic method for naturalizing the protocol.

It seems reasonable to assume that the unwitting interpretations used by the analyst to make sense of the material must be related, in some way, to the gloss needed to naturalize a transcript. The glossing comment may be thought of as some kind of transformation of the unwitting interpretation. In more technical language, we might think of the gloss as representing a set of fully naturalized, unwitting interpretations; we begin with the assumptions made by the analyst when he first heard the utterance and expand on this information to make it coherent to an outsider with a different set of background assumptions. We now see with more clarity why we must begin to unpack the transcript immediately after it is recorded; the need for haste stems from the fact that the unwitting interpretations are particularly vulnerable to the passage of time.

We noted earlier in the chapter how active listening tends to occur in response to loosely organized associations, and we can use this rule to help to identify the passages most in need of unpacking. If large portions of the transcript are more or less readable as they stand, we would assume that the analyst was, in fact, listening with evenly hovering attention and making the minimum of background assumptions. But if the transcript begins to change and the patient begins to speak in a more fragmented, nonsequential fashion, we can assume that unwitting interpretations are being formed by the analyst, and these need to be recovered and elaborated upon to make up the final gloss.

The need to provide the full context before an utterance can be understood points to the poverty of our theoretical language by showing how vulnerable our descriptions are to background assumptions. If we can only convey the sense of an hour by simulating the experience of the treating analyst, then it follows that we still lack the necessary concepts needed to unambiguously identify and describe our subject matter. Our technical terms convey both too much and too little; they make a pretense of explaining or describing without completing the task; the "understanding," when it comes, is partly misunderstanding, the result of active attempts on the part of the reader to read his own meaning into the message. We have seen how the concept of therapeutic alliance, for example, takes on different meanings in the hands of different authors; it appears to refer to *something,* but a comparison of representative papers shows that it has no single referent. Thus it serves more as a metaphor than a piece of descriptive language; each reader supplies his preferred meaning, usually without realizing what he is contributing.

Schafer's action language (1976), designed to become the "native tongue of psychoanalysis," can be seen as one attempt to solve this problem. By reformulating our terms so that they refer exclusively to observable actions, we make it possible to minimize the effects of context. If a piece of behavior can be seen and touched, we have a tangible referent and need to be less concerned about the meanings that are being read into the description. But even visible behavior is not entirely unambiguous, as Searle demonstrated by ringing changes on the target sentence "The cat is on the mat" (see Chapter IX). And action language raises other problems of its own. By substituting actions for intentions and by placing the emphasis on conscious rather than on unconscious thoughts and feelings, action language threatens to rob psychoanalysis of its most distinctive concepts (see Meissner, 1979). We may have partly solved the problem of zero context but at the cost of restricting ourselves to the less significant data. To grapple with issues of the most clinical importance, we must find other ways of dealing with ambiguity.

PRIVATE AND PUBLIC ASSUMPTIONS

If we assume that we have no automatic way of decoding the patient's associations and argue, on the contrary, that understanding is an active process that requires an unending supply of unwitting interpretations, then we might ask where these interpretations come from. We can group them into two categories—public and private. Public assumptions come from the shared psychoanalytic theory which every analyst learns during his training and which he supplements through subsequent formal and informal clinical encounters; as we pointed out in Chapter VI, much of this theory is not heavily dependent on actual data. We will discuss the specific impact of this theory on understanding later in this chapter; here it is only necessary to point out that it colors the way the analyst listens by emphasizing certain kinds of themes and, in general, by influencing the particular texture of his analytic competence. Once it becomes clear that the analyst is engaged in constructive listening much of the time, then the role of background theory changes from that of an abstract superstructure, to be distinguished from the so-called "clinical" theory (see Klein, 1973), to an active presence in the clinical encounter which specifically affects what he hears and how he chooses to respond. Once we give up the idea of "evenly-hovering attention," then it becomes all the more important to know what assumptions the analyst is making to supplement the patient's associations.

Private assumptions come from the analyst's hopes and fears—which brings us to a new understanding of countertransference. In the usual view of the analytic interchange, countertransference is seen as a possible source of error, something to be "analyzed away" so as not to contaminate the therapeutic conversation. From our point of view, we would argue that countertransference may be a necessary part of active listening and that unless the analyst is continually supplying his own private associations, he can never hope to understand the clinical encounter. This does not mean that the analyst's private assumptions should not be treated as interfering; on the contrary, it argues more than ever for keeping careful track of exactly what unwitting interpretations are being formed during each part of the session so that they can be made available to the outside reader. As we have seen, only by being supplied with the relevant context can he hope to understand the full meaning of the session. But this requirement places special demands on the treating analyst. We need to know the private meaning of each interpretation because what the analyst was intending to convey and what led to his intention may be quite different from its surface appearance.

This requirement becomes especially important if we view an interpretation as a pragmatic utterance that is to be judged primarily in terms of what it intended to achieve. Such a formulation would lead us away from the interpretation as a literal proposition and emphasize instead what might be called its rhetorical presence. We can easily think of statements that assume a different meaning with a change of inflection, and if we are deprived of the inflection, we can hardly interpret the statement. The same principle applies to context. Just as we need the sound and phrasing of the utterance to allow us to understand its lexical message, so we need the background assumptions and countertransference pressures leading to the unwitting interpretation that helped to form the spoken interpretation. We have seen in Chapter II how misunderstanding follows from poorly crafted texts. The same principle applies to the analytic conversation. Analyst and patient can hardly claim to be professional wordsmiths, and it, therefore, follows that without additional help from both speakers our understanding is only partial.

Because the treating analyst must always be a participant in the discovery process, it follows that any analysis of the text alone, without his participation, is an exercise in half truths. Now that tape recording is becoming almost commonplace, it becomes all the more tempting to treat the recorded hour or case as a fully transparent text that can be judged, rated, and otherwise explicated *sui generis*. Studies by Dahl et al. (1978) and Weiss et al. (1980) are only two of a growing number of attempts to ignore context and treat the recorded text as a fully naturalized—and, therefore, public—document. Thus Dahl et al. (1978) have used linguistic procedures to understand a sample of analyst statements, and while their findings may be suggestive, can they be conclusive? What conclusions can be drawn from the syntactic parsing of an interpretation without knowing its paralinguistic surround, what the analyst was intending to convey (which may, in fact, have differed from his actual utterance), and something about the shared history of the words and phrases used in the interpretation? Deprived of the actual context, the explicator of such a text must supply his own, and the resulting interpretation may shed less light on the analytic process than on the hopes and fears of the explicator.

Interpretation, furthermore, may be the least important unit in the dialogue. The traditional *explication de la psychanalyse* has tended to focus on formal interpretations because they are visible and because they seem to be the prime movers of the analytic process. But for a full understanding of the process, we should probably concentrate on the underlying preparatory beliefs—the unwitting interpretations—which give rise to the visible interpretations, and for these we need the cooperation of the treating analyst. Because of the importance of unwitting interpretations, the treating analyst must participate in the discovery process at a time when all private associations are still available, because only then can he give us the full range of background information necessary for understanding each utterance. One way of describing our task is to say that for any given segment of the analytic space we must have access to the full range of background assumptions that lay the ground-work for the full set of unwitting interpretations that lead finally to the formal interpretation. It can be readily seen that neither of the first two sets can be derived from the tape-recorded transcript—no matter how good the equipment may be.

If we listen actively and creatively much of the time, there is no longer any clear line where reconstruction stops and con-struction begins. We have seen that ours is an archeology of descriptions, not of images, and that language is always get-ting in the way between what the patient saw or felt and the way this experience appears (variously transformed) in the analytic conversation. We never make contact with the actual memory or dream; language is always the elusive go-between. As a result of the multiple meanings of much of our data and as a result of the fact that we have no systematic means of decoding these meanings, we must always assume that for any given interpretation actually made there are any number of other candidates that could be made and have equal claim on our attention. We are only just beginning to understand how unwitting interpretation and background assumption combine to produce a particular interpretation at a particular time; as we understand the process in more detail, we will become more sensitive to the way in which context can influence content. As we come to understand the role of context, we will begin to understand the relative nature of meaning and appreciate, with Viderman, the unlimited possibilities in any given situation. Rather than speak in terms of exact and inexact interpretations (following Glover), we should think in terms of relative effect and ask ourselves how this particular interpretation in this particular analytic space would further the analytic process, much as we might look at a chess position in the middle game and ask about the effects of a particular move. But analysis, of course, is not chess, because to understand a game we need only the sequence of moves, whereas to understand a clinical encounter we need much more than the sequence of utterances.

THE PROBLEM OF VALIDATION

We have described a formal interpretation as an artistic and pragmatic creation that is always oriented toward the future. From this point of view, it no longer makes sense to speak of the historical validation of an interpretation. How does this position bear on the recent concern, raised by Grünbaum (1979), that clinical findings may have no particular epistemological status and that perhaps the clinical data cannot be used to validate psychoanalytic theory?

Grünbaum begins his argument with the following summary of the psychoanalytic process:

The success of an analysis is emphatically held to require that the patient's principal conscious acts, thoughts, and feelings be traced to their *actual* unconscious determinants, both genetic and dynamic. Thus, if successful, an analysis is claimed to comprise a *veridical reconstruction* of the causally relevant events in the patient's early and current life. Therefore we must ask: What reason do orthodox analysts offer for expecting that their intra-clinical procedures can attain such a veridical reconstruction? Their reason is none other than that the general genetic and dynamic hypotheses of Freudian theory, which they invoke at every turn in their interpretations, are either true or well supported observationally. (p. 458)

We have seen reason to question the assumption that we can ever translate the patient's associations into the actual unconscious determinants because we have no method of systematically working backward from effect to cause. We found that the method of free association would not necessarily unravel the dream into its constituent parts, and the fragments that did emerge required supplementary assumptions, contributed by the analyst, before they began to make sense. We also found that the shape of memories could be heavily influenced by the way in which they were described and that what looked like confirmation or recovery might be no more than the effect of an aptly worded description. Freud opened for us his Pandora's box of ambiguity, but he was somewhat overoptimistic about the extent to which the treatment method would discover the "true" meaning of any piece of behavior.

As a result of these uncertainties, we concluded that it is more appropriate to think of construction rather than reconstruction; to give up the archeological model; to think of an interpretation as a pragmatic statement that has no necessary referent in the past; and to replace historical truth by narrative truth. But this formulation raises problems with what Grünbaum has called Freud's "tally argument" (1979, p. 465)— that an interpretation, to be effective, must *tally* with what is real in the patient—and that only accurate interpretation, so defined, can mediate veridical insight and only such insight can cure the neurosis. What are the implications of creative interpretation for the theory of cure? If Grünbaum is right in his assertion that the tally argument is central to psychoanalytic theory, then we seem to have argued ourselves into an awkward position.

Freud's "tally" argument is first cited in one of the introductory lectures (Freud, 1917b) written at a time when Freud was convinced of the truth of the archeological model. It was written shortly before he published the Wolf Man case, in which he reports his most famous reconstruction. But as he became more clinically experienced, he began to back away from this model and adopt a more moderate stand about the historical truth value of his analytic work, and in his final paper on the topic, he seems to have taken the position (as noted in the preceding chapter) that "an assured conviction of the truth of the construction . . . achieves the same therapeutic result as a recaptured memory" (1937, p. 266). If a creative interpretation can bring about that kind of assurance, then perhaps a strict correspondence with the specific past event is no longer necessary.

We spoke earlier of the difference between historical and artistic truth and examined the argument that truth was not a necessary part of beauty. If an interpretation is seen as an artistic product, we might argue further that it achieves its effect through something analogous to the well-known *suspension of disbelief*. An interpretation may produce the desired result because the patient, supported by a belief in the analyst and reinforced by the power of the transference, may allow himself to suspend disbelief in the literal meaning of a given interpretation and thereby make himself accessible to its artistic and rhetorical surround. We have suggested (in Chapter V) that the primal-scene interpretation applied to Mondrian's career was compelling because it reduced a series of complex life events to a single cause and because it grounded a unique life and a revolutionary style of painting in a traditional body of theory. An interpretation, then, may bring about a positive effect not because it corresponds to a specific piece of the past but because it appears to relate the known to the unknown, to provide explanation in place of uncertainty. We have come to see that certain kinds of pragmatic statements can produce changes in behavior simply by virtue of being stated; given this assumption, we no longer need to hold, with Grünbaum, in the tally argument and its implications. Specifically, we would suggest that the "tally" argument is something of a straw man and that interpretations may be effective without necessarily being "true" in a strict historical sense.

The problem of matching patient report with the historical past is further complicated by the fact that the same event (historical fact) can be given multiple explanations. Consider a male patient who refused to wear glasses even though he was very nearsighted. In telling about this period in the analysis, he remembered his concern about being different from his friends and being singled out as the one with glasses. But as the events of his high-school years were remembered in more detail and as his feelings about these facts came into sharper focus, it became clear that the use of glasses carried overtones of being found feminine, girlish, and (at a deeper level) castrated; thus to avoid the glasses was to emphasize his masculinity. Not long after this narrative began to unfold, the patient began to remember that he had heard stories that wearing glasses might actually weaken his eyes (perhaps another reference to castration); thus the avoidance of glasses might actually improve his vision over the long run. As the wish behind this belief was explored, the patient remembered that one of his goals during high school was to enlist in the Air Force and become a pilot; thus the avoidance of glasses became one way of preparing to become a hero. Other contributing factors included the fact that neither parent wore glasses; thus a matter of identification was also involved.

Which narrative is true? Each story shares a piece of the truth—but not necessarily the historical truth. The skeptical historian, in all likelihood, could validate only the fact that the patient was nearsighted, that he did not wear glasses, and that his parents had normal vision—all these facts could be checked. On the other hand, data confirming any one of the explanatory narratives listed above are probably out of reach. What, then, is the truth of these explanations? Pieces of each story may have emerged now and then in the patient's awareness as he was growing up; the latent structure of each narrative might well have served as an organizing scheme during specific periods in the patient's life; but it seems unlikely that any of the narratives could be corroborated.

It may be helpful at this point to introduce the distinction between *plain* and *significant* narrative, which was first proposed by Walsh (1958). The first is a "description of the facts restricted to a straightforward statement of what occurred." The second is an account of the facts "which brought out their connections" (p. 480). The *plain* narrative is clearly dependent on historical truth and the *significant* narrative on narrative truth. Walsh makes clear that the validity of a *significant* narrative (its narrative truth) cannot be checked by making an appeal to the known facts because "the connections between events are not open to inspection in the way the events themselves are. . . . Causal language is of a different logical order from observation language; the former presupposes the latter, and is not just an extension of it" (p. 483). This way of putting the difference captures very nicely the case of the nearsighted patient. Many of the significant narratives left no trace in the past because the "connection between events" was outwardly invisible (inside the head of the growing adolescent) and inwardly variable, appearing and disappearing in bits and pieces but never fully in awareness as a fully rounded story. Once again, we see that narrative truth cannot be validated by appeal to historical fact. On the contrary, it speaks to a different domain, a domain that only comes alive within the analytic situation.

To a significant degree, the narrative that emerges from the analytic work can be regarded as a kind of theory, and to an important extent, theories remain independent of facts. A recent discussion by Gergen (1981) makes the point very clearly. He points out that a theory represents an interpretation of a particular meaning of an action, and that this meaning cannot be observed per se. "The symbolic meaning of observables is, either on the level of mundane discussion or on the broad theoretical level, not open to objective verification or falsification. There is no observable referent to which the investigator can reliably point. The meaning of human action is dependent on the observer's system of interpretation. The observer must bring to the event a conceptual system through which behavioral observations may be rendered meaningful. There is no means of verifying or falsifying a 'mode of interpretation' " (p. 335).

If we view the analytic work in this light, we see that the narrative truth of an interpretation or construction can never be verified by pieces of the past. This conclusion represents a direct contradiction to Grünbaum's assertion that a successful analysis "is claimed to comprise a *veridical reconstruction* of the causally relevant events in the patient's early and current life" (Grünbaum, 1979, p. 458). Significant tallies can never be achieved because the assumed causes leave no traces.

NARRATIVE TRUTH AND HISTORICAL TRUTH

If validation seems out of reach, how do we arrive at a general theory? The answer may be a long time coming—because of the particular nature of narrative truth. If interpretations are creative rather than veridical and if the analyst functions more as a pattern maker than a pattern finder, then we may be faced with a glaring absence of general rules. What rules there are, moreover, may pertain mainly to the more trivial aspects of our clinical material. If the impact of a particular interpretation is contingent, as we noted in the last chapter, on the specific texture of time and place, the rules for it being true are just as much out of reach as the rules for any other kind of artistic masterpiece. It may be comforting to assume, as is the custom, that we have a general theory waiting in the wings, waiting to be confirmed; but the fact that after almost one hundred years we are still waiting for a set of confirmed postulates should give us a good grasp of future prospects.

The widespread belief in this general theory may actually interfere with our clinical work. To the extent that the analyst is guided by certain kinds of presuppositions, he will tend to understand the material in a more restricted fashion. He is handicapped in his task of constructive listening by the search for certain kinds of universals, and if some of these universals never appear, or appear in somewhat different forms, he is handicapped even further. He may, for example, miss the interpretative opportunities of the moment while waiting for some vague shape of the future. One of the problems in going from normative to privileged competence is that in the absence of detailed knowledge about the particulars of a clinical happening, the outside observer will tend to see it in terms of vague stereotypes; thus the received theory will be mistakenly reinforced. Since all of our cases are incomplete, it is relatively easy to insert pieces of the theory whenever we need to explain a discontinuity.

The more serious interference, however, comes from pseudo confirmations during the course of treatment. If we are right in assuming that much of the time the analyst listens in a constructive, hypothesis-generating manner, and that the source of many of these hypotheses is a received theory that is only partially confirmed from sources outside of the psychoanalytic situation, then we are in danger of trying to build lasting conclusions from mostly soft pattern matches. We have seen how any narrative is almost infinitely flexible and can accommodate any number of additions; and we have seen how any given detail takes on a kind of protected status once it has acquired a narrative home. It would follow that the same kind of acceptance would apply to a piece of theory which has apparently been supported by the clinical material. Working within a tradition of narrative truth, this kind of accommodation would present no problem because we would not assume that we are establishing general laws—but working within a tradition of historical truth, the consequences are much more serious. Every time a piece of theory is apparently supported by the clinical material, it tends to maintain our belief in established assumptions and discourage the search for new explanations. So long as psychoanalysis is seen as a kind of archeology in which patterns *emerge* from the material, then any pattern that even roughly corresponds to what the theory might predict is cause for excitement and satisfaction—the received theory is (mistakenly) confirmed.

If there is less established theory than we like to assume, we can think of two important consequences. First, it makes each analyst even more alone than he is already; if there are almost no guidelines, then the risk of going wrong is sizably increased. If Viderman and Loch are correct in seeing an interpretation as primarily a creative act, then the analyst, like it or not, is engaged in an artistic struggle with the patient and with all of his colleagues. Seen in this light, the impossible profession becomes even more so.

The second consequence bears on the form of the general theory. In one of his last papers, Freud returned to the importance of theory vis-à-vis method. "I have told you," he wrote, "that psychoanalysis began as a method of treatment; but I did not want to commend it to your interest as a method of treatment but on account of the truths it contains, on account of the information it gives us about what concerns human beings most of all—their own nature—and on account of the connections it discloses between the most different of their activities" (1932, p. 156). He was clearly thinking of truth in the traditional sense, and believed that psychoanalysis contained a set of general laws that could be applied to specific cases. But if we are shifting to a more relativistic notion of truth, then the discoveries we make in our clinical work, even though they may have direct therapeutic implications, do not necessarily generalize to other patients. Our discoveries, in other words, may be highly situational and need to be understood in their immediate context; it would be a mistake to reduce them to some general law because, by so doing, we might lose the very ingredient that made them effective in the specific case.

In the hands of our most gifted colleagues, the discovery and creation of narrative truth may, in fact, operate so smoothly and so successfully that it appears lawful, giving the impression that our general theory is more advanced than is actually the case. It may be that Freud's own clinical genius may have fooled him into assuming that most of the theoretical problems had been resolved, that associations follow naturally from unconscious ideas, and that these ideas can be systematically decoded from the associations. We see the familiar mark of the projective fallacy: What was obvious to Freud did not lie in the clinical material but came from the particular structure he imposed on it. Because connections between associations can always be found, we lose sight of how much we contribute to the discovery process and how far we are, in fact, from having at our fingertips a fully fledged theory to account for the individual case.

If the specific detail of the clinical happening is what makes all the difference, then it becomes all the more important to carry out a systematic unpacking of each clinical encounter; our significant contributions would seem to lie in the complexity of the particular event, and these can never be communicated in the conventional abstract formulation. With this in mind, it becomes all the more important to find ways of naturalizing each encounter in a routine and systematic manner and to take precautions *not* to reduce a complicated happening to a stereotyped "law" that may be only an empty metaphor. If narrative truth is the source of our clinical success, then it should be taken seriously in all of its specific detail; it will not survive translation into something more general.

This view of the psychoanalytic enterprise, with its emphasis on narrative truth, raises serious questions about how we go about constructing a general theory. Many of Freud's initial constructs were designed to serve as tentative formulations—what he called "nebulous, scarcely imaginable basic concepts, which it [the science of psychoanalysis] hopes to apprehend more clearly in the course of its development, or which it is even prepared to replace by others. For these ideas are not the foundation of science, upon which everything rests: that foundation is observation alone. They are not the bottom but the top of the whole structure, and they can be replaced and discarded without damaging it" (1914, p. 77). Constructs were meant to be provisional; observation was the key.

In the intervening years, observation has been slighted and constructs have become reified; the combination of incomplete evidence and stereotyped theory makes for near-inevitable confirmation. It may be time, once again, to reaffirm the tentative nature of our theory, thinking of it more as metaphor than established fact; to spend less time searching for confirmation (which is usually based on soft pattern matches) and more time accumulating data; and to begin to look at particular clinical events—events that come as close as possible to representing the original encounter of analyst and patient in all of its complexity. As we learn the ways in which truth emerges from the psychoanalytic dialogue and leads to changes in understanding, we may slowly replace our metaphors with something more substantial and make a beginning toward formulating a science of the mind.

References

Adams, H. 1918. *The education of Henry Adams*. New York: Houghton Mifflin.

Aiken, H. D. 1951. The aesthetic relevance of belief. *Journal of Aesthetics and Art Criticism* 4:301–15.

Arendt, H. 1977. *The life of the mind. Vol. I. Thinking*. New York: Harcourt Brace Jovanovich.

Arlow, J. A. 1979. The genesis of interpretation. *Journal of the American Psychoanalytic Association* 27 (Suppl.):193–206.

Atkinson, R. F. 1978. *Knowledge and explanation in history*. Ithaca: Cornell University Press.

Bally, C. 1944. *Linguistique générale et linguistique française*. Paris: Leroux.

Barthes, R. 1973. *Le plaisir du texte*. Paris: Éditions de Seuil.

———. 1977. *Image, music, text*. New York: Hill & Wang.

Brenner, C. 1977. Working alliance, therapeutic alliance, and transference. *Journal of the American Psychoanalytic Association* 27 (Suppl.):137–57.

Browne, N. D. F. 1980. Mirroring in the analysis of an artist. *International Journal of Psycho-Analysis* 61:493–503.

Culler, J. 1975. *Structuralist poetics*. Ithaca: Cornell University Press.

Dahl, H.; Teller, V.; Moss, D.; and Trujillo, M. 1978. Countertransference examples of the syntactic expression of warded-off contents. *Psychoanalytic Quarterly* 47:339–63.

Dewald, P. A. 1972. *The psychoanalytic process.* New York: Basic Books.

Dewey, J. 1934. *Art as experience.* New York: Milton, Balch.

Dillon, G. L. 1978. *Language processing and the reading of literature.* Bloomington, Ill.: Indiana University Press.

Edelson, M. 1975. *Language and interpretation in psychoanalysis.* New Haven: Yale University Press.

Farrell, B. A.; Wisdom, J. O.; and Turquet, P. M. 1962. The criteria for a psychoanalytic interpretation. In *The Proceedings of the Aristotelian Society.* Suppl. vol. XXXVI. London: Harrison & Sons.

Finke, R. A. 1980. Levels of equivalence in imagery and perception. *Psychological Review* 87:113–32.

Foucault, M. 1973. *The order of things.* New York: Vintage.

Freud, S. 1899. Screen memories. In *The complete psychological works.* Standard ed. Vol. 3. Ed. and trans. James Strachey. New York: Norton, 1976.

———. 1900. The interpretation of dreams. In *The complete psychological works.* Standard ed. Vols. 4 and 5. Ed. and trans. James Strachey. New York: Norton, 1976.

———. 1901. *On dreams.* Trans. James Strachey. New York: Norton, 1952.

———. 1905. Fragment of an analysis of a case of hysteria. In *The complete psychological works.* Standard ed. Vol. 7. Ed. and trans. James Strachey. New York: Norton, 1976.

———. 1912. Recommendations to physicians practicing psychoanalysis. In *The complete psychological works.* Standard ed. Vol. 12. Ed. and trans. James Strachey. New York: Norton, 1976.

———. 1913. On beginning the treatment. In *The complete psychological works.* Standard ed. Vol. 12. Ed. and trans. James Strachey. New York: Norton, 1976.

———. 1914. On narcissism: an introduction. In *The complete psychological works.* Standard ed. Vol. 14. Ed. and trans. James Strachey. New York: Norton, 1976.

———. 1917a. The paths to the formation of symptoms. In *Introductory lectures on psychoanalysis.* Ed. and trans. James Strachey. New York: Norton, 1966.

———. 1917b. Analytic therapy. In *Introductory lectures on psychoanalysis.* Ed. and trans. James Strachey. New York: Norton, 1966.

―――. 1918. From the history of an infantile neurosis. In *The complete psychological works*. Standard ed. Vol. 17. Ed. and trans. James Strachey. New York: Norton, 1976.

―――. 1932. *New introductory lectures on psychoanalysis*. Ed. and trans. James Strachey. New York: Norton, 1965.

―――. 1937. Constructions in analysis. In *The complete psychological works*. Standard ed. Vol. 23. Ed. and trans. James Strachey. New York: Norton, 1976.

Friedman, L. 1969. The therapeutic alliance. *International Journal of Psycho-Analysis* 50:139–53.

Gergen, K. 1981. The meagre voice of empiricist affirmation. *Personality and Social Psychology Bulletin* 7:333–37.

Gill, M. M. 1979. The analysis of the transference. *Journal of the American Psychoanalytic Association* 27 (Suppl.):263–87.

Gill, M. M.; Simon, J.; Fink, G.; Endicott, N. A.; and Paul, I. H. 1968. Studies in audio-recorded psychoanalysis. I. General considerations. *Journal of the American Psychoanalytic Association* 16:230–44.

Glover, E. 1931. The therapeutic effect of inexact interpretation. *International Journal of Psycho-Analysis* 12:397–411.

Gombrich, E. H. 1969. *Art and illusion*. Princeton: Princeton University Press.

―――. 1972. *Symbolic images*. New York: Phaidon.

Goodman, N. 1968. *Languages of art*. Indianapolis: Bobbs-Merrill.

Gray, P. 1973. Psychoanalytic technique and the ego's capacity for viewing intrapsychic activity. *Journal of the American Psychoanalytic Association* 21:474–94.

Greenacre, P. 1973. The primal scene and the sense of reality. *Psychoanalytic Quarterly* 42:10–41.

Greenson, R. R. 1967. *The technique and practice of psychoanalysis*. New York: International Universities Press.

Grice, H. P. 1967. *Logic and conversation*. Unpub. manuscript, William James Lectures at Harvard.

Grünbaum, A. 1979. Epistemological liabilities of the clinical appraisal of psychoanalytic theory. *Psychoanalysis and Contemporary Thought* 2:451–526.

Harding, D. W. 1963. *Experience into words*. London: Chatto & Windus.

Hirsch, E. D., Jr. 1967. *Validity in interpretation*. New Haven: Yale University Press.

Holt, R. R. 1975. Drive or wish? A reconsideration of the psychoanalytic theory of motivation. In *Psychology vs. metapsychology: psychoanalytic essays in honor of George S. Klein,* ed. M. M. Gill and P. S. Holzman. New York: International Universities Press.

Isenberg, A. 1955. The problem of belief. *Journal of Aesthetics and Art Criticism* 13:395–407.

Jacobsen, P. B., and Steele, R. S. 1979. From present to past: Freudian archaeology. *International Review of Psycho-Analysis* 6:349–62.

James, H. 1902. *The ambassadors.* New York: Harper & Brothers.

Kammerman, M., ed. 1977. *Sensory isolation and personality change.* Springfield: Charles C. Thomas.

Kanzer, M. 1975. The therapeutic and working alliances. *International Journal of Psychoanalytic Psychotherapy* 4:48–68.

Klein, G. S. 1973. Two theories or one? *Bulletin of the Menninger Clinic* 37: 102–32.

Kohut, H. 1977. *The restoration of the self.* New York: International Universities Press.

Kris, E. 1956a. The recovery of childhood memories in psychoanalysis. *The Psychoanalytic Study of the Child* 11:54–88.

———. 1956b. On some vicissitudes of insight. *International Journal of Psychoanalysis* 37:445–55.

Kuhn, T. S. 1962. *The structure of scientific revolutions.* Chicago: University of Chicago Press.

Lacan, J. 1977. *Écrits: a selection.* New York: Norton.

Langer, S. K. 1942. *Philosophy in a new key.* Cambridge: Harvard University Press.

Langs, R. J. 1975. Therapeutic misalliances. *International Journal of Psychoanalytic Psychotherapy* 4:77–105.

Loch, W. 1977. Some comments on the subject of psychoanalysis and truth. In *Thought, consciousness and reality,* ed. J. Smith. New Haven: Yale University Press.

Loewenstein, R. 1951. The problem of interpretation. *Psychoanalytic Quarterly* 20:1–14.

Loftus, E. F. 1979. *Eyewitness testimony.* Cambridge, Mass.: Harvard University Press.

Loftus, E. F., and Loftus, G. R. 1980. On the permanence of stored information in the human brain. *American Psychologist* 35:409–20.

Luborsky, L., and Spence, D. P. 1978. Quantitative research in psychoanalytic therapy. In *Handbook of psychotherapy and behav-*

ior change: an empirical analysis. 2d ed. Ed. S. L. Garfield and A. E. Bergin. New York: Wiley.

Mahony, P. 1980. Toward the understanding of translation in psychoanalysis. *Journal of the American Psychoanalytic Association* 28:461–75.

Major, R. 1980. The logical process of interpretation. *International Review of Psycho-Analysis* 7:397–403.

Meissner, W. W. 1979. Methodological critique of the action language in psychoanalysis. *Journal of the American Psychoanalytic Association* 27:79–105.

Merleau-Ponty, M. 1964. *Signs.* Trans. R. C. McCleary. Evanston, Ill.: Northwestern University Press. Originally published by Librairie Gallimard, Paris, 1960.

Neiderland, W. 1965. Memory and repression. *Journal of the American Psychoanalytic Association* 13:619–33.

Oliver, H. 1980. *Flaubert and an English governess.* New York: Oxford University Press.

Popper, K. 1959. *The logic of scientific discovery.* London: Hutchinson.

Quine, W. V., and Ullian, J. S. 1970. *The web of belief.* 2d ed. New York: Random House.

Ramzy, I. 1974. How the mind of the psychoanalyst works: an essay on psychoanalytic inference. *International Journal of Psycho-Analysis* 55:543–50.

Reich, A. 1973. *Annie Reich: psychoanalytic contributions.* New York: International Universities Press.

Reichenbach, H. 1951. *The rise of scientific philosophy.* Berkeley: University of California Press.

Ricoeur, P. 1970. *Freud and philosophy.* New Haven: Yale University Press.

———. 1977. The question of proof in Freud's psychoanalytic writings. *Journal of the American Psychoanalytic Association* 25:835–71.

Rosenberg, H. 1975. *Art on the edge.* New York: Macmillan.

Schachtel, E. G. 1947. On memory and childhood amnesia. *Psychiatry* 10:1–26.

Schafer, R. 1976. *A new language for psychoanalysis.* New Haven: Yale University Press.

———. 1979. The appreciative analytic attitude and the construction of multiple histories. *Psychoanalysis and Contemporary Thought* 2:3–24.

————. 1980. Narration in the psychoanalytic dialogue. *Critical Inquiry* 7:29–53.

Schorer, M. 1961. Technique as discovery. In *Approaches to the novel,* ed. R. Scholes. San Francisco: Chandler.

Schulkind, J., ed. 1976. *Virginia Woolf: moments of being.* New York: Harcourt Brace Jovanovich.

Schwaber, E. 1979. On the 'self' within the matrix of analytic theory—some clinical reflections and reconsiderations. *International Journal of Psycho-Analysis* 60:467–79.

Searle, J. R. 1979. *Expression and meaning.* Cambridge: Cambridge University Press.

Shapiro, A. K., and Morris, L. A. 1978. The placebo effect in medical and psychological therapies. In *Handbook of psychotherapy and behavior change: an empirical analysis,* ed. S. L. Garfield and A. E. Bergin. 2d ed. New York: Wiley.

Shapiro, T. 1970. Interpretation and naming. *Journal of the American Psychoanalytic Association* 18:399–421.

Sherwood, M. 1969. *The logic of explanation in psychoanalysis.* New York: Academic Press.

Simon, J.; Fink, G.; Gill, M. M.; Endicott, N. A.; and Paul, I. H. 1970. Studies in audio-recorded psychoanalysis. II. The effect of recording upon the analyst. *Journal of the American Psychoanalytic Association* 18:86–101.

Singer, M. G. 1971. The pragmatic use of language and the will to believe. *American Philosophical Quarterly* 8:24–34.

Spence, D. P. 1973. Analog and digital descriptions of behavior. *American Psychologist* 28:479–88.

————. 1976. Clinical interpretation: some comments on the nature of the evidence. In *Psychoanalysis and contemporary science,* ed. T. Shapiro. Vol. V. New York: International Universities Press.

Steiner, G. 1967. *Language and silence.* New York: Atheneum.

————. 1975. *After Babel.* New York: Oxford University Press.

Sternberg, M. 1974. What is exposition? In *The theory of the novel,* ed. J. Halperin. New York: Oxford University Press.

Stevenson, R. L. 1911. *Treasure Island.* New York: Scribner.

Stoppard, T. 1972. *Jumpers.* New York: Grove Press.

Viderman, S. 1979. The analytic space: Meaning and problems. *Psychoanalytic Quarterly* 48:257–91.

Waelder, R. 1936. The principle of multiple function. *Psychoanalytic Quarterly* 5:45–62.

Wallerstein, R. S., and Sampson, H. 1971. Issues in research in the psychoanalytic process. *International Journal of Psycho-Analysis* 52:11–50.

Walsh, W. H. 1958. "Plain" and "significant" narrative in history. *Journal of Philosophy* 55:479–84.

Watt, I. 1969. The first paragraph of *The Ambassadors:* an explication. In *Contemporary essays in style,* ed. G. L. Love and M. Payne. Glenview, Ill.: Scott Foresman.

Weiss, J.; Sampson H.; Gassner, S.; and Caston, J. 1980. Further research on the psychoanalytic process. *Bulletin #4,* Mount Zion Hospital and Medical Center, San Francisco, Calif.

Whorf, B. L. 1956. *Language, thought and reality: selected writings of Benjamin Lee Whorf,* ed. John B. Carroll. Cambridge, Mass.: MIT Press.

Zetzel, E. R. 1966. The analytic situation. In *Psychoanalysis in the Americas,* ed. R. E. Litman. New York: International Universities Press.

Index